D1357136

THE QUEEN'S LAST MAP-MAKER

RICHARD BARTLETT IN IRELAND, 1600-3

J.H. ANDREWS

Published in Ireland by
Geography Publications, Kennington Road, Templeogue, Dublin 6W.

ISBN 978-0906602-430

Design and typesetting by Keystrokes Digital, Dublin.
Printed by Betaprint, Dublin.

Contents

List of plates

List of figures

Abbreviations

BL British Library, London

CSPI Calendar of state papers, Ireland

NMM National Maritime Museum, Greenwich

PRO National Archives, London (formerly Public Record Office)

SP State papers in PRO

TCD Trinity College, Dublin

Preface

Richard Bartlett was a talented cartographer and topographical draughtsman who practised in Ireland at the beginning of the seventeenth century. Although his life and career are poorly documented, he left what for this period must be reckoned a substantial output comprising between nineteen and twenty-seven items depending on how they are counted. These magnificent maps and drawings might be thought capable of speaking for themselves, especially as nearly all of them have already been reproduced in print. My answer is that Bartlett's contributions to Irish geography and topography are important enough to be celebrated verbally and in a book exclusively their own.

The need for such a publication might seem to have been already met by Gerard Hayes McCoy's masterly introduction to *Ulster and other Irish maps* (Irish Manuscripts Commission, 1964), a volume containing facsimiles of all Bartlett's maps in the National Library of Ireland. In the last forty-five years a few additional facts and opinions have emerged about the maps in question; but the main limitation of Hayes-McCoy's essay is that although he did a major service to scholarship by identifying Bartlett's work at smaller scales in British repositories and in Trinity College, Dublin, his editorial commitment to the National Library collection prevented him from devoting much space to this less familiar material.

The present study, which gives more attention to Bartlett's undervalued regional maps, has developed from a long-running interest in the Elizabethan cartography of Ireland. I have already written about most of the better-known map-makers of the period in the form of single essays or part-essays on Baptista Boazio, the two John Brownes, Francis Jobson, Brian Fitzwilliam, William Jones, Robert Lythe, John Norden and John Thomas. After so much effort, not doing the same for Bartlett might look like a deliberate act of disparagement. It therefore seems advisable to fill the gap, though I am conscious of being poorly qualified to pronounce on certain aspects of his work.

Where exact quotation is appropriate I have followed the spelling of whatever map is under discussion. Otherwise, since I am writing in English, I have adopted existing anglicised place-names, and in certain cases not recorded by the Ordnance Survey I have even followed the example of John O'Donovan by inventing new English forms on the analogy of old ones.

Many people have helped me with this book. In attempting to trace the earlier history of Richard Bartlett's large-scale maps I owe a considerable debt to Rose Mitchell of the British National Archives. On their later history I have been advised by Mark Curtoys, Val Gildea, Mervyn Miller and James Peters, and especially by Sir Richard Bowlby, the only living person known to have handled the maps before their return to Ireland. In Dublin Sharon Weadick has traced their story in detail from their acquisition by the National Museum until the appearance of Hayes-McCoy's book. A large number of other research problems have been investigated for me in Dublin by Beatrice Coughlan. My own study of the maps has been greatly facilitated by two National Library staff-members, first Noel Kissane and more recently Elizabeth Kirwan. On questions of interpretation I have benefited from access to unpublished map-historical work by Annaleigh Margey and Felim McGrath, and from the expert knowledge of Paul Kerrigan on Tudor Irish fortifications and Kay Muhr on Ulster placenames. Sources of information on various other subjects have been made known to me by Patrick J. Duffy, Thomas Herron, Arnold Horner, Bernhard Klein, Mic Moroney, Jane Ohlmeyer, Anngret Simms and William J. Smyth; a computer programme for map accuracy assessment was supplied by Rob Kitchin; and various aspects of the topography of Ulster and north Connacht have been elucidated by Anne Connon, Bill Crawford, Sarah Gearty and Patrick O'Brien. My own maps have been expertly redrawn by Stephen Hannon. William Nolan, as well as doing everything a first-class publisher could be expected to do, has kindly taken over the whole business of assembling and processing facsimiles of Bartlett's maps. The Heritage Council has given a generous grant towards the cost of publication. Thanks to them all.

J. H. A.

J.H. ANDREWS was born in England and educated at the universities of Cambridge and London. From 1954 to 1990 he taught historical geography at Trinity College, Dublin, where he became a Fellow of the College in 1969 and associate professor in 1977. He is a past-president and honorary life member of the Geographical Society of Ireland and a member of the Royal Irish Academy. He has been involved in two major Academy publications, as secretary to the editorial committee of the *Atlas of Ireland* from 1971 to 1979, and as co-editor of the *Irish historic towns atlas* from 1981 to 1992. He has served as review editor for the map-historical journal *Imago Mundi*, and as editorial adviser to *The history of cartography* published by the University of Chicago Press. Professor Andrews has written many papers and several books on historical geography and the history of cartography, including *A paper landscape: the Ordnance Survey in nineteenth-century Ireland* (1975); *Plantation acres: an historical study of the Irish land surveyor and his maps* (1985), and *Shapes of Ireland. Maps and their makers* (1997). *The Queen's last map-maker. Richard Bartlett in Ireland, 1600-3* is based on studies and researches in Ireland and England spread over a long working career.

Chapter 1

Unexplored Landscapes

Richard Bartlett's map-making activities in the opening years of the seventeenth century command attention as the embodiment of three virtues not often present in the same individual — geographical judgement, cartographic professionalism and artistic flair. Although his recorded output was confined to one small country, these gifts should have made him a figure of international importance. Until very recently they have failed to do so, and the present book was conceived as a remonstrance against this state of affairs. Accordingly its first chapter, setting the scene for Bartlett's brief career, is addressed to English-speaking readers at large rather than to those already familiar with the course of Irish history.

TWO KINDS OF TERRITORIALITY

At one time it was widely thought that the famous Tudor cartographer Christopher Saxton had personally surveyed a small area near Belfast and left a map of it for posterity.[1] That theory is now discredited, but we may still ask ourselves what Saxton would have thought if he had really visited Ireland during the reign of Elizabeth I. At least it was a kingdom with the same monarch as his native England, represented in Dublin by a lord deputy or lord lieutenant and served by what was meant to be a comparable apparatus of state. But there were also a number of crucial differences, some of them highly relevant to a cartographer's own profession. The unit of mapping that Saxton had found most convenient for England in the 1570s was the shire or county. Ireland was big enough to make twenty or thirty English shires and it would have taken several years to map an area this size even at Saxton's impressively rapid work-rate.[2] The smaller kingdom had its own counties but they did not yet form a comprehensive network. (The modern county names will be used as convenient territorial indicators throughout this book, however.) Some of their boundaries remained uncertain, and some counties that existed on paper had not yet become fully operational as units of local government. It is hard to imagine Irish county officials organising guides to local hill-tops from which a visiting surveyor could make his observations, as the sheriffs of Wales were expected to do for Saxton.[3]

In Irish geographical thinking the place of the English county was taken, for some purposes at least, by a kind of territory that had no counterpart in England. As we shall see, the five provinces of Leinster, Meath, Munster, Connacht and Ulster were often treated as independent for cartographic purposes, whereas Irish county maps were comparatively rare until the late seventeenth century.[4] The boundaries of provinces, like those of counties, were not always clearly defined, and where contemporaries agreed among themselves on this subject they sometimes differed from modern opinion. From 1569 to the end of Elizabeth's reign Munster and Connacht possessed their own presidents or governors. Leinster and Meath needed no president because they could be administered from Dublin, a fact that increasingly led them to be regarded as a single province. Ulster was too remote to be treated in this way, but also too rebellious for any form of devolution to be attempted there.

Each English county was composed of historic subdivisions usually known as hundreds or wapentakes. In a few cases Saxton had contrived to map these territories, probably by using written lists of parishes that allowed the boundaries to be threaded between places he had already surveyed. His successor John Speed finished mapping the hundreds throughout most of the kingdom.[5] In Irish counties, both old and new, the official equivalent of the English hundred was the barony. Many baronies were adopted ready-made from pre-existing native territories which had once possessed their own chiefs or 'captains' and which remained important elements in the political geography of the north and west. Irish lordships presented two complications to the foreign observer: they possessed a hierarchical structure of their own, and at any given level of the hierarchy the name of each region had to be distinguished from that of its dominant family or sept. The north of Ireland will be further considered from this standpoint in a later chapter.

CHURCH AND PEOPLE

Below the hundred or barony in both kingdoms was the parish. In England this was a social and administrative reality familiar to everyone, and English parishes were now acquiring various non-religious local-government functions, among them poor relief and the maintenance of roads, while most parish churches asserted their importance by standing amidst a substantial village. Saxton made no attempt to delineate parish boundaries, but church sites were a pervasive feature of his maps. In much of Ireland the parishes were larger than those of England, the churches smaller and more dilapidated (some of them altogether ruinous), and often unaccompanied by any substantial number of nearby dwelling houses. In Connacht, for instance, it was complained in 1574 that the existence of many former parishes had been forgotten and in 1600 there was 'scarce any church standing' for sixty miles between Dublin and Athlone.[6] These regrettable facts were easily explained. The ecclesiastical reformation decreed by Queen Elizabeth's father had converted Ireland's parish churches to protestant use while leaving the mass of the people steadfastly catholic. In consequence medieval parish centres now played little part in the life of the country.

Ireland and England also differed in their experience of monasticism. The medieval religious houses of both kingdoms had been officially closed at the time of the reformation, though in remote parts of Ireland some of the buildings were still serving their original purpose. As late as 1590 it was thought necessary to extract an undertaking from an ostensibly well-affected Irish lord not to maintain any monks or friars in his country.[7] The older monastic sites, with roots in pre-Norman Christianity, continued to function as centres of pilgrimage and devotion; and even when deserted and ruined, many Irish abbeys were known to travellers as landmarks, chiefly because there were so few other buildings large enough to compete for attention.

Outside the monasteries, two kinds of secular habitation need to be distinguished. Irish towns, with municipal corporations, tholsels or town halls, courts of law, large well-built churches, market places and other trading facilities, were similar to those of England except for being less uniformly distributed over the country and more dependent for their security on a circuit of defensive municipal walls and gates. In rural areas the contrasts were more striking. The prevailing settlement form for the gentry of Gaelic Ireland had been an unfortified house protected by a small circular enclosure, sometimes of earth and timber, sometimes of dry stone masonry.[8] These sites are prominent in Irish toponymy as raths, lisses and cashels, but can seldom be found on early maps. More conspicuous cartographically, as we shall see, were the crannogs or inhabited artificial lake islands particularly common in Ulster.

In the landscape raths had been giving way since late medieval times to residential towers built of stone. These more conspicuous structures, usually and justifiably called castles, were still being built throughout Elizabeth's reign. Together with their less defensible outhouses and perhaps a cluster of adjacent tenants' and labourers' cabins, they often had the appearance of a small village. Some were occupied by influential landowning families loyal to the crown; others, increasingly, by Irishmen of more rebellious disposition.[9]

This brings us to the lowest levels of the territorial and settlement hierarchies. In all habitable parts of Ireland, the smallest territorial divisions were areas smaller than a parish and larger than a family farm, known by various generic names (for instance ballibоes, ploughlands, cartrons and tates) and later collectively designated as townlands.[10] Each had an individual name and boundary that were generally familiar to the local inhabitants. A typical townland might be as small as two or three hundred acres. Castles would take their name from the townland in which they were situated. Where there was no castle, a small community of farmers would live in cabins which, by analogy with later and better-documented periods, we can picture as single-storey thatch-roofed dwellings, comfortable enough perhaps, but easily destroyed and easily replaced, not always on the same site. In Saxton's England such settlements would have been beneath a cartographer's notice.

REALMS OF NATURE

The most striking feature of the Irish landscape, however, was the obtrusiveness of nature.[11] Mountain masses were found in all parts of the island, not just in the north and west as in Britain. The climate, cool, wet and misty even on the lowlands, deteriorated sharply with increasing altitude and little land above 500 feet was cultivated. Rivers were broad and rarely fordable, some of them obstructed by unnavigable rapids. Lakes of all shapes and sizes abounded, especially in the midlands and the north. Many streams changed direction unpredictably and confusingly between their upper and lower courses, a phenomenon for which Ireland was later to become well known among physical geographers. No wonder Irish rivers were so often wrongly shown on early maps as interconnected, with the same stream apparently flowing in opposite directions at the same place. Bridges were rare enough to be worth mapping, even when the roads that led to them were ignored. (The omission of roads was common on regional maps in England and indeed throughout western Europe at this period.) Much of the lowland between the rivers was occupied by peat bogs, penetrable only to those who knew their secret paths. Elsewhere, woods were dense and threatening. Both bogs and woods were usually irregular in shape and therefore difficult to map with precision. The neat stockaded parks familiar on Speed's county maps were almost unknown in Ireland.

The foregoing generalisations were by no means uniformly applicable to the whole country. In much of Leinster and east Munster (apart from the Wicklow mountains and the boglands of Leix and Offaly) conditions were more favourable, especially in the area round Dublin known as the English Pale. In this south-eastern quadrant the lowlands were less encumbered by bog, the river system simpler, the climate slightly kinder, nucleated settlements more abundant and communications easier. Regions of special difficulty, by contrast, were the mountains that dominated the peninsulas of west Munster, west Connacht and Donegal, together with smaller uplands in the Glens of Antrim, the Mountains of Mourne and the Wicklow Mountains. Another intractable terrain-type was the drumlin belt that stretched across the north midland counties, from Down through Armagh, Monaghan, Cavan, Fermanagh, Leitrim and Sligo. This mass of intermingled small clay hills, woods, lakes and bogs was particularly unattractive to the surveyor, blocking off Ulster from the rest of the country. Its southern boundary plays a major role in the story of Irish maps.

CARTOGRAPHIC IMPLICATIONS

For every landscape there is an ideal map-scale. In much of the modern era, the most convenient scale for travellers in Ireland has been reckoned at half an inch to one statute mile. It is interesting that this was approximately the scale of the most successful topographical representation of any territory in Elizabethan Ireland, the celebrated Leix-Offaly map of the 1560s.[12] This map approximates to what might be called the 'carpet' style, in which bogs, woods, hills and farmland are all distinctively shaded or coloured, a fitting background for the territorial divisions that were later adopted as baronies. For most of the Elizabethan period such detailed coverage was beyond the resources of Anglo-Irish cartography. A more practicable approach was that of Saxton himself, in which individual names and symbols were positioned on an agnostical white background. For a provincial map in this less ambitious style the Leix-Offaly scale might be halved or halved again, varying between 1:250,000 and 1:500,000. For present purposes such scales may be described as small.

The reign of Queen Elizabeth was a time of almost continuous English effort to pacify and civilise Ireland by a mixture of war-making, colonisation and administrative reform. Yet, seen at the kind of map-scale we have been discussing, there was remarkably little change in the country's human geography, especially by comparison with the achievements of the Norman period or the decades that followed the restoration of King Charles II. This must have made it seem hardly worthwhile for maps to carry a date. It is consequently difficult to arrange surviving examples in any kind of sequence or to demonstrate their links with political or military events. From modern historical atlases it might be expected that the creation of new Irish counties in Elizabeth's reign would provide a useful chronological marker, especially in the north and west,[13] but most of these territories were so ineffective as units of local administration that cartographers tended to ignore them. For instance, Antrim and Down are thought to have been shired in about 1570, but seldom appear with county labels on maps of the 1590s and 1600s.

The physical processes of conquest and settlement were similarly inscrutable. Almost until the accession of James I, troop movements left no permanent mark on the Irish countryside. Architectural changes to defensive sites were too small to be cartographically significant, with a few rare exceptions such as Corkbeg, Co. Cork (1569),[14] and the Blackwater fort in Co. Armagh (1575).[15] The same was true of new civil settlements, which were almost invariably located at places (old monastic centres, for instance) whose names were likely to have appeared on earlier maps. When Richard Bartlett first came to notice, in 1600, this situation had finally begun to change.

REFERENCES

1. J.H. Andrews, 'Christopher Saxton and Belfast Lough', *Irish Geography*, v, 2 (1965), pp 1-6.
2. Ifor M. Evans and Heather Lawrence, *Christopher Saxton, Elizabethan map-maker* (Wakefield, 1979); William Ravenhill (ed.), *Christopher Saxton's 16th century maps: the counties of England and Wales* (Shrewsbury, 1992).
3. William Ravenhill, 'Christopher Saxton's surveying: an enigma' in Sarah Tyacke (ed.), *English map-making 1500-1650* (London, 1983), pp 112-19.
4. For examples of the earliest Irish county maps see Patrick J. O'Connor, *Seeing through counties: geography and identity in Ireland* (Newcastle West, 2006), pp 23-35.
5. John Speed, *The theatre of the empire of Great Britaine* (London, 1612).
6. Fynes Moryson, *An itinerary, containing his ten yeeres travel ...* (4 volumes, Glasgow, 1907-8), ii, p. 332.
7. Moryson, *Itinerary*, ii, p. 183.
8. Matthew Stout, *The Irish ringfort* (Dublin, 1997).
9. Tom McNeill, *Castles in Ireland: feudal power in a Gaelic world* (London, 1997).
10. T. McErlean, 'The Irish townland system of landscape organisation' in T. Reeves-Smyth and F. Hammond (eds), *Landscape archaeology of Ireland* (Oxford, 1983), pp 315-39.
11. J.P. Haughton, 'The physical environment' in Dáibhí Ó Cróinín (ed.), *A new history of Ireland*, i (Oxford, 2005), pp 32-48.
12. J.H. Andrews and Rolf Loeber, 'An Elizabethan map of Leix and Offaly: cartography, topography and architecture' in William Nolan and Timothy P. O'Neill (eds), *Offaly: history and society: interdisciplinary essays on the history of an Irish county* (Dublin, 1998), pp 243-85.
13. K.W. Nicholls, Map 5, Counties 1543-1613, in T.W. Moody, F.X. Martin and F.J. Byrne (eds), *A new history of Ireland*, ix (Oxford, 1984), p. 43.
14. PRO, MPF 1/85; Paul M. Kerrigan, *Castles and fortifications in Ireland, 1485-1945* (Cork, 1995), p. 35.
15. PRO, MPF 1/99; Kerrigan, *Castles and fortifications*, p. 5.

Chapter 2

Reluctant Geographers

The European renaissance brought a great increase in the making and use of maps for both scholarly and practical purposes. Although this trend reached England in the time of Henry VIII, the Gaelic inhabitants of Ireland were largely unaffected by it: they still had little interest in travelling to distant countries, and their native land was small enough to be familiar from first-hand knowledge or by word of mouth. In the Pale and the larger towns, where many people were of Anglo-Norman descent, English was widely spoken and English culture familiar to varying degrees. The Anglo-Irish community developed an interest in studying its own history but not, apparently, in mapping its own territory. At any rate no early map of Ireland or anywhere else has been discovered in an Irish archival context suggestive of 'old English' origin. The country was certainly devoid of instrument-makers, engravers, printers and publishers. When Queen Elizabeth's governor of Connacht recommended to the English authorities that a map of the province should be printed, it never entered his head to arrange for this to be done himself.[1] The neglect of organised geographical studies among the Palesmen was reflected in the small number of statements about the size and configuration of Ireland that emanated from this group, one of them being Edmund Campion's less than realistic assertion that the country was shaped like an egg.[2] Even when maps became important as items of display or acquisitiveness, and not just as aids to study or decision-making, no Elizabethan inhabitant of the Pale is known to have started a collection.

The people who did consult maps of Tudor Ireland were foreigners who aspired first to conquer the country and then to govern it. Continental invaders never penetrated more than a few miles inland. Their ships might carry small-scale coastal charts of western Europe, but this was a type of map that English sailors could afford to ignore, knowing the voyage to Ireland as they did from experience. When the Spaniards or Italians landed, they sometimes made localised sketch-maps of ports and harbours, a handful of which have been preserved in European record repositories.[3] For the most part, however, map historians of Elizabethan Ireland can safely concentrate their attention upon the queen's government in London, whose members and employees have left us a total of well over two hundred Irish maps. Probably a comparable number from the same period have disappeared.

GEOGRAPHY AND GOVERNMENT

Even in a civilised country, 'map-mindedness' is an attribute whose incidence varies widely and unpredictably among the population. But as England became a colonial power the development of cartographic sensitivity was encouraged by the fact that although senior members of its governing establishment spoke and wrote about Ireland at great length, few of them ever travelled there. If anyone needed maps, it was this kind of armchair expert, but the history of map-commissioning and its consequences is difficult to trace. Although the subject is mentioned in numerous official letters and despatches, such references are often seriously obscure or misleading. Thus the word 'plot' sometimes meant a map, but a plot could also be a scheme or proposal devoid of graphic content; similarly a 'description' could be either cartographic or purely verbal according to its context. However geographically informative a document may be in other respects, then, we may simply not know whether maps were used in its preparation; but in general the evidence is consistent with an increasing reliance upon cartographic aids among English public servants involved with Ireland. One small linguistic clue to this effect is a shift from the particular to the general in the application of the definite article. Thus a reader could be advised to consult 'your map', that is to say a certain map known to be in his possession, or he could be referred to 'the map', meaning any one of the relevant maps that the writer thought were available to him. The second formula suggests more strongly than the first that maps were widely available. A difficulty in collecting and evaluating such references is that as maps became more familiar, so their existence was increasingly taken for granted as simply not worth mentioning — any more than a letter-writer would mention the clerk who transcribed his original draft. This trend was fully established by the end of Elizabeth's reign. For instance, in Fynes Moryson's account of the Irish wars, a major source for the next two chapters of this book, there is not a single reference to any of the maps that must surely have been consulted by the people he was writing about and presumably by himself.[4]

To Henry VIII, maps were both novel and important. For the cartographic attitudes of Edward VI and Mary I there is little evidence either way. In Elizabeth's case the verdict is mixed.[5] The queen was sometimes said to have asked her Irish ministers for maps, but this may simply have reflected the wishes of those who drafted her letters, and it must be significant that no strictly royal collection survives from her reign, or even any references to such a collection. Maps assumed to have been meant for the queen are now found, if at all, in the 'state papers' preserved by her privy council, or among the personal possessions of individual statesmen. The best documented member of this group was the queen's secretary and later lord treasurer, William Cecil (also known as Lord Burghley from the barony he acquired in 1571), who was the mainstay of Elizabeth's government from the beginning of her reign until his death in 1598. Burghley's pleasure in map-reading was inherited to some degree and in a slightly different form by his son and successor, Robert Cecil.[6] Without these two powerful enthusiasts, present-day cartographic historians of Tudor Ireland would have disappointingly little raw material.

Among English administrators resident in Dublin, differences of map-consciousness are even more striking. This makes it unfortunate that their terms of office were comparatively short, partly no doubt because most Englishmen disliked having to live in Ireland. Some of them were cartographic philistines whose spatial thought-processes fed on memories or mental images derived from travelling through the country or listening to verbal testimony. If these officials ever called for cartographic assistance it was probably at the request of Burghley and his fellow councillors rather than on their own initiative. Some of their Irish-based colleagues were more sympathetic. Lord deputies with varying degrees of positive interest in maps were the earl of Sussex (1558-65), Sir Henry Sidney (1565-71, 1575-80), Sir William Fitzwilliam (1571-5, 1588-94) and Sir John Perrot (1584-8). Among Irish secretaries of state the leader in this respect appears to have been the unusually long-serving Sir Geoffrey Fenton. Map-minded provincial governors were Sir Richard Bingham in Connacht (1584-96) and the brothers Sir John and Sir Thomas Norris in Munster (1597-9) — the province whose future governor, Sir George Carew (1600-3), eventually outstripped them all.[7] However modern their cartographic philosophy in other ways, none of these pundits ever tried to establish a permanent national map-making department in anticipation of the Ordnance Survey. What they usually did when the demand for maps exceeded the supply was complain.

PROBLEMS OF CLASSIFICATION

We must now ask what kinds of cartography Elizabethan officialdom considered useful, and what kinds of skill were needed to produce them. Here the principal danger to historians is anachronism. Thus one problem in studying this early period is that little attention had yet been paid to classifying maps. Consider for instance the volume described in a list of state papers as 'an old book of maps of Ireland that was my lord treasurer Burghley's'.[8] Luckily we know the contents of this book, at least by their titles. Its compiler had refrained from juxtaposing representations of different countries, but otherwise he seems to have worked at random, interspersing individual Irish counties with baronies, provinces, castles and in one case the whole kingdom. (Burghley's concern for counties reflected his experience of the Saxton era in England: in other collections, as already noted, Irish county maps were comparatively rare.) Carew in the 1600s was a more methodical curator and cataloguer. His categories were, in order: Ireland in general, the provinces, miscellaneous small regions (including counties), forts, cities, towns, castles, military actions.[9] This taxonomy is paralleled, in Carew's collection and elsewhere, by the titles of Elizabethan Irish maps extant today, and also in surviving cross-channel correspondence requesting, promising or enclosing maps. Such sources show how cartographers almost always chose their title from the name of a single pre-existing region, usually a political or administrative unit, native or colonial, old or new. Natural entities, such as Lough Neagh or the Bays of Donegal and Sligo, are less common though by no means unknown.

Maps might occasionally be criticised by contemporaries for inaccuracy but never for their design or subject-matter. The nearest anyone came to thematic analysis on such occasions was a request for 'some larger and more particular description topographically' than was in 'the usual chards'.[10] As for praise, the award for explicitness must go to Humphrey Willis's map of Inishowen, Co. Donegal, in which the recipient could see 'both how the forces are dispersed in several garrisons, and also how strongly it is enclosed with rivers, loughs, bogs and forts'.[11] These comments suggest, by what they omit as well as what they include, a lack of any clear distinction between military and political approaches to map-making. Ireland's lord deputies and provincial governors were expected to be equally competent at presiding over councils of state and at leading troops against the enemy — doubtless consulting the same kind of small- or medium-scale map in either case. Hills, bogs and forests were equally significant politically (as boundary-markers) and strategically (as obstacles to movement); also economically, as guides to local resources, though economic productivity was never much of an issue in Ireland. Such maps cannot be pigeonholed: the only way to characterise them is as 'regional'.

MOTIVES AND METHODS IN REGIONAL CARTOGRAPHY

How were regional maps produced? Not by taking measurements, except in a few unusual cases mentioned elsewhere. The mere act of travel, whatever its immediate purpose, would yield a ready impression of regional topology in the sequence of landmarks along each route, and for off-route landmarks the observer could record the distinction between left and right, near and far. Estimates of distance could be derived from travel times, compass directions from the position of the sun and stars (with scale lines and north-indicators inserted accordingly) — though it is unlikely that Irish travellers gave any thought to astronomical latitude at this period, let alone longitude. All this could be supplemented by similar information supplied in speech or writing by other travellers. Careful observers might be suspicious of maps made 'by report' rather than 'by view', but most readers could probably see little difference, and some cartographers made no attempt to hide their dependence on other witnesses. Thomas Cusack is a good example. In 1564 he told William Cecil how he 'got the dean of Armagh and others of knowledge to confer with me for making of a perfect plat and description of every part of that country'.[12] Two years later, his 'description' of Ulster (presumably a map) was said to be 'in as good order and sort as I could call to my remembrance'.[13] Testimony and memory were hardly the best of cartographic sources, but they were better than nothing.

Regional mapping along these lines may appear simple enough, but it needed a genuine geographical talent, perhaps as much inherited as acquired, and most likely to be found among merchants and soldiers — in Ireland more often the latter. Certainly the output of Irish regional maps appears to have grown with the size of the occupying army. Nobody won fame by practising this rather basic kind of cartography. Some senior officers almost went out of their way to avoid naming the juniors who did the work, while not above claiming most of the credit for themselves. Not even cartographers of the highest calibre were immune from anonymity. When English privy councillors were drafting a letter about Robert Lythe in 1568 nobody could remember his name, only that he was 'skilful in the description of countries by measure according to the rules of cosmography'.[14] Unfortunately, many surveyors and draughtsmen took the hint and refrained from signing their maps. If names do occur it is seldom more than once, hardly a token of sustained professional commitment. Such loners were John Tomkin, Captain John Baxter, John Thomas, Captain Nicholas Dawtrey, Captain James Carlyle, Thomas Fleming and James Grafton — none of whom has found his way into any modern carto-biographical reference book.[15] This rather dispersed pattern of recruitment helps to explain the absence of a distinctively Irish cartographic style.

The presence of three army captains in the foregoing group raises the issue of social class. A cartographically active member of a propertied family was more likely to figure in his own writings or those of his contemporaries than a practitioner with nothing to offer but his talent. A case in point is John Browne, whose survey of Mayo dates from 1584. Without his possession of a landed estate in the area he was mapping, we should probably never have known his name.[16] As it is, he and his nephew (also a cartographer) are familiar figures.

MAPS FOR SPECIALISTS

After the region, the second most common map-subject in Elizabethan Ireland was the single strongpoint — perhaps a walled town, perhaps a free-standing castle or, increasingly towards the end of the reign, an earth-banked artillery fort. Plans of defensive works were drawn to seek expert military approval for their design; also to estimate the cost of construction and maintenance and the size of the necessary garrison. Such plans were often made by the engineers who supervised the building of the fort. They required a carefully measured survey with accurate instruments and a large scale of protraction. Their authors were highly skilled professionals, following the tide of war from one theatre to another, no doubt looking forward to early retirement and a more peaceful way of life. Engineers' names were correspondingly better known than those of map-compilers, both to contemporaries and to historians. Robert Lythe, Edmund York, and Paul Ivy were all employed to map fortifications in both Ireland and England. Lythe had also worked in Calais.[17]

Less familiar in sixteenth-century Ireland (though later to become overwhelmingly plentiful) was the property map. The normal method of dealing with the various rebellions of the Tudor and Stuart periods was by confiscating land from actual or potential rebels and redistributing it among new proprietors loyal to the English crown, usually with the object of encouraging settlement by British immigrants. Inventories of landed property formed an essential part of such transactions and it eventually became usual for these to include the taking of precise measurements and the drawing of large-scale maps. In fact the Irish official establishment had included a 'surveyor-general' since the 1540s but for a long time his duties were archival, inquisitorial and legal rather than cartographic. Nor did Ireland share in the tradition of estate mapping that was to develop quite rapidly in Christopher Saxton's England. It was not until the Munster confiscations of the 1580s that we hear of any Irish property maps, and then there were only four surveyors engaged in making them. Of these John Lawson and Richard Whittaker disappeared after a few months, while Arthur Robins was dead from unknown causes by 1591. Only Francis Jobson remained in the public eye.[18]

Narrative maps, our fourth and last category, were usually records of a military campaign, a siege or a battle. Such memorials were comparatively uncommon, especially since the army could not be relied upon to record failures as comprehensively as successes. The truth is that Irish warfare gave the cartographer few spectacular set-pieces of any kind. All the same, the best of our few narrative maps are invaluable additions to historical knowledge, whatever their shortcomings geographically and artistically.

With respect to the foregoing classification we must note that once a competent surveyor had been enticed to Ireland, it would be worth employing him on any task that might present itself regardless of his original speciality. This may help to explain a certain tendency for cartographers to become personally associated with individual officers of the highest seniority: Robert Lythe with Sir Henry Sidney; the two John Brownes (uncle and nephew) with Sir Richard Bingham; on a more localised scale, John Thomas with Captain (later Sir) John Dowdall, William Jones with Sir George Carew and, as we shall see, Richard Bartlett with Lord Mountjoy. In general, Irish cartography was at its most successful when a surveyor trained in measuring small areas was given reason and opportunity to adapt his technique for an all-purpose regional map — more accurate and perhaps covering a larger area than the 'topological' outlines described above. The best example was Lythe, who arrived in 1567 to map 'the north' but was soon defeated by its prevailing insecurity. Whereupon Sidney, with rare foresight, set him to survey the rest of the country, which he did to great effect, impressing posterity as the Irish equivalent of Christopher Saxton, whom he actually preceded by several years. Poor health drove Lythe back to England in 1571, apparently for good, without having carried his surveys very far into the northern drumlin belt or beyond. At home he recovered sufficiently to map the Isle of Sheppey and its fortifications.[19]

The best-known immigrant specialist in property mapping was Francis Jobson, who differed from Lythe in having taken up permanent residence among the Irish. He hoped to become accepted as a military engineer and the commander of a fort, though he failed to convince at least one English expert of his abilities in this sphere.[20] Jobson also suffered from never managing to attach himself to any senior office-holder for any length of time. On a purely cartographic plane, he showed unusual talent in reducing, combining and augmenting his patchy Munster surveys to make a general map of the province,[21] but his more conventional achievement took place further north. It stemmed from an attempt by successive lord deputies to regularise the administration of Ulster, and particularly to define the territorial jurisdictions of Hugh O'Neill and his neighbour

Turlough O'Neill in the heart of the province. This naturally prompted Burghley to request a map of the affected area.[22] In 1590, as it happened, the circumstances were unusually favourable: Hugh O'Neill had been proclaiming his loyalty to the crown (he was encouraged by being made earl of Tyrone five years earlier), and he apparently agreed to furnish the government's surveyor with guides and escorts. Even so, Jobson reported being 'every hour' in fear of his life and was unable to put either Fermanagh or Donegal convincingly upon the map.[23]

Elizabethan narrative cartography was well represented by John Thomas, who drew lively picture-plans of the battle of Ballyshannon in the autumn of 1593 and the siege of Enniskillen Castle in the following year.[24] Less successfully, he also mapped Fermanagh and its lakes, the adjacent territories being 'left as blanks, for that I never viewed them'.[25]

THE PERSONNEL FACTOR

Nobody was available to finish what Lythe, Jobson and Thomas had started, and indeed the shortage of cartographers in Ireland is a motif that runs through the whole of Elizabeth's reign. Here are a few comments on it, all addressed either individually to Burghley or to the English privy council as a whole. [26]

(1) Earl of Essex, 8 May 1575: 'I cannot send your lordship the plot of Ulster.'

(2) Sir Warham St. Leger, 20 April 1582: 'There is no man here skilful to make a map as it ought to be.'

(3) Munster commissioners, 16 February 1587: 'We have no other skilful measurers now in this land, but the said Mr Robins & Jobson.'

(4) Sir John Perrot, 27 March 1587: 'Neither is there anyone thereabout can draw the plot.'

(5) Sir William Fitzwilliam, 20 July 1593. 'Touching your honour's pleasure for a plot of Ulster there is not any here that can do it ... .'

(6) Sir William Fitzwilliam, 31 July 1593: '... truly I know not yet how to get your lordship another [map of Ulster], since was now never a man that can do it.'

(7) Lord Burgh, September 1597: 'It is not in my power to send your lordship a topographical description of the places, none that I can meet being skilful in lines with pencil and by scale to describe them.'

There is nothing unexpected about any of these complaints. Hazards for strangers surveying in Ireland make a formidable list: the wet climate and poor visibility; the bad state of the roads; the lack of comfortable accommodation; the threat of violence from the local population; the difficulty of obtaining guides and interpreters; and the uncertainty of prompt and adequate remuneration for work not routinely covered by the government's regular annual expenditure. Other problems were more professional in character. Then as later, there seems to have been no shortage of ink and paper in Ireland, but remote areas like Connacht were 'subject to the want of many instruments & colours fit for the same, which indeed is not to be had'.[27] However well equipped for field work, surveyors often lacked confidence in their ability as draughtsmen or colourists. Lythe found that 'here is no good painter in the land to set it so well forth as I would have it, save only to be done of mine own hands'.[28] Others confessed their maps to be 'crudely handled', 'rough hewn', 'wrought in some haste' and 'not ... artificially done'.[29]

MAPPING FROM MAPS

All the more reason, then, for maximising the effectiveness of what had actually been achieved, and in particular for combining fragmentary or unfinished maps into the least unsatisfactory attainable synthesis. Compilation needed a different kind of skill from normal surveying, and some field-workers may have preferred to avoid it for fear of introducing new errors. To judge from the many maps annotated in his handwriting, Burghley himself was influenced by this rather pessimistic philosophy. Faced with yet another Irish crisis, his custom was to request an original map of the trouble-spot in question, at the same time consulting as many older maps as he could find of the same area. He never arranged for these maps to be digested into a single Irish atlas. In fact it is noticeable that the most active periods of secondary Irish map compilation fell outside the years of Burghley's greatest authority. One was in the 1550s and early 1560s, when serviceable all-Ireland maps were pieced together by Laurence Nowell and Gerard Mercator. The other was after Burghley's replacement as England's chief minister by his son Robert, inaugurating the heyday of two able compilers who may never have set foot in Ireland, John Norden and John Speed.[30]

Official attitudes aside, two conditions were required for success as a compiler. One was residence in Ireland, if not for field work then at least to pick the brains of possible informants. The other was access to a full range of cartographic raw materials. It would have been difficult to meet both these requirements if the witnesses were in one country and the maps in another. We know that many Irish maps made their way to England at an early stage. How many remained in Ireland? Direct evidence on this subject is interesting, but limited in quantity. In Connacht Bingham was apparently unable in 1592 to provide Burghley with a duplicate of John Browne's recently-supplied provincial map.[31] Less than a year later, the lord deputy declared himself unable to produce a replacement for Jobson's Ulster. Of course, not relinquishing a map and not possessing it might be two different things, but since the deputy wrongly described the Ulster map as including 'part of Maguire's country', it does seem unlikely that he still had access to a copy.[32] Later evidence points to the continued or renewed availability of Jobsonian maps — in the possession of their original author, for instance. All in all, it seems clear from these divergent examples that no comprehensive lord deputy's map library was acknowledged to exist in Dublin.

Then there is the testimony of surviving specimens, which show beyond doubt how few of Ireland's cartographers were able to profit fully from the work of their predecessors. Thus the representation of Leix and Offaly in Lythe's national map of 1571 differs considerably — and for the worse — from an excellent anonymous regional map of those territories that can be safely dated about ten years earlier.[33] The maps of Munster based on Jobson's plantation surveys show many large areas of unconfiscated land as almost blank, no use having been made of Lythe's excellent 'Single draght of Mounster'. Browne's Connacht, with its admirably realistic western 'bulge', was obviously unknown to Mercator, Boazio, Norden, Speed and all their contemporaries. John Thomas knew little or nothing of earlier maps, and his own version of the Fermanagh lakes had no influence on later representations of Ulster. Speed was apparently unaware of Norden's Irish achievements. Lythe by contrast left an indelible mark on later Irish cartography but most of his influence was exercised at several removes, and his disciples fell into two groups who seemed to be unaware of each other's existence.[34] By Bartlett's time the fog appears to have been lifting, as we shall see.

REFERENCES

1. J.H. Andrews, 'Sir Richard Bingham and the mapping of western Ireland', *Proceedings of the Royal Irish Academy*, ciii C, 3 (2003), p. 85.
2. Edmund Campion, *A historie of Ireland written in the yeare 1571* (Dublin, 1809), p. 1.
3. Frederick M. Jones, 'The plan of the Golden Fort at Smerwick, 1580', *The Irish Sword*, ii (1954), pp 41-2; Enrique García Hernán, 'Philip II's forgotten armada' in Hiram Morgan (ed.), *The battle of Kinsale* (Bray, 2004), p. 54; Ciaran O'Scea, 'Spanish map of the siege of Kinsale', ibid., pp 364-5.
4. Fynes Moryson, *An itinerary containing his ten yeeres travel ...*, 4 volumes (Glasgow, 1907-8). On Moryson's reticence about maps in general, see Catherine Delano-Smith, 'Milieus of mobility: itineraries, route maps, and road maps' in James R. Akerman (ed.), *Cartographies of travel and navigation* (Chicago, 2006), pp 25-6.
5. Peter Barber, 'Was Elizabeth I interested in maps — did it matter?', *Transactions of the Royal Historical Society*, xiv (2004), pp 185-98.
6. R.A. Skelton and John Summerson, *A description of maps and architectural drawings in the collection made by William Cecil, first Baron Burghley now at Hatfield House* (Oxford, 1971).
7. William O'Sullivan, 'George Carew's Irish maps', *Long Room (Bulletin of the Friends of the Library of Trinity College, Dublin)*, xxvi-xxvii (1983), pp 15-25.
8. Lambeth Palace, MS 619/153: 'A note of Mr. Wilson's mappes of Irland'.
9. Lambeth Palace, MS 637; T.D. Hardy and J.S. Brewer, *Report to the Right Hon. the master of the rolls upon the Carte and Carew papers in the Bodleian and Lambeth libraries* (London, 1864), pp 94-5.
10. SP 63/27/2, William Cecil to Sidney, 6 January 1569.
11. Humphrey Willis to Robert Cecil, 15 May 1601, *CSPI, 1600-1*, p. 339.
12. SP 63/10/38.
13. SP 63/18/21.
14. SP 63/24/29.
15. PRO, MPF 1/277 (Tomkin, *c.*1571); SP 63/179/72 (Carlyle, 1595); *CSPI, 1586-8*, p. 253 (Grafton, 1587); *1588-92*, p. 230 (Fleming, 1589); *1598-9*, pp 162-4 (Dawtrey); NMM, MS P.49/7 (Baxter, *c.*1600); MS P.49/21 (Thomas, 1594).
16. Martin J. Blake, 'A map of part of the county of Mayo in 1584: with notes thereon, and an account of the author, and his descendants', *Journal of the Galway Archaeological and Historical Society*, v, 3 (1905), pp 145-58.
17. Sarah Bendall, *Dictionary of land surveyors and local map-makers of Great Britain and Ireland, 1530-1850*, 2 vols (London, 1997).
18. J.H. Andrews, *Plantation acres: an historical study of the Irish land surveyor and his maps* (Belfast, 1985), ch. 2.
19. J.H. Andrews, 'The Irish surveys of Robert Lythe', *Imago Mundi*, xix (1965), pp 22-31.
20. Edmund York to lord deputy, 6 August 1591, SP 63/160/7 I.
21. Earlier version: TCD, MS 1209/36; NMM, MS P.49/22. Later version: NLI, 16 B. 13; TCD, MS 1209/37; NMM, MS P.49/18; NMM, MS P.49/20; NMM, MS P.49/27.
22. Lord deputy to Burghley, 9 August 1590, SP 63/154/3.
23. Jobson to Queen Elizabeth, [*c.*1598], SP 63/202iv/83.
24. BL, Cotton MS Aug. I, ii, 38 (Belleek); Cotton MS Aug. I, ii, 39 (Enniskillen).

25. NMM, MS P.49/21. Other quasi-cartographic representations of military engagements in Elizabethan Ireland include Bearhaven 1602, *Pacata Hibernia; or, a history of the wars in Ireland ...* (Dublin, 1810), iii, p. 526; Blackwater fort 1597, TCD, MS 1209/34; Caher castle 1599, *Pacata Hibernia*, i, p. 76; Carrigfoyle 1580, *Pacata Hibernia*, i, p. 120; Castlemaine 1572, PRO, MPF 1/78; Dunboy 1602, *Pacata Hibernia*, iii, p. 558; Glin castle 1600, TCD, MS 1209/60; Smerwick 1580, NMM, MS P.49/31 and PRO, MPF 1/75; Wicklow, 1599, TCD, MS 1209/12 (for which see Timothy R. Jackson, 'A Wicklow skirmish in word and image: time and space in TCD MS 1209/12', *Word and Image*, xxi, 1 (2005), pp 56-78); Yellow Ford 1598, TCD, MS 1209/35.
26. (1) SP 63/51/9; (2) SP 63/91/41; (3) SP 63/128/44; (4) SP 65/5/12; (5) SP 63/170/47; (6) SP 63/170/58; (7) SP 63/200/118.
27. Bingham to Burghley, 8 February 1587, SP 63/128/34.
28. SP 63/31/36.
29. William Wynter to Burghley, Smerwick, 24 December 1580, SP 63/79/35; John Browne to Francis Walsingham, Co. Mayo, 10 June 1585, SP 63/117/16; Bingham to Burghley, Ardnaree, 8 February 1587, SP 63/128/34; Bingham to Burghley, Connacht, 8 February 1591, SP 63/157/11.
30. J.H. Andrews, *Shapes of Ireland: maps and their makers 1564-1839* (Dublin, 1997), chs 2, 4; J.H. Andrews, 'John Norden's maps of Ireland', *Proceedings of the Royal Irish Academy*, c, C, 5 (2000), pp 159-206.
31. George Bingham to Burghley, 25 October 1592, SP 63/167/11.
32. Lord deputy to Burghley, 20 July 1593, SP 63/170/47.
33. J.H. Andrews and Rolf Loeber, 'An Elizabethan map of Leix and Offaly: cartography, topography and architecture' in William Nolan and Timothy P. O'Neill (eds), *Offaly: history and society: interdisciplinary essays on the history of an Irish county* (Dublin, 1998), pp 243-85.
34. J.H. Andrews, 'Baptista Boazio's map of Ireland', *Long Room*, i (1970), pp 29-36.

Chapter 3

A Bartlett Chronology: the First Two Years

Cartographers in Elizabethan Ireland differed greatly in talent and experience, but in one respect they are all the same: almost nothing is known of their private lives. The subject of this book is one more case in point. Outside his maps, only two indubitable contemporary or near-contemporary references to Richard Bartlett have ever been discovered. Luckily, as Gerard Hayes-McCoy was the first to point out, Bartlett's work can be identified from its distinctive style, so in one respect it hardly matters that only four of his maps are signed.[1] Each of these signatures is spelt 'Barthelet' or 'Bartheletus', which might be taken as indicative of a French origin. Equally interesting is the fact that three of the signatures carry the suffix 'Norf'. At this time Norfolk was the most prosperous county in England and also the second-furthest county from Dublin. Perhaps Bartlett's references to it are a hint that crossing the Irish Sea had given him something of a 'culture shock'. It could also be a sign that he had left home in the comparatively recent past.

Hayes-McCoy looked hard for Bartlett family antecedents in England, concentrating particularly on the county of Norfolk and on professions associated with the graphic arts. No convincing candidates emerged. In Ireland the most likely possibility at first sight was one Mr. Bartlett, the lord deputy's cornet or subaltern of horse referred to in 1601.[2] This theory has had its supporters, but the full name of the officer in question is later given as Henry Barkeley.[3] There is another case that Hayes-McCoy does not mention. Sir Thomas Norris, lord president of Munster, writing to Robert Cecil on 14 May 1597 from Shandon near Cork, recommended 'Richard Bartelett, a young English gentleman', who had spent the last four or five years in Spain. Since becoming known to Norris, he had shown himself 'very skilful and conformable to Her Majesty's laws in coming to service and sermons, not refusing to take the oath of supremacy, and giving many other good testimonies of his loyal disposition'.[4] What was the nature of this Bartlett's 'skill'? Was he a Catholic or former Catholic, or did it just appear possible that he might be? And what had he been doing in Spain? It seems unlikely that an Englishman would have had much chance of practising cartography there when the two countries were officially at war. But here at least is a person of the right name and age-group who had apparently achieved some kind of official recognition in Ireland. After a period of residence in Spain, and with his loyalty in need of proof, such a man might well call himself 'Norfolkiensis' as a credible but not-too-emphatic method of affirming his Englishness.

THE COTTON MAP

It was during the war against Hugh O'Neill, second earl of Tyrone, that Richard Bartlett's identity as a cartographer first emerged. At this time English strategy for pacifying the province of Ulster was composed of three elements. One was an invasion from the south-east personally led by Charles Blount, Baron Mountjoy, who had become the queen's deputy for Ireland in February 1600; the other lines of attack were from the east at Carrickfergus, where Sir Arthur Chichester had been installed as governor a year earlier; and from Lough Foyle, where Sir Henry Docwra established a new English base in May 1600. Docwra had his own map-makers, effective enough without being in Bartlett's league.[5] No maps are mentioned in Chichester's correspondence, but there is one, of Lough Neagh, that may possibly be connected with his campaign.

Bartlett's association was with Mountjoy. His first surviving production is an uncoloured but finely drawn map signed 'Rich. Barthelet Norf desc:

A°1600', here designated as 'Cotton' after its early seventeenth-century owner (plate 1).[6] It has a scale and a compass indicator (with north at the top) but no title. The area represented stretches from Dromore westwards to a point near the present town of Caledon and latitudinally from the neighbourhood of Dundalk to the southern end of Lough Neagh, stopping short of O'Neill's principal base at Dungannon, which was presumably regarded as out of reach. The north-westward thrust of the map is emphasised by the flanking positions of the two insets: one standing vacant in the upper right corner; another, diagonally opposite and with its own scale-line, showing the new English fort of Mountnorris.

Before drawing this map Bartlett had obviously acquired a certain amount of cartographic experience. One of his personal trademarks — the scale-bar drawn as a picture of a three-dimensional block rather than a simple rectangle — was already in evidence. Other features of his style were still evolving: the Cotton map is fussier in both script and settlement-symbolism than his later work, and gives little hint of his mature talent for hill-shading. This suggestion of rapid development, such as it is, seems consistent with our picture of a relatively young man.

Bartlett seems unlikely to have been present when rebel forces were engaged in the Moyry pass on 17 May 1600. At any rate his treatment of this critical area is rather sketchy. It includes short detached stretches of the Threemile Water and Fourmile Water where they intersect the road, but not the upper or lower courses of these streams — the only occurrence in his work of linear features deliberately left unfinished. He also omits the woods encumbering the pass, which received substantial attention in at least one contemporary account of the action,[7] and he is wrong in making the main road into Ulster run east rather than west of Faughart Hill, an error he corrected in the following year.

Apart from passes through the woods, the only lines of communication in the Cotton map are apparently routes followed on some particular occasion rather than elements in a general system of highways. Thus the Faughart and other roads are best interpreted as Mountjoy's route from Dundalk to Newry and thence north-westwards, probably not in May but on a second journey several months later. The mapped line ends about half way along the direct route from Newry to Armagh at a new fort that was named Mountnorris after one of the lord deputy's military heroes. The fort was actually built between September and November; it may have been still incomplete when Bartlett drew the Cotton map, which differs somewhat at this point from the plan he devoted to it two years later, notably in the absence of a central angle-bastion on the fort's eastern perimeter. Mountjoy scored no decisive victory in 1600. His return journey took him to Narrow Water castle at the head of Carlingford Lough, and thence to the walled town of Carlingford, where the routes traced by Bartlett come to an end. Perhaps this is where the map was drawn.[8]

Mountnorris appears well represented in Bartlett's inset but it was Captain Richard Hansard who took credit for drawing 'divers plots' of the fort and it is possible that the Cotton version was a copy of Hansard's work.[9] Mountjoy's failure to mention Bartlett on this occasion anticipates an incident of May 1602 when the general, preparing for another northern journey (and having now had several opportunities for observing his cartographer's talents), complained that the only available engineer was 'a Dutchman whom I have suffered to go to Connacht'.[10] Again no names are given. Two months later, the only experts mentioned as capable of designing harbour fortifications in Ireland were Josias Bodley and Paul Ivy.[11] Although described by at least one modern historian as an engineer,[12] Bartlett was evidently a recorder of fortifications rather than a creator.

Another witness who ignores Bartlett is Mountjoy's secretary. It was during this first Ulster campaign that the deputy decided to employ Fynes Moryson 'in the writing of the history or journal of Irish affairs'.[13] Perhaps at the same time he also thought of getting someone else to provide this document with a complementary graphic record of forthcoming events.[14] Unfortunately there is no evidence of any collaboration between writer and map-maker. Not expecting readers to consult a good map, Moryson generally avoided minor placenames, and when he did use them it was without checking whether or not Bartlett had done so. Examples are Newcastle in O'Dogherty's country, Loughlurken near Armagh, Clancarvell somewhere in south Co. Armagh or south Co. Monaghan, St. Patrick's Well and Russellstown near Downpatrick, Donanury near Newry, Rawlaghtany near Armagh, and Dunnman near Derry, all of them absent from Bartlett's maps.[15]

EXCURSIONS SOUTH AND NORTH

During the winter of 1600-1 Mountjoy led his troops in a complicated series of expeditions through Meath, Kildare, Westmeath, King's County and Louth. If Bartlett was present on these occasions he left no sign. There is nothing odd about his silence. An end-of-century cartographic hiatus for the area in question is broadly consistent with the previous course of events in Ireland: since the surveys of Robert Lythe, thirty years earlier, most government officers would have regarded the Pale and its borderlands as sufficiently well known for practical purposes.

The question of Bartlett's employment between map-making assignments brings us to the first of his two appearances in the contemporary or near-contemporary written record. It comes from the Irish treasurer at war's accounts for the period 1 April 1601 to 31 March 1602.

> Gifts and rewards. Richard Bartlett late lieutenant to Sir John Brockett Knight in reward for his charges being sent for from Duncannon and employed both in the north and at the siege of Kinsale and giving his attendance on the lord deputy till his return to Dublin. £20.[16]

Here, once and for all, Bartlett's credentials are plain to see. So far, at any rate, he had acted not as a civilian specialist with a loose attachment to the army in the manner of doctors, chaplains and secretaries, but as a serving soldier, presumably employed on ordinary regimental duties whenever there was no call upon his special skills. There is no need to infer that 'giving attendance' involved anything more than this. Bartlett's comparatively modest rank also explains the lack of other references to the man himself, because only captains and above were customarily named in Elizabethan army lists. Nor was he senior enough to address letters to the kind of exalted personage whose correspondence would be preserved for posterity — differing in this respect from freelance practitioners such as Lythe and Jobson. Whether the phrase 'late lieutenant' implied a change of rank or status (as distinct from a change of posting) is impossible to say. Bartlett might have been expected to achieve promotion in the course of the war, but no captain of his name is known to appear in any army list.[17] Yet if he had given up regular service after the battle of Kinsale we might have hoped to find evidence of further 'gifts and rewards' for his later maps.

Bartlett's next two subjects, Duncannon and Lough Neagh, will have to be considered together. Duncannon in Co. Wexford was an English fort built between 1587 and 1590 on the east side of Waterford harbour, using a natural promontory generally regarded for military purposes as part of Munster rather than Leinster. In June 1601 Sir John Brockett was on his way to take command of this post and Lieutenant Bartlett might have been expected to arrive there at about the same time. Was he directed to practise his craft in this strategically important area? It was ten years since Duncannon is known to have been mapped,[18] so perhaps the time had come for something more up-to-date. On 25 July Brockett drew Robert Cecil's attention to just this point: 'That your honour may the better take knowledge of the fort, the harbour, with every creek [and] the country wherein the fort doth stand with every village within eight or ten miles, ... I will make you an exact plot or map truly made to a scale.'[19] As Elizabethan cartographic promises go, this was impressively definite. If it ever existed, Brockett's map would have been bounded by limits in the neighbourhood of Waterford city, Hook Head and Bannow Bay (fig. 1). The words 'truly made to a scale' laid claim to professional competence and 'every village' seemed to promise a kind of topographical map that was actually rather uncommon in Ireland. It is typical of high-level military

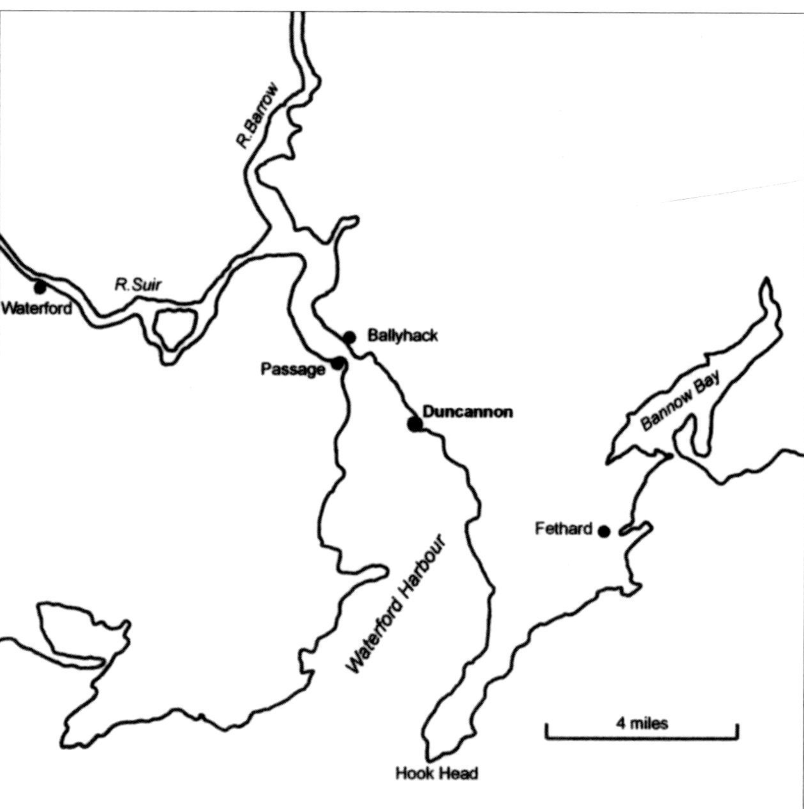

Fig. 1: Waterford Harbour and Duncannon fort.

correspondence that no cartographer's name appears, but surely the lieutenant and not the constable may be assumed to have done the work. In fact the only map that survives from the time and place in question is a scaled plan of the fort (sadly without the surrounding countryside), unsigned and undated but indisputably from Bartlett's hand, and well up to his later standard apart from the absence of colour — an understandable omission at this distance from urban amenities (plate 2).[20]

Chronologically, the foregoing interpretation is hard to reconcile with one of the two representations of Lough Neagh that survive from this period. Although without date or signature, this parchment map was almost certainly drawn by Bartlett (plate 3).[21] Its most explicit inscription associates Sir Arthur Chichester with the river of Massareene, 'out of which the Governor of Knockfergus disembarketh for the Clanno [Clonoe]'. Here then is a celebration in miniature of English naval power with echoes of Chichester's earlier war service at sea. The map in question is unornamented and rapidly drawn, as if the author was saving himself for the lord deputy's achievements rather than those of a subordinate commander. Another sign of haste is that the scale appears to have been wrongly calculated.

Since it says nothing of an English presence at Toome or of the new fort ('Mountjoy') on the western shore, Bartlett's Lough Neagh map must date from before July 1602. Early in September of the previous year Chichester took a 'perfect view' of the most convenient loughside situation for a new base, but Bartlett makes no attempt to pin-point the locality in question (wherever it was), which might reasonably have been expected to appear on any contemporaneous map of the lake.[22] This map also omits Charlemont, overlooking the east bank of the Blackwater since June 1602, but it does record a fort across the river. The latter might be 'Fort Burroughs' built by lord deputy Thomas Burgh in 1597 but shown by Bartlett five years later as ruined; alternatively, it might be Mountjoy's new Blackwater fort of 'the Mullin', an identification that would give the Lough Neagh map a useful *terminus post quem* at mid-July 1601. Any cartographer's portrayal of single fortifications on a small- or medium-scale regional map must obviously be treated with suspicion as a record of architectural detail; one can only say that Bartlett's fort-symbol, with its two bastions pointing away from the river, resembles Burgh's earlier construction rather than the Mullin. This interpretation leaves us free to date the map either before or after July 1601.

Present or future crossings of Lough Neagh from east to west were a *leitmotif* of Chichester's correspondence in 1601-2, though he never entered into topographical detail and we can only assume that the unnamed Irish forts or sconces that he mentions on 14 May 1601 are those described by Bartlett as 'lately built' west of the lake.[23] At that time Chichester's attacks had not yet become a routine, to judge from the content of the map — and indeed from its existence, because Bartlett has singled out one particular occasion without seeing any need to distinguish it from earlier or later events. It is also significant that only one boat is shown, a galley with ten sets of oars. This may have been 'the great boat' or queen's boat of 14 May, but it does not look like the thirty-ton barque that Chichester had available in the following year.[24] Considered in isolation, the most likely date for the Lough Neagh map is May 1601, but in the light of other circumstances it may have to be placed a few weeks later.

In any attempt to correlate the Duncannon and Lough Neagh maps, the following hypotheses are best avoided. (1) Bartlett travelled from Ulster to Co. Wexford and back again before making his appearance at Kinsale. Objection: this is an awkwardly complicated sequence of events that finds no warrant in the treasurer's account quoted above. (2) The missing map of the Duncannon district was drawn by somebody else after Bartlett's departure from the fort. Objection: cartographers were not so plentiful in Ireland that we should willingly postulate two of them at work within the same few weeks in the same remote corner of the country. (3) Bartlett had already drawn the Duncannon map some time before Brockett offered it to Cecil. Objection: if the map already existed, Brockett would surely just have sent it, without first promising to 'make' it. A more likely scenario would be that Bartlett drew the Duncannon fort plan before 25 July, that Brockett's announcement drew attention to a talented cartographer available for more important service, and that Bartlett was accordingly summoned to Ulster, abandoning his unfinished map of the Duncannon environs — which after all does not survive. In August he would have completed two assignments, first the hastily drawn Lough Neagh map and then the map of south-east Ulster discussed below.

These difficulties may be mitigated by examining the second of the two Lough Neagh maps that belong to the period under consideration.[25] This is not in Bartlett's style. It may be called the 'Fugos' map after its name for three small islands that Bartlett leaves anonymous in Brookish Bay.[26] Though by no means identical, the two maps have several non-essential features in common. Both make the Rabbit Point and Stanierds Point peninsulas longer and sharper than they should be, both introduce a fictitious river connecting the Bann and the Blackwater, and both name a relatively unimportant church (Mauhern) in the neighbourhood of this river. The Fugos map is almost certainly earlier than Bartlett's. It identifies certain sites west of the lake as 'where Tyrone fortifieth'; Bartlett describes the same forts as 'lately erected'. It therefore seems possible that Bartlett's 'Description of Lough Eaugh' was a heavily edited version of the Fugos map. This would explain why, contrary to what became his normal practice, he failed to define the miles in his scale line. It would also explain why he was able to map the lake so quickly.[27]

THE TRINITY MAP

Bartlett's next contribution, referred to here as the Trinity map (plate 4), made the most of his personal attachment to the commander-in-chief. It was entitled 'The description of a part of Ulster containing the particular places of the Right Honourable the Lord Mountjoy now Lord Deputy of Ireland his journeys and services on the north part of that kingdom, from his entry thereinto until this present August 1601'.[28] The date suggests a cartographic valediction, prompted by Mountjoy's awareness that the war in Ulster was drawing to a temporary close as he travelled south to meet the Spaniards in Munster. In its brief northern campaign of 1601 his army had penetrated no further into the O'Neill heartland than Benburb on the Blackwater, and Bartlett's new map was little more extensive than its Cotton predecessor, though at least he now found room for the rebel fortress at Dungannon castle. The Trinity map is carefully drawn and coloured, though Bartlett's palette was still limited — to blue, red and yellow. Perhaps it was produced in Dublin. It carries two coats of arms, one of Sir George Carew, president of Munster, the other of Sir Richard Wingfield, marshal of the English army, neither of whom had served in Ulster. Possibly Bartlett was engaged in a morale-raising exercise to show senior officers how their commander-in-chief had been employed (and perhaps to hint that their own exploits might be similarly commemorated), but it seems strange that they were expected to share the same map. Perhaps there were two copies of it, each including both heraldic devices to be on the safe side.

In the area he was now covering for the second time Bartlett included little information that he had not recorded in the Cotton map of 1600, but his style had become markedly less idiosyncratic. There are about half a dozen new names that could have been inserted from a master map drawn in the previous year if for some reason they had been overlooked in the first copy. New linear features are even fewer: they include a correction to the Threemilewater near the Moyry Pass and a new lake (the Ordnance Survey's 'Cashel'?) west of Newry. Like Mountjoy's campaigning in the same season, the Trinity map was not much of an advance.

THE SIEGE OF KINSALE

Far to the south, the walled seaport town of Kinsale was occupied by Spanish troops on 21 September 1601 and quickly besieged by the English army under the command of Mountjoy with the support of Carew as president of Munster and the earl of Thomond from the same province. Irish forces led by Hugh O'Neill and Hugh Roe O'Donnell came south to support the Spaniards but were comprehensively defeated on Christmas Eve in what proved to be the crucial battle of the war. Bereft of native support, the Spaniards surrendered on 2 January 1602. There had been much digging and banking of earthworks around the town and several extramural locations played a critical role in the campaign, notably Castle Park and Rincorran. The result was a burst of urban and suburban cartography without precedent in Ireland. Five small manuscript English maps of this area survive from 1601, including one by Paul Ivy and one by Baptista Boazio.[29] None of them looks like Bartlett's work.

This brings us to the enormous oil painting preserved in Trinity College, Dublin, which gives a bird's eye view of the siege and battle, combining successive stages of the campaign (distinguished by numerous inset written commentaries) in one elaborate synthesis, and purporting to continue the story until 9 January 1602. A similar though much smaller view was engraved for *Pacata Hibernia*, a history of the rebellion in Munster written by Carew's putative natural son Thomas Stafford and published in 1633 (plates 5(a)–(b)).[30] Some authorities suggest that the painting was enlarged from the engraving, others — more plausibly — that the engraving was reduced from the painting, which not surprisingly contains a number of details for which the engraver had no space.[31] However, it is also possible that both extant versions were directly or indirectly descended from some common archetype now lost. This last hypothesis absolves us from explaining how the engraver managed to copy a model that is unlikely to have been generally accessible.

The Kinsale painting has recently been attributed to Bartlett and dated to 'the days and weeks after the battle'. It has also been described by the same author as 'easily the best topographical painting of its day anywhere in Europe'.[32] From these assessments we might expect it to have figured more specifically in Bartlett's entry for 'gifts and rewards' quoted above. However that may be, in subject matter and overall conception it certainly shows a strong generic resemblance to his other work, where infantry and cavalry are more than once depicted in action against a background that was part panorama and part plan.[33] The painting also echoes some of his Ulster maps in its oblique representations of low hills and in its sharply defined leaf-like outlines of river flood plains. In detail, however, it is less schematic, more carefully executed, and (at first sight) more realistic-looking than the other maps considered in this essay. Yet for all its superior handling of light, shade and colour the picture lacks Bartlett's gift for evoking the destruction and neglect that were already part of Ireland's medieval heritage. Its smooth-surfaced castles, churches and curtain walls, even where partially ruined, all look as if they had been built within the last few weeks. Doors, windows and battlements seem wrongly proportioned, and the church in particular appears too high for its length and breadth. In one patch of open country west of the lord deputy's camp at New Mills, a river misses its valley and runs instead down a nearby open hillside — an unlikely disposition for a topographer as skilled as Bartlett. The trees around Kinsale are also out of character, their huge leaves more suggestive of an ornamental garden shrub than of anything to be seen in the Irish countryside. (These are mainly matters of artistic convention: they do not necessarily detract from the painting's reliability as a record of troop movements.)[34] Equally problematic are the Kinsale inscriptions. Unfortunately there are no good opportunities for a comparative assessment of their orthography apart from the spelling 'castell', used three times out of four in the painting, as against 'castle' in all twenty unabbreviated occurrences among Bartlett's Ulster maps. But at least we can say that the script of the painting is too regular and formal to carry conviction as evidence for Bartlett's authorship.

Perhaps the least unlikely interpretation of these facts is that Bartlett produced the original representation of the battle from which the painting was worked up by some other artist. No one else with the requisite ability is known to have observed the siege with this motive; the army's engineers, Josias Bodley and Paul Ivy, would have been too busy for such a task. And Kinsale would not have been mentioned by the treasurer at war as partly justifying Bartlett's twenty-pound gratuity if he was there for the same reason as every other infantry officer. As for the idiosyncrasies of the painting already mentioned, one cannot expect copyists to reproduce the small stylistic peculiarities of their model when working in a different medium. Nevertheless, the authorship of our hypothetical Kinsale source-map remains too doubtful to justify giving it any more space in the present book.

REFERENCES

1. G.A. Hayes-McCoy, *Ulster and other Irish maps c.1600* (Dublin, 1964).
2. *CSPI, 1601-3*, p. 200: 4 December 1601; Caoimhín Ó Danachair, 'Representations of houses on some Irish maps of *c.*1600' in Geraint Jenkins (ed.), *Studies in folk life: essays in honour of Iowerth C. Peate* (London, 1969), p. 92; John Mulcahy, 'The arts in Louth: surveying the territory manuscripts', *Irish Arts Review*, xxiv, 3 (2007), pp 88-91.
3. Fynes Moryson, *An itinerary, containing his ten yeeres travel ...* (4 volumes, Glasgow, 1907-8), iii, p. 2.
4. *CSPI, 1596-7*, p. 290.
5. Maps of Docwra's theatre of operations from 1600-1 include: Lough Foyle and Lough Swilly, PRO, MPF 1/335(1); River Foyle, NLI, MS 2656/16; River Foyle, Sir Basil McFarland (formerly Dartmouth collection); Burt Castle, PRO, MPF 1/335(2); Derry, PRO, MPF 1/335(1); Derry, TCD, MS 1209/14; Dunnalong, SP 63/207vi/84ii; Dunnalong, TCD, MS 1209/14; Lifford, SP 63/207vi/84iii; Lifford, TCD, MS 1209/14. Documentary references: *CSPI, 1600*, p. 194; *1600-1*, pp 92-5, 292, 339; Henry Docwra, 'A narration of the services done by the Army ymployed to Loghe-Foyle, under the leadinge of mee Sr Henry Docwra Knight' in John O'Donovan (ed.), *Miscellany of the Celtic Society* (Dublin, 1849). See also W.S. Ferguson, *Maps & views of Derry, 1600-1914, a catalogue* (Dublin, 2005), pp 1-5.
6. BL, Cotton MS Aug. I, ii, 37.
7. Moryson, *Itinerary*, ii, pp 305-6.
8. Moryson, *Itinerary*, ii, pp 336-42.
9. *CSPI, 1600-1*, pp 20, 30, 41, 330, 359, 447.
10. *Calendar of Carew MSS, 1601-2*, p. 233.
11. Moryson, *Itinerary*, iii, pp 169-70.
12. John McGurk, *The Elizabethan conquest of Ireland: the 1590s crisis* (Manchester, 1997), p. 8.
13. Moryson, *Itinerary*, ii, p. 343.
14. Mercedes Camino, '(Un)folding the map of early modern Ireland: Spenser, Moryson, Bartlett, and Ortelius', *Cartographica*, xxxiv, 4 (1997), p. 10; Thomas Herron, 'Orpheus in Ulster: Richard Bartlett's colonial art' in Thomas Herron and Michael Potterton (eds), *Ireland in the renaissance* (Dublin, 2007), p. 294.
15. Moryson, *Itinerary*, ii, pp 305, 307, 377, 400, 404, 415; iii, pp 149, 167. At Kinsale, Moryson's names Knock Robin (iii, p. 1) and West Fort (iii, p. 54) are omitted from a map (discussed below) that may be based on Bartlett's work.
16. PRO, AO1/288/1082; J.H. Andrews, review of G.A. Hayes-McCoy, *Ulster and other Irish maps, c.1600* in *Irish Historical Studies*, xiv (1965), p. 269.
17. Moryson, *Itinerary*, iii, pp 146-51, 249-50.
18. Hatfield House, Cecil papers, 186/75.

19. Sir John Brockett to Sir Robert Cecil, 25 July 1601, *CSPI, 1600-1*, p. 450.
20. Lambeth Palace, MS 635/193.
21. PRO, MPF 1/133. This map's previous archival reference (SP 63/208/48) does not help to establish its date.
22. *CSPI, 1601-3*, p. 64. R.G. Morton, 'Naval activity on Lough Neagh, 1558-1603', *The Irish Sword*, viii (1967-8), pp 288-93, does not discuss the map evidence, or any issues of precise chronology.
23. *CSPI, 1601-3*, p. 356.
24. *CSPI, 1601-3*, p. 396; C.L. Falkiner, 'William Farmer's chronicles of Ireland from 1594 to 1613', *English Historical Review*, xxii (1907), p. 128.
25. NLI, MS 2656/19, discussed in Hayes-McCoy, *Ulster and other Irish maps*, p. 30.
26. These are now known simply as The Three Islands (Patrick McKay and Kay Muhr, *Lough Neagh places: their names and origins* (Belfast, 2007), p. 125).
27. One significant difference is that the Fugos map show three of O'Neill's fort-sites west of Lough Neagh (Clanno, Ballinderry and Toome) whereas Bartlett shows four, one of them unnamed. This could be a copying error, another sign of haste.
28. TCD, MS 2379.
29. NMM, MS P.49/17; NLI, MS 2656/22; Hatfield House, Maps II/38 (Boazio); Hatfield House, Maps II/40 (Ivy); Lambeth Palace, MS 635. Ivy's plan of Castle Park is TCD, MS 1209/55. For contemporary foreign maps of Kinsale see Hiram Morgan (ed.), *The battle of Kinsale* (Bray, 2005), pp 109, 364-5.
30. 'The armie of the kinge of Spayne comaunded by Don John de Aguila besieged in the towne, of Kinsale ...' in *Pacata Hibernia; or, a history of the wars in Ireland* ... (London, 1633) ii, pp 188-9. This does not differ in any significant respect from the re-engraving in the Dublin (1810) edition of the *Pacata* (ii, pp 334-5).
31. Anne Crookshank and David Webb, *Paintings and sculptures in Trinity College, Dublin* (Dublin, 1990), p. 166; Anne Crookshank and the Knight of Glin, *Ireland's painters, 1600-1940* (New Haven, 2002), p. 64; Morgan, *Battle of Kinsale*, pp 360-61. These issues are more fully discussed in Felim McGrath, 'The TCD oil painting of the siege and battle of Kinsale', B.A. dissertation, Department of History, Trinity College, Dublin, 2008.
32. Hiram Morgan, 'Picturing the battlefield', *Irish Times Weekend Review*, 15 December 2007. The possibility of a link between Bartlett and the Kinsale painting had already been ventilated in Andrews, review of Hayes-McCoy, p. 269; see also Mic Moroney in Crawford Art Gallery, *[C]artography: map-making as artform* (Cork, 2007), p. 17.
33. NLI, MS 2656, va and xi.
34. Damien Shiels, 'The Kinsale battlefield project', *Irish Post-Medieval Archaeology Group Newsletter*, vi (2007), pp 4-7.

Chapter 4

A Bartlett Chronology: the Last Two Years

We now reach the summit-level of Bartlett's career, a series of maps and views to be cited here under the name Bowlby in honour of their twentieth-century discoverers.[1] They are almost uniform in size, style and colouring, and in four cases carry an unusual kind of overlapping scrollwork decoration, suggesting joint involvement in the same artistic enterprise. Altogether there are sixteen subjects occupying twelve numbered pages, the whole collection celebrating Mountjoy's final assault on the O'Neill heartland. Although some of these sites had been visited by the deputy in 1600 and 1601, it seems probable on grounds of stylistic uniformity that all or nearly all of them were mapped in quick succession, leaving their most likely date as the summer of 1602. At this time Mountjoy made two journeys through the region depicted, in each case starting and finishing at either Dundalk or Newry. One lasted from 1 June to 30 July, the other from 20 August to 11 September.[2] Our main authorities for these events are (a) letters written at the time by the English military commanders, (b) Fynes Moryson's near-contemporary account of the rebellion in Ireland, and (c) routes and camp-sites shown on one of Bartlett's regional maps in the British National Archives (MPF 1/36, to be considered in more detail later), which is here given the name of 'the campaign map'.

A disappointing feature of the Bowlby maps is that with a single exception their title-panels are empty. This phenomenon is surprisingly common in Elizabethan cartography and no one has offered a plausible explanation of it. In some cases a cartouche may have been left to await the attention of a superior penman who never materialised, but Bartlett was quite capable of writing a reasonably neat inscription. A second hypothesis is that he meant to fill the gaps himself but never got round to doing so; after all, he may not have expected his career to end as it did in sudden catastrophe. But would he have embarked on other time-consuming maps (discussed below) when it need have taken no more than a day's work to finish these? Another possibility is that Mountjoy might have preferred to insert his own narrative text, perhaps with the intention of employing Moryson as scribe, but this too is not very convincing: some of the blank panels are too small to hold anything more than a bare title. The emptiness of the Bowlby cartouches is made especially frustrating by the paucity of names and descriptions within the body of the maps. So detailed and circumstantial is the art-work, however, that Hayes-McCoy had little difficulty in identifying most of the locations.

ACROSS THE BLACKWATER: THE FIRST JOURNEY

The Bowlby maps will now be itemised, roughly according to the pagination of the volume in which they first appeared. They are arranged in approximate geographical order from south-east to north-west, and also in approximate chronological order of visitation by the English forces in 1602. It must be noted however that the marginal roman numerals quoted by Hayes-McCoy are in a later hand and may not coincide exactly with the original sequence.[3] The first page shows two subjects: (Ia) the Cooley peninsula together with Dundalk and the southern extremities of County Down; (Ib) on a larger scale, Moyry castle and fort (plate 6). Of these the former, henceforth identified as the 'Cooley map', is the only true regional portrait in the series, and in later chapters of this book it will be grouped with Bartlett's other small-scale work and not with the Bowlby fort plans. The Cooley map aligns the peninsula more correctly than those of 1600 and 1601, supporting the already well-founded hypothesis of a later date. Perhaps Bartlett intended a number of such small-scale maps to cover Mountjoy's theatre of operations and then abandoned this project as over-ambitious, contenting himself for the present and immediate future with plans of more localised subjects. Cooley aside, the other Bowlby items have much in common and their individual peculiarities, such as they are, do little or nothing to elucidate their temporal succession.

Mountjoy's Moyry fort (Ib) with its 'tower or keep of stone' was built in June 1601.[4] Bartlett found it flying the English flag but with no sign of armament or a garrison and no buildings except the castle, which was presumably housing the warders at the time. In most of Mountjoy's later forts the plans record a number of thatched cabins, but these structures could be built so quickly that their presence or absence has no obvious chronological import. It might however be claimed that the Moyry map looks like a quick sketch, as if its author was anxious to move on.

The plan of Mountnorris (II) is also later than Mountjoy's initial occupation of its site, as can be seen from certain changes to the layout of the fort (plate 7). Originally there were two compartments: an ancient circular enclosure or rath of supposedly Danish origin, and a straight-sided trident-shaped annex built in 1600. Now there was a further extension, polygonal in shape with four angle-bastions; this was laid out in the summer of 1601, perhaps in August when the lord deputy is known to have spent some time in and around the fort.

In the ruined city of Armagh (IIIa) the most recent researchers have identified all ten of Bartlett's medieval sites with varying degrees of certainty,[5] but the Elizabethan history of the site has attracted less attention (plate 8). Up to 1601 this had been the principal English objective in south Ulster and it is noticeable that a year later Bartlett's otherwise extraordinarily vivid and evocative map-view shows none of the lord deputy's proposed fortifications. The only exception, according to Hayes-McCoy, was some kind of firing platform partly blocking the east window of the medieval cathedral. Other half-finished fortifications may have been omitted as unwelcome evidence of previous English military failures. They would also have spoiled the traumatic effect of a civil community in ruins, awaiting a heroic commander to rescue it, though whether Bartlett was influenced by such considerations must be open to doubt. Hayes-McCoy also noticed Bartlett's first human figure, a sentry perched on the wall of a ruined church. It is not clear who was meant to receive this person's warning signals, unless it was the artist himself.

The next subject (IIIb) is a three-cornered fort beside the River Blackwater, built by Mountjoy in July 1601. It is the first Bowlby plan to carry a title, which reads rather oddly 'New fort or of the Mullin' — evidently a conflation of two possibilities, New Fort and Fort of the Mullin. No one else is known to have used the latter name, which may have been Bartlett's own invention. Maps I to III were probably drawn in June 1602. 'Drawn' here refers to the original record of the artist's observations: the fair copies as they survive may have been made at a somewhat later date.

In the Blackwater valley, the new designation 'Charlemont' (IV) was a play on Mountjoy's Christian name and his baronial title (plate 9). This is the first Bowlby map that can be indisputably dated. Admittedly the site had been chosen a year in advance, marking the terminus of a newly discovered route from Armagh to the Blackwater, but the deputy's letters make clear that the fort and bridge were not built until late June 1602. Bartlett evidently spent some time beside the Blackwater, as we shall see, but he produced no large-scale representation of Essex's fort of 1575, now 'all ruinated',[6] or of 'the Ruins of Fort Burroughs'.[7] Apart from their broken-down condition, these had not been Mountjoy creations and were doubtless thought to lie outside the cartographer's brief.

The next page (V) is a quadripartite image showing (a) an unnamed crannog or lake-island under attack; (b) Dungannon castle flying the flag of St. George; (c) the rath of Tullaghoge with the uncomfortable-looking stone inauguration-chair of the O'Neills and, some distance away, an English military camp; (d) an enlarged view of the famous chair (plate 10). The castle was occupied on 23 June 1602. The chair was demolished on Mountjoy's orders as a symbolic gesture at some time towards the end of August; in Bartlett's drawing it is still intact. As for the crannog, by 22 June, according to Sir Arthur Chichester, O'Neill had abandoned most of his islands in the vicinity of Dungannon, 'keeping only a ward in Lough Rewgh'.[8] This was probably the scene of the operations shown in Va. On one of Bartlett's small-scale maps it appears as 'Lo. Rehou' close to the deputy's line of march. It is now known as Roughan Lough.

The crannog and Tullaghoge drawings are the first of the series in which transitory objects or occurrences — rows of soldiers' tents and the soldiers themselves in action — make clear that Bartlett had finally caught up with the war. He may previously have remained some distance in the rear, not getting close to the centre of events until Mountjoy reached

Dungannon. Perhaps he had fallen behind schedule by experimenting with the kind of regional map he had drawn for Cooley.

Mountjoy fort (VII) was built in the first week of July 1602 near the coast of Lough Neagh five miles east of Roughan, not in fact a very promising site from an offensive point of view (plate 11). The plan itself was on the largest scale that Bartlett had yet chosen, leaving room for considerable architectural detail but no sign of life except the smoke rising from some of the chimneys. No doubt it was the choice of name for this impressive new settlement-site that inspired the cartographer to copy the lord deputy's armorial bearings as a knight of the garter. This is the only obvious basis for one historian's 'heraldic' interpretation of Bartlett's plans.[9]

On 14 July it was reported that the deputy had withdrawn to replenish his stock of provisions, probably at Charlemont rather than Newry, and that he now intended to establish a garrison at Monaghan. This venture presumably explains the looping route to and from Monaghan shown in Bartlett's campaign map (fig. 2). Whether Mountjoy followed this curve in a clockwise or anticlockwise direction is not immediately obvious. He is known to have conducted one or two minor operations en route, because in Moryson's words he 'marched back towards Monaghan, and in the way taking some islands and strong places'.[10] ('Back' may refer to the temporary stationing of troops at Monaghan two months earlier.) Then, having garrisoned the fort, he 'took, burned and spoiled all the islands in those parts of greatest strength, placing wards in some of them'.[11] The road passed near lakes and islands both east and west of Monaghan, so none of this does much to help determine the soldiers' direction of movement. Here special interest attaches to Rooskey Lough, some seven statute miles to the west. Beside the lake Bartlett's later campaign map shows a fort which is apparently unrecorded in the Bowlby series but which at first sight is likely to have been built shortly before or after the one at Monaghan. On the other hand it was eight weeks after taking Monaghan that Mountjoy wrote of 'Ruske, where I have planted a garrison' as if this had been done quite recently — perhaps by a subordinate commander, in which case there might seem to be less need for a separate plan of it.[12]

In support of the anticlockwise option for the Monaghan detour, one would expect the deputy to secure Monaghan itself before moving west to fortify the less important site at Rooskey. On the other hand, if we take Bartlett's road-drawing literally an anticlockwise route through Monaghan would include an awkward and improbable hairpin bend in the

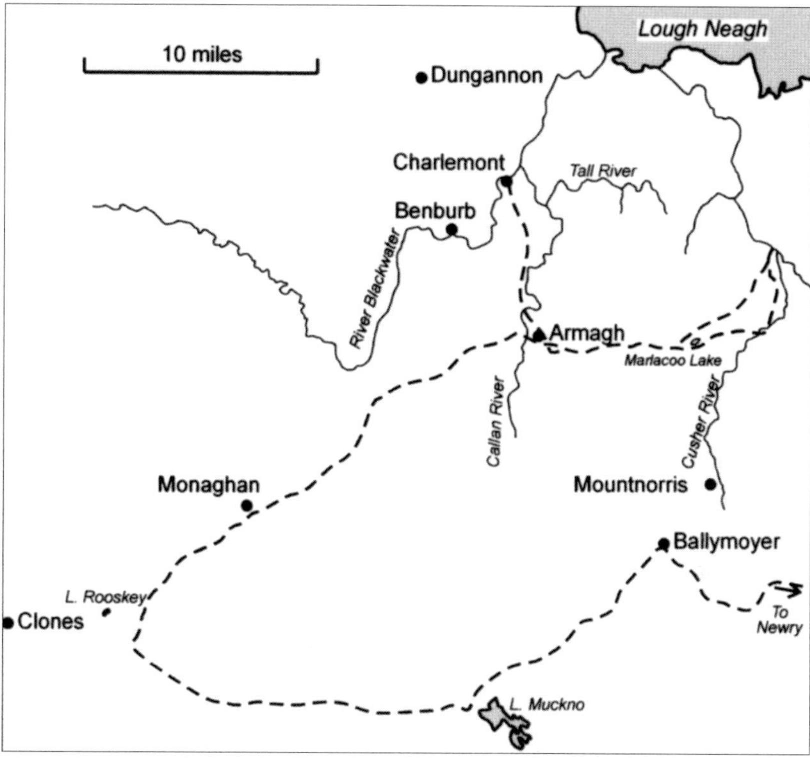

Fig. 2: Mountjoy's journey to Monaghan, July 1602 (roads from PRO, MPF 1/36).

neighbourhood of Armagh city. This can be avoided by making the excursion part of a longer and (locally) more direct route that runs first from Charlemont eastwards to the Bann and then westwards again straight across the Blackwater. Such an extended sequence would give point to Mountjoy's wide-ranging claim, on 29 July, to have 'cleared all the country from the Bann to the Dartree'.[13]

Whatever his route into Monaghan, the deputy is known to have been present there on 19 July. Here Bartlett drew two plans (IX), one partly superimposed on the other. The larger (a) shows the new star-shaped English fort; the smaller (b) a kidney-shaped lake with two crannogs (plate 12). Hayes-McCoy interprets the crannogs as the original stronghold of the MacMahon chiefs lying a short distance south of the new fort, a suggestion supported by the size and complexity, apt for a chief, of the cruciform-planned house that occupies the larger enclosure. It may be significant in this connection that the campaign map treats 'Monoghan' and 'The Forte of Monoghan' as two different places. On the other hand the lake in IXb is very much like Rooskey Lough as depicted on Bartlett's smaller-scale regional map; resemblances include the shape, the presence of two islands, and the position of a nearby stream. This lake also contained an important residence belonging to the Dartree branch of the MacMahons.[14] So perhaps Bartlett did make a separate plan of Rooskey after all — omitting the adjacent fort because it had not yet been built.

ACROSS THE BLACKWATER: THE SECOND JOURNEY

At the end of July 1602 Mountjoy was back in Newry. Then after three weeks' recuperation he again moved north and by the last week of August had crossed the Blackwater for a mopping-up exercise that included the destruction of O'Neill's chair. Only now did Bartlett have the leisure to produce an overview of the middle Blackwater valley from just below Charlemont upstream to Benburb, including five forts and three camp-sites with a complex pattern of rivers and roads (VIII: plate 13). These details generated a large number of *in-situ* reference-letters which could hardly be left without explanation and which appear in a unique 220-word marginal commentary that partly makes up for the paucity of writing in all the other Bowlby cartouches. Amid much else of importance, the Blackwater caption provides a rare example of a Bartlett date, 'this year 1602'. Better still, it refers to Mountjoy's passing the river in his '2 jornie', that is to say in August rather than July. It was appropriate that this masterpiece of topographical portraiture should be one of the only two maps in the Bowlby series that Bartlett chose to sign.

With the Irish fort of Inisloughan (VI: plate 14) we take a long geographical step backwards from the Blackwater to a point some ten miles to the east. It was captured on 15 or 16 August 1602, not by Mountjoy himself but by Sir Henry Davers, which doubtless explains why there is no route leading to it on the campaign map. Here for a change the cartographer was separated from his employer, for it is clear from the display of tents and weaponry that Bartlett was eye-witness to a siege, however short: perhaps it was considered particularly desirable to make a record of native fort-building styles. The ripe corn in the foreground confirms a date in August. Bartlett's plan shows no means of entering or leaving the enclosure. This is an odd omission (especially at a time when Englishmen's anti-Irish jokes had not yet assumed their modern form), perhaps to be explained by the occupants having blocked the fort's perimeter in a last desperate attempt at impregnability.

Next in chronological order is Augher (X: plate 15) fifteen miles south-west of Dungannon on a route of its own, a northern 'loop' west of Charlemont that was almost entirely separate from all the earlier lines of movement shown on the campaign map. The Augher island fortress was occupied by the English on 7 September and augmented with a new bastioned earthwork on the adjacent mainland. This is another enclosure that was mapped without an entrance, apart from the possibility of squeezing in along the lake shore; perhaps the plan was drawn half-conjecturally, before the building was finished.

The most puzzling of the Bowlby maps is Bartlett's third representation of an unnamed crannog (XI: plate 16) almost at the end of the series in a context that does little to reveal its geographical position. Hayes-McCoy found a number of resemblances between this site and the one near Dungannon already mentioned (Va), and his final conclusion was that they were probably the same place. Both crannogs lie towards one end of their respective lakes, both contain three houses, and both are directing six rounds of small-arms fire at English troops on the mainland. The attackers, armed in both cases with muskets and a single cannon, occupy earthworks of similar size and shape on the shore of the lake. However, there are also some significant differences between V and XI. One lake is considerably longer than the other, and the patterns of woods, hills, bogs, streams, roads and houses in the surrounding area are different. Also, it is only the later (presumptively) of the two maps that carries a scale line. Would Bartlett have returned to this site with the sole purpose of measuring a distance for his scale? More to the point, in such a carefully assembled composition as the Bowlby atlas it would seem improbably maladroit for the same incident to be represented on two different pages without good reason. After all, when the enemy could be housed in three cabins this was hardly a battle of Napoleonic proportions. The only other lake named among Mountjoy's conquests was 'Magherlowni', said to have been captured in early July.[15] Having already found some degree of irregularity in the Bowlby time-sequence, we cannot immediately dismiss this date as too early for the penultimate page of the atlas. However, Bartlett's campaign map also records several other lakes and islands close to its various routeways (the most notable being Lough O Donallie, at a site later known as Castlecaulfield on the approach to Augher) so perhaps the subject of map XI had better be left uncertain.

The last Bowlby plan (XII: plate 17) is almost equally puzzling in a different way. At least Bartlett's inscriptions make clear that it represents a lake on the River Shannon, so there is no danger of confusing 'Muck rusk' with the 'Ruske' (Rooskey) garrisoned by Mountjoy in County Monaghan. It seems impossible to disagree with Hayes-McCoy that the subject of XII is Lough Bofin between Counties Leitrim and Roscommon (fig. 3). On the island of Muckruske there is a small ruined church and part of a churchyard, with an ancient-looking outer enclosure (the hachures of the bank drawn only faintly as if to throw doubt on its tactical value) of a kind familiar almost everywhere in Ireland. The question is why the island should have been surveyed at all when it was devoid of military features. Perhaps this is one plan consistent with the theory that the entire Bowlby series was made 'for possible future use' rather than as a record of events.[16] But that is not the end of the matter. To a native Irish cartographer, if any such person had existed, a site like 'Muck Rusk' might have seemed worth mapping for its potential as a modern defence post, but from an English standpoint the fortification of small islands remote from the sea would have been considered strategically unrewarding. In any case, this island lay nearly fifty miles from any of the other eleven locations under review, and it seems unlikely that Bartlett would have undertaken a special journey as long as that. Nor is it very probable that he surveyed other possible military subjects at varying distances from the main series and that only one of these conjectured peripheral maps remains in the Bowlby atlas; one notices, all the same, that Map XII has a slightly different colour scheme from the other maps and that it is the only member of the series to be drawn in 'landscape' rather than 'portrait' format.

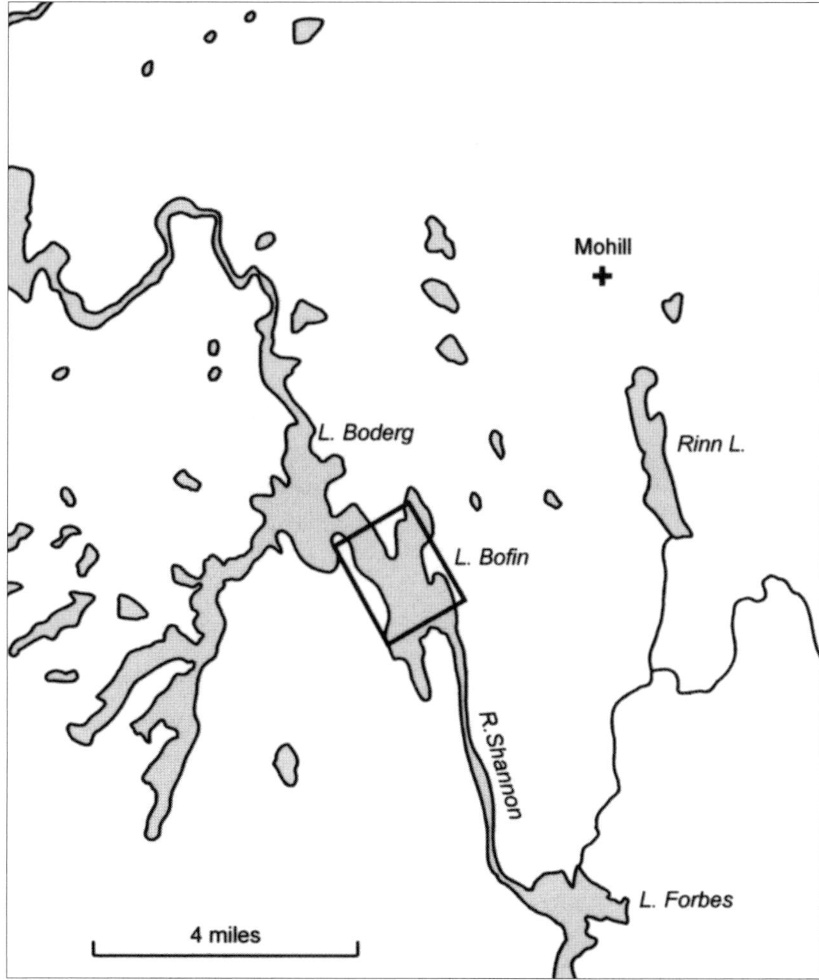

Fig. 3: Lough Bofin and the upper Shannon. The rectangle shows the approximate area covered by NLI, MS 2656/12.

Documentary sources do little to resolve the problem. No forts or garrisons are listed anywhere near Lough Bofin at the period in question and it is by no means clear what was happening there. In September 1602 Mountjoy noted that O'Neill and his supporters 'had a way into O'Rourke's country, to which the army could not pass'. Whatever blocked the army's path, it did not keep out the governor of Connacht, Sir Oliver Lambert, who at about the same time was 'called back from the prosecution of O'Rourke' by the threat of another Spanish invasion.[17] In the following spring Lambert was said to have 'of late done very well' in O'Rourke's country, but by that time Bartlett was probably engaged elsewhere.[18] It remains possible, however, that he had accompanied the governor to this region in the autumn and left at about the same time soon after his visit to Lough Bofin.

A RETURN TO REGIONAL MAPPING

Attention must now be turned to a set of three quite different Mountjoy-dedicated maps archivally distinct from the Bowlby group but closely related to each other — not least in their style of execution, which is coarser than in Bartlett's earliest work, though equally effective. Unlike the Bowlby plans these maps were evidently not conceived as a series. They are customarily listed in the order traditional for atlases, that is a small-scale general map followed by larger-scale regional maps. In this case, however, the general map seems to belong in the second place, chronologically at least. These items are not signed or dated, but nobody has disputed Hayes-McCoy's attribution to Bartlett.

The campaign map (PRO, MPF 1/36: plate 18), already cited more than once, covers the whole of Mountjoy's personal acquaintance with Ulster in 1602, showing a complex pattern of roads (the same length of road sometimes being duplicated as two double lines drawn side by side) that was no doubt meant to trace at least some of the English army's movements, with schematically drawn tents representing its overnight camp sites. The relatively unsuccessful seasons of 1600 and 1601 were omitted, so there are no routes through Carlingford or into Iveagh. On the other hand, the campaign map post-dates the key events of August and September 1602 — the occupation of Augher, the destruction of the Tullaghoge chair and the capture of Inisloughan — and was probably intended to mark the cessation of hostilities, with the English ship on Lough Neagh firing its guns rather as a victory celebration than as an act of war. Needless to say, it was the commander and not the cartographer who was being honoured here: routes followed by Bartlett but not by Mountjoy were omitted.

There are several indications that the campaign map may have been finished quickly to meet a pressing deadline. More hills, trees and buildings have been accidentally left uncoloured than on the later maps. A serious omission is Mountjoy's new fort at the Mullin, of which he was no doubt deservedly proud. The fort appears on Bartlett's general map of Ulster, but only as an afterthought, to judge from its lack of colour and the awkward alignment of its name. If the campaign map had already passed out of its author's possession, this would explain why he was unable to make the same correction there. Finally, in the campaign map, unlike its two companions, some of the colours are 'offset' from one side to the other, as if the sheet had been folded for urgent despatch to its recipient before being thoroughly dry.

The second post-Bowlby regional map (PRO, MPF 1/35: plate 19) embodies similar indications of date to those of the campaign map. It also contains a rare example of a Bartlett title. The word 'general' in 'A generalle description of Ulster' no doubt referred to territorial extent rather than thematic range of subject-matter, but in fact this map could qualify in both respects. Though always placed first in references to the regional trio, typologically and no doubt chronologically it should come second, offering a small-scale geographical portrait, detached and almost academic in spirit, with no travel notes and no obvious reference to recent events — an impression strengthened by introducing the tribal names from Ptolemy's map of the British Isles in A.D. *c.*150. With its carefully balanced distribution of detail among the regions of the province, the map also recalls Richard Hadsor's hope of 'an uniform civil government' in Ireland.[19] In more practical terms, it shows some evidence of having been handled and, presumably, studied, the two halves having become separated along part of the central fold.[20]

The campaign and Ulster maps both carry England's royal coat of arms, the absence of a Scottish lion and an Irish harp indicating a date before the death of Queen Elizabeth on 14 March 1603.[21] Finally, and less predictably, there is a map outlining Donegal Bay and Sligo Bay from near Rossan Point to the west side of Killala Bay, henceforth cited as the 'Bays map' (PRO, MPF 1/37: plate 20). Like the 'Generalle description' it looks more like a neutral account of spatial relations than a military despatch. This time the royal arms are absent: perhaps Bartlett had now learned of the queen's death without having yet been shown the insignia of James I. At any rate his excursion into new territory, with much original detail in south-west Donegal and elsewhere, seems likely to be later than the two last-mentioned maps. The *terminus ante quem* for its origin is Mountjoy's resignation as lord deputy of Ireland at the end of May 1603 and his replacement by Sir George Carey, an officer not known for any special interest in cartography whose previous experience had been administrative rather than military. The Bays map apparently owes much to first-hand knowledge but its *raison d'être* is obscure. Sligo and Mayo lay outside Mountjoy's personal command and were not particularly under threat. Theoretically, of course, this was a possible invasion route into Ulster, perhaps justifying a western equivalent of the campaign map — except that here there was no campaign. However, this interpretation is supported by an approximate similarity in the scales of the two maps, that of the Bays being slightly larger than seems warranted by its content. Whatever the reason for mapping it, the region depicted has no obvious natural unity — it seldom stretches more than ten miles inland — though as it happened several cartographers had paid special attention to it and one of Bartlett's motives may have been to put them right with a precursor of Mountjoy's scheme for mapping 'the north part of Ulster', to which we must now turn.

THE FINAL FRONTIER

The second and last of our documentary references to Bartlett is one of the most famous passages in the history of Irish map-making. It comes from six years after the event, a time when another generation of surveyors, led by Josias Bodley, was toiling through the six escheated counties of Ulster to lay the groundwork for James I's ambitious post-war plantation project. Legal aspects of the inquiry were dealt with by the attorney general of Ireland, Sir John Davies, one of the most cartographically-minded Irish members of his profession then or later (not that this is saying much), whose letters to Robert Cecil provide a running commentary on the progress of the Bodley survey. In September 1609 Davies wrote: 'Our geographers do not forget what entertainment the Irish of Tyrconnell gave to a mapmaker about the end of the late rebellion for one Barkeley being appointed by the late earl of Devonshire to draw a true and perfect map of the north part of Ulster (the old maps of Tyrconnell being false and defective) when he came to Tyrconnell the inhabitants took off his head, because they would not have their country discovered.'[22] It was a violent end to a violent era: future Anglo-Irish map-makers' aims and methods would be very different.

So, unusually for an office-holder of his status, Davies not only recognised that there were such people as map-makers but knew what had happened to one particular member of this profession and even made a creditable attempt at the man's name. (He was not the only Elizabethan writer to confuse 'Bartlett' and 'Barkeley'.) There can be no chronological significance in his identifying Mountjoy as earl of Devonshire: Bartlett's appointment must have been arranged before the creation of the earldom in July 1603, and indeed before Mountjoy relinquished the office of lord deputy in May, though it is unlikely that the next deputy would have wished to rescind it. We may wonder whether Davies would have been more likely to remember the murder if it happened after the beginning of his attorneyship in November 1603. His phrase 'about the end of the late rebellion' might in a medium-term retrospect be extended about as far forward as that, though hardly much further. However, it may be more convincing to place Bartlett's last journey in the summer months.

Even after several centuries, it is impossible not to feel a sense of tragedy at this point. Nevertheless a number of unpleasant questions must be raised. How did Davies know what happened to Bartlett? How did he know why it happened? Was death in Donegal a fate reserved for strangers as such, or for Englishmen in general, or for government employees in particular — or perhaps just for cartographers? Would Bartlett have been left unmolested if he had come with a different motive, like developing the fisheries or prospecting for minerals? Was he tried by some kind of kangaroo court? Were his servants or assistants allowed to go free? What happened to the tools of his trade? Might a Bartlett theodolite be one day unearthed in the mountains, like Samuel de Champlain's astrolabe among the lakes of upper Canada centuries after being lost? And was Davies's reference to the 'discovery' of Tyrconnell merely a rhetorical flourish, or were the killers acting on the theory (common among later cartographic historians) that a country mapped must also be a country subjugated, oppressed, exploited and enslaved? Even more distasteful: does it matter how this death was achieved? In 1590 an earlier surveyor of Ulster, Francis Jobson, had felt 'in every hour in danger to lose my head'.[23] In a later cartographic enterprise Edward Brookes had been 'not without danger of his head at sundry times'.[24] For the victim of decapitation, it was posthumously degrading to provide one's executioners with a portable trophy; nor was there much consolation in the fact that severed heads could occasionally themselves make an appearance in contemporary maps.[25] On the other hand, beheading in England was a recognition of superior social status and Bartlett may have thought himself lucky not to be hanged. Were cartographers regarded, literally in the last analysis, as people of some importance after all?

It is also fair to ask how far Donegal could be considered a special case. Its chief, Hugh O'Donnell, who died in 1602, had made fewer submissive gestures than O'Neill, and its status was less determined by precedent than that of O'Neill's Tyrone. Apparently indeed there was no record of a royal title for this region before 1603, though we may doubt whether Bartlett's murderers were influenced by such legalistic niceties.[26] The situation was regularised in September of that year by granting an earldom to the recently insurgent Rory O'Donnell (son of Hugh), a notable manifestation of the government's more accommodating postwar policy. Was it part of this policy to send a cartographer into Donegal without an adequate bodyguard? One historian considers it unpardonably negligent of Mountjoy to have done so.[27]

The deputy himself had many other problems to worry him in 1603 — most of them, as it happened, arising outside Ulster. This makes it all the more surprising for him to commission such an ambitious map without having some particular reason in mind — though we must also note that, true to the gradualistic spirit of the age, he did not ask for a map of all Ireland. Perhaps Bartlett's appointment was a passing impulse. It is also possible that the initiative came from the cartographer himself, who must have been well aware that the 'Generalle description of Ulster' was by no means free from faults.

As it turned out Bartlett's death brought little good to anyone. In the same year William Parsons was employed for no less than seventy-seven days in surveying the territories of Tyrconnell.[28] Government lawyers, including Davies, toured the county in the summer of 1604 and again in 1607-8.[29] In 1607 Sir Richard Hansard was proposing to survey 'all that seacoast'. This probably referred to individual sites rather than to the whole region, but it was still a demanding programme and we know that Hansard managed to cover Teelin, Killybegs, Donegal, and Ballyshannon.[30] Two years later Donegal was mapped on schedule as one of King James's six escheated counties, and although its barony maps do not survive, it seems clear from reduced versions of them that the work was competently done.[31]

REFERENCES

1. G.A. Hayes-McCoy, *Ulster and other Irish maps* c.*1600* (Dublin, 1964). See also ch. 12 below.
2. Except in the case of *verbatim* quotations, endnotes will not be supplied for military events documented in Moryson's *Itinerary* and the *Calendars* of state papers and Carew manuscripts.
3. I have added letters to these numbers where appropriate. Smaller and more nearly contemporary arabic numbers occur within or adjoining the upper border-strips of Monaghan, Augher, Dungannon and Charlemont. These bear no relation to the present sequence of the maps or to their probable chronological order.
4. Fynes Moryson, *An itinerary, containing his ten yeeres travel ...* (4 volumes, Glasgow, 1907-8), ii, p. 399.
5. Catherine McCullough and W.H. Crawford, *Irish historic towns atlas no. 18: Armagh* (Dublin, 2007), pp 3, 12-13. The *Atlas* identifications differ from Hayes-McCoy's in two respects. His Franciscan friary at the left-hand (southern) edge of the map is identified by McCullough and Crawford as the Priory of Culdees, his Augustinian abbey west of the cathedral as the archbishop's residence. The *Atlas* suggests no modern equivalents for Bartlett's streets and paths.
6. Earlier maps: PRO, MPF 1/99 (1587), copy of 1600 in BL, Cotton MS Aug. I, ii, 32; TCD, MS 10837, pp iv-ix.
7. Earlier maps: TCD, MS 1209/34; PRO, MPF 1/311.
8. Chichester to Robert Cecil, 22 June 1602, *CSPI, 1601-3*, p. 415.
9. R.D. E[dwards], obituary notice of Gerard Anthony Hayes-McCoy, *Analecta Hibernica*, xxviii (1978), p. xvi. The obituarist refers to Hayes-McCoy's 'perhaps underestimating slightly the heraldic significance of the whole collection'.
10. Moryson, *Itinerary*, iii, p. 178.
11. Moryson, *Itinerary*, iii, p. 182.
12. Moryson, *Itinerary*, iii, p. 216 (12 September 1602).
13. *CSPI, 1601-3*, p. 459.
14. Aidan O'Sullivan, 'Crannogs in late medieval Gaelic Ireland, *c*.1350-*c*.1650' in Patrick J. Duffy, David Edwards and Elizabeth FitzPatrick (eds), *Gaelic Ireland* c.*1250*-c.*1650: land, lordship and settlement* (Dublin, 2001), p. 414.
15. Moryson, *Itinerary*, iii, p. 167.
16. Caoimhín Ó Danachair, 'Representations of houses on some Irish maps of *c*.1600' in Geraint Jenkins (ed.), *Studies in folk life: essays in honour of Iowerth C. Peate* (London, 1969), p. 92.
17. Moryson, *Itinerary*, iii, pp 206-7.
18. *CSPI, 1603-6*, p. 55.
19. Joseph McLaughlin, 'Richard Hadsor's "Discourse" on the Irish state', *Irish Historical Studies*, xxx (1997), p. 350.
20. In facsimiles this is especially evident in the Inishowen peninsula, where some of the names divided by the fold do not quite fit together.
21. Bartlett does not mention the 'warning fires' (lit by the Scots to summon help from their fellow countrymen) which had been mapped by Francis Jobson near Fair Head in Co. Antrim. His tactful silence might be thought to suggest a date later than the accession of the king of Scotland to the English throne, but this argument seems less compelling than the heraldic evidence.
22. *CSPI, 1608-10*, p. 280.
23. SP 63/202iv/83.
24. Ralph Lane to Robert Cecil, 24 March 1602, SP 63/210/72.
25. Map of Cork city, *c*.1587, *Pacata Hibernia; or, a history of the wars in Ireland*, iii (Dublin, 1810), pp 692-3; John Thomas, siege of Enniskillen, 1594, BL, Cotton MS Aug. I, ii, 39.
26. Hans S. Pawlisch, *Sir John Davies and the conquest of Ireland: a study in legal imperialism* (Cambridge, 1985), p. 37.
27. George Hill, *An historical account of the plantation in Ulster at the commencement of the seventeenth century 1608-1620* (Belfast, 1877), p. 170, n. 23.
28. PRO, AO1/289/1085.
29. John McCavitt, *The lord deputyship of Sir Arthur Chichester in Ireland, 1605-16*, Ph. D. thesis, Queen's University, Belfast, 1988, pp 195, 201.
30. Hansard to Cecil, 1 November 1607, *CSPI, 1606-8*, p. 315.
31. [Josias Bodley?], 'A generall mapp of the six excheated Counties in Ulster', *c*.1610, Hatfield House, CPM supp. 2; 'A plott of the six escheated counties of Ulster', BL, Cotton MS Aug. I, ii, 44, reproduced *Analecta Hibernica*, viii (1938), following p. 298.

Chapter 5

The Hidden Archive

While there can be no doubt that Bartlett's large-scale plans and views of 1602 were derived from his own observations, the origin of his small-scale regional maps is not so clear. In discussing their sources it may first be asked how much of the author's time between the autumn of 1600 and the spring of 1603 is *not* known to have been spent on field work directly related to Lord Mountjoy's campaigns. A roughly estimated aggregate would be about nine months — a period that might conceivably have been spent surveying other parts of Ulster for inclusion in the 'Generalle description'. And of course this time-span could be lengthened indefinitely if Bartlett is thought to have been working unnoticed in northern Ireland before 1600. The last suggestion seems distinctly improbable, and altogether it is unlikely that he was ever in a position to map the whole of Ulster entirely from first-hand experience.

One suggestive feature of Bartlett's earliest maps may be mentioned before we go further. This is his habit, regardless of the task in hand, of filling each map-frame up to the neat line with topographical detail — that is except towards the south-west corner, an area that could legitimately be ignored as lying outside Ulster. Thus when recording Mountjoy's movements of 1600-1 he incorporated the Lagan valley into the Cotton map, and much of the Ards peninsula into the Trinity map, in both cases unnecessarily. So it seems that at the beginning of his career Bartlett already had a map of Ulster from which he could extract appropriate rectangles as a base for his own more recent information, which in turn increases the likelihood that he was borrowing from the work of earlier cartographers.

PATTERNS OF DESCENT

These speculations must now draw us into the cartographic history of the whole province over a period of several decades. First, however, a general comment is needed on the theoretical problem of descent and ancestry among derivative maps. Hitherto 'cartogenealogical' studies of Tudor Ireland have focused on Robert Lythe's travels through the southern provinces.[1] Most maps descended from these pioneering surveys were drawn by English or foreign copyists mainly resident outside Ireland who possessed little or no independent knowledge of the country and who were probably each following a single cartographic source rather than attempting any kind of synthesis. Moreover, in Lythe's case certain logically possible relationships are conveniently excluded by the fact that his own maps are known in advance to be earlier than any of those that resemble them. In such circumstances 'family' structures can be profitably studied from internal evidence and particularly through an analysis of common errors.

In late Elizabethan Ulster the situation was different. We do not always know whether Bartlett followed or preceded the cartographers from whom he might be thought to have drawn part of his information. Furthermore, copyists of Ulster maps were more likely than Lythe's disciples to consult two or more sources, and some of them were capable of combining these sources with authentic new detail derived from their own experience of the landscape. In this kind of open-ended cartographic environment, textual analysis is inevitably less rewarding. And if Bartlett copied different maps for different regions, some geometrical distortion would almost certainly be introduced by the merger of separate outlines, thus reducing the similarity between source and derivative in any individual case and so frustrating the efforts of the textual analyst.

To make matters worse, the evidence for Ulster is full of gaps. There are many contemporary notices of maps that can no longer be found, and many extant maps of unknown date and authorship that seem to be ignored in all surviving documents — which makes it all too probable that some maps have disappeared without leaving any trace whatever. Such difficulties are only to be expected after four hundred years, but some of our most pressing historiographical questions may well have been unanswerable even in Bartlett's own time. At least it seems clear enough that here, as elsewhere in Ireland, even the best Elizabethan cartographic efforts were unsatisfactorily dispersed and intermittent. In particular, not all map-makers were familiar with the achievements of their predecessors, which meant that progress, though perceptible in the long run, was a good deal slower than it need have been.

Most early Elizabethan maps of Ulster exhibit a number of what look like family resemblances, though some of their common features are diagrammatic enough to have been excogitated from verbal evidence by mapmakers working independently of one another. They include a squarish shape for the whole province; coastal detail more or less correct along the Irish Sea, notably in the Ards peninsula and Strangford Lough; a long east-west Lough Erne; and a longish Lough Neagh aligned from north to south. These characteristics may be seen in maps of Ireland by Laurence Nowell (*c.*1564) and Gerard Mercator (1564) as well as in the outline adopted from an unknown source by Robert Lythe in 1571 for those northern territories that he had been unable to survey himself.[2] Another good example is a map of Ulster in the British National Archives, henceforth called the 'Burghley' map from the lord treasurer's numerous additions to it.[3]

This 'square' conception of Ulster was disseminated in a large number of manuscript and printed maps of Ireland directly or indirectly descended from Lythe's, including those of Jodocus Hondius (1591, 1592), Peter Plancius (1592), Gerard Mercator (1595) and Baptista Boazio (1599). It seems natural, in the absence of other information, to assume that the lost maps of the same period were of no better quality than the survivors. Their authors included Thomas Cusack (1564), John Denton (1567), Rowland White (1569 or 1573) and Nicholas Dawtrey (*c.*1590).[4] If these men had made surveys as detailed as Lythe's, they would probably have requested and perhaps received payment, in which case we would expect their efforts to have left more documentary traces than the few brief references available.

Improvements to this early Elizabethan version of Ulster fell into two categories. First, there were intensive surveys or sketches of restricted areas, usually smaller than a county, most of them spread along the coast from Lough Foyle to Carlingford Lough. Some were connected with identifiable non-cartographic situations or events, as with Lythe's survey of the Bagenal lands in Lecale, Mourne, Omeath and Cooley,[5] or the map made to illustrate Sir Thomas Smith's intended plantation in the Ards peninsula.[6] Other local maps had no recognisably specific purpose, though the endemic threat of invasion from the western highlands and islands of Scotland made the whole Ulster coastline a zone of persistent governmental concern. Although such maps varied widely in merit, their territorial coverage was too limited to make much difference to a small–scale and highly selective composition like Bartlett's 'Generalle description of Ulster'.[7] But while no particular maps of this type can be shown to have affected his work, he may still have left occasional signs of extraneous influence — the use of circled dots as location markers around Downpatrick in the Trinity map, for example, and the flagged castles overlooking Strangford Lough in the 'Generalle description', both of them uncharacteristic of Bartlett's other work.

A different kind of late Elizabethan improvement came from introducing piecemeal alterations to provincial maps at a scale that was unlikely to be any larger than Bartlett's. These were probably contributed by travellers engaging in various kinds of non-cartographic activity rather than by the leaders of *ad hoc* surveying expeditions. The likeliest insertions were small named features such as settlement sites, islands, lakes or hills. For instance the inscriptions 'Monestrhull' (Inishtrahull, north of Inishowen), 'Shipp Iland' (Sheep Island, Co. Antrim) and 'Ocanes chief house called Lameuade' (Limavady) all appear, apparently for the first time, on a small, simplified and generally unoriginal representation of Ulster, here called the 'Greenwich map', that probably dates from the mid 1590s.[8] No one would have visited the north coast of Ireland with the sole object of collecting details like these. A similar argument may apply to certain more ambitious innovations that were beginning to appear on maps at the same period, of which the most important was the westward projection of Donegal, still badly mis-shapen in the 1590s but recognisably different from Lythe's model.[9]

Bartlett himself gives a possible example of this process. In his general map of Ulster 'Mo Kells', Co. Antrim, is drawn and named in a darker ink than the surrounding detail, while the church symbol has been left uncoloured, an unusual omission in such cases. So perhaps Kells was added as a rather hasty afterthought, especially as it does not appear on any survivors from the group of maps that Bartlett is most likely to have consulted. Furthermore, its symbol lies noticeably too near the River Main (Bartlett's River Braid), very much as if it was inserted 'by eye'.

JOBSON AND LANE

So much for generalities about the cartography of Elizabethan Ulster. There remain for closer attention a small number of particularly accurate and detailed maps. The first is a manuscript version of Ulster that identifies itself as 'described and plotted for Her Majesty in anno 1590 by Francis Jobson'.[10] Unlike most of the original cartographers mentioned in this chapter, Jobson was better known elsewhere in Ireland, and his 'Provence of Ulster' is perhaps the most underrated map of northern Ireland still extant.[11] It is commendably informative from the east coast across to and including the Foyle-Mourne-Strule valleys, its most noticeable characteristic in this area being the reconstruction of Lough Neagh: though much improved, the lake was if anything now slightly too wide, as well as extending too far and with too much angularity towards the south-east. Beyond the Foyle basin, as Jobson admitted, his Donegal and Fermanagh are grossly inferior to the rest of the province, with one particularly glaring error where the Erne drainage reaches Donegal Bay through Bundrowes instead of Ballyshannon. This last anomaly almost looks like a deliberate mistake, flaunted to disclaim responsibility for information outside the author's survey area.

We next meet someone who stands opposite to Bartlett on the spectrum between fame and obscurity. Sir Ralph Lane had served with Francis Drake and John Hawkins, and later as governor of the English colony in Virginia. Like several other Elizabethan public servants with overseas experience he displayed a marked affinity for maps, and in 1595, writing as muster-master to the army in Ireland, he addressed separate letters to Burghley and to the queen, offering 'a card of Ulster, very exactly set down'.[12] The last phrase need not imply a measured survey, but it must certainly put the historian on his mettle. An experienced traveller like Lane would hardly have applied it to most of the Ulster maps that survive from the 1580s and 1590s. His 'exact' cartographer was either Captain James Carlyle or a member of Carlyle's staff (Lane contradicts himself on this point), but in either case the map was based on long experience of living and travelling in Ulster, and also, adds Lane, on a close acquaintance with the local septs and factions — always a useful qualification for drawing maps of Ireland.

Regrettably none of Carlyle's handiwork can now be identified. However, in March 1602 Lane wrote twice to Robert Cecil on the subject of Strangford Lough, a location whose strategic importance he said he had come to appreciate by studying the twelfth-century conqueror of Ulster, John de Courcy.[13] Again Lane promised a map and this time we have, not the original 'card of Ulster', but what looks like a close relation — complete with numerous marginal references to de Courcy including a full-length portrait — which unfortunately confines itself to the area east of a line between Lough Foyle and Benburb.[14] Lacking both date and signature, this map has been attributed to Bartlett,[15] but its handwriting is much neater than his (seven of its nine cartouches are fully inscribed, itself an un-Bartlettian feature) and the incidental drawings are less competent though certainly more imaginative, even if the colour scheme is more restrained than Bartlett's. It is also hard to imagine the practical and down-to-earth Bartlett filling one cartouche after another with a beautifully written disquisition on dubiously relevant *minutiae* of medieval history. Anyway, the map in question will henceforth be accredited to Lane.

Lane's geography seems to be partly based on that of Jobson. However, the precise relations linking the extant Jobson and Lane maps with Bartlett remain obscure. Several anomalous features are present in all three. Examples are the exaggerated bend of the River Lagan near Dromore in County Down, the east-west (instead of almost north-south) alignment of the coast at the head of Strangford Lough, and the Blackstaff River that nearly or completely divides the Ards peninsula in two. Then there is a rather suspicious-looking group of three bridges in a province otherwise almost devoid of such amenities, one on the River Bann and the other two on the not very important Clanrye River east of Newry; common to Jobson and Lane, these structures are faithfully copied on Bartlett's maps of 1600 and 1601, though later he evidently found them to have been demolished, or perhaps never to have existed.[16] The same switch from acceptance to rejection appears in Bartlett's successive responses to the abnormal river-widths characteristic of the two other maps. Another habit shared by all three cartographers was to represent 'passes' by lines of trees on either side of a road — without showing the rest of the adjacent wood and without continuing the road into open country at its ends. This practice, apparently unknown in English maps of

England, seems to have been pioneered by Jobson and later adopted by Lane.[17] Like the excessively wide rivers, it is more characteristic of Bartlett's earlier than his later maps.

It is place-names, however, that provide our most abundant evidence of genealogical relationships. In the area that these cartographers have in common, much toponymy is shared by Lane and Bartlett alone, very little by Jobson and Bartlett alone. This must mean something, though not much can be deduced from the exact spelling of the names, a matter on which Bartlett seems often to have taken his own decisions. There are also several more specific links between Lane and Bartlett. One is their inclusion of names no longer current among the general public. They both associate 'Logia' (Lough Foyle) with the ancient Greek geographer Ptolemy, and they both recognise 'Promontor Isanium' (St. John's Point, Co. Down), and 'Ricnea' (Rathlin Island), though it is only Lane who adds explanatory glosses for these two names, which suggests that the introduction of ancient nomenclature was Lane's idea rather than Bartlett's.[18] It is true that Bartlett seems to assert his independence by quoting four Ptolemaic tribal names apparently new to Anglo-Irish cartography (Robogdii, Voluntii, Darnii, Erdini), together with the equally obsolete though non-Ptolemaic 'Ins Eugenia' for Inishowen; but these might have come from Lane's lost 'card of Ulster'. Among other uses such names helped to signal that Bartlett's 'Generalle description of Ulster' was essentially a compilation, and not altogether based on the author's own surveys.

Another common feature appears in the scale bars. Jobson, Lane and Bartlett are all unusual in reckoning 1.25 English miles to one Irish mile. A less substantial but still cartogenealogically promising feature, mentioned in a previous chapter, concerns the presentation of these scales. Bartlett usually drew a marginal scale bar not as a flat rectangle but in simulation of a three-dimensional block with writing on two or more sides. This is exactly how the scale appears on Lane's map. So who had been copying from whom? Lane drops several chronological hints. One is 'a fort erected by [the earl of] Tyrone against Terlogh Lenogh', a member of the O'Neill family who died in 1595. The fort appears to have been built in 1587-8[19] and Lane's caption must still have been fairly topical when it was first written, so perhaps the Lane map was compiled over a period of several years. Other fort-symbols tell the same story. Thus Lane's Mountnorris seems to fall between the building operations of autumn 1600 and those of mid-1601. His portrayal of the Blackwater, on the other hand, appears to predate O'Neill's 'razing' of the fort in May 1600.[20] But at least both dates are earlier than Bartlett's 'Generalle description'.

It is not suggested that Bartlett ever saw the only surviving copy of Lane's map, only that he may have used some less idiosyncratic version of it than the one we have.[21] Another hint of a connection between the two men is the occurrence of 'Sir Ralf Lane' as a landowner at two places on Bartlett's Trinity map. Less obvious, in the same map, is his apparently superfluous caption 'Penins[ula]' below the name of the castle at Sketrick to which Lane attached so much strategic importance. This was perhaps intended to correct the phrase 'Isle of Scattericke' in one of the Lane map's historical notes. (In fact Sketrick is usually counted as an island, despite having been at some periods linked to the mainland by a causeway.)

BOAZIO AND GRIFFIN-COCKET

Next come two closely similar maps of Ulster and its borderlands that apparently owe little or nothing to those already mentioned. One is foreshadowed in a letter of 17 July 1601 written to Robert Cecil by Captain Charles Plessington of the queen's ship *Tremontane*. Cruising off the coast of Mayo, Plessington reported having 'viewed and taken perfect notes of all the rivers & havens hereabouts'. In particular he claimed the discovery of a hitherto unmapped 'river', probably either Broadhaven or Blacksod Bay. He also rashly promised Cecil a chart showing the whole circuit of Ireland in 'better form' than ever before.[22] Unsurprisingly, no such chart can now be found, but we do have a map of northern Ireland purporting to have been drawn by 'Mr Griffin-Cocket master' of the *Tremontane*.[23] (Nobody seems to know whether 'cocket' was a personal name or some obscure naval classification. In its most familiar signification a cocket was a customs document associated with commercial imports and exports rather than with the management of warships.) Here then is a probable author for at least part of the Griffin-Cocket coastline, though a ship's master can hardly have supplied its interior content from his own observations, and any reconstruction of this map's history must therefore find room for another editor knowledgeable about the territories of Ulster and their chiefs. There is one sign, indeed, that the original map may have portrayed the interior in more detail than its surviving representative: this is the word 'causey' (causeway) for a short length of road that was clearly not important enough to have been included by an original cartographer working at the Griffin-Cocket scale.

The *terminus post quem* for this map is May 1601, when the *Tremontane* was first sent to Lough Foyle. It could have been drawn at any time up to Plessington's replacement in August 1603, but is unlikely to post-date the end of organised hostilities in the spring of that year. In its only surviving form the map is accompanied by separate large-scale insets showing Derry, Lifford and Dunnalong, and it is conceivable that future research might help to date these plans more precisely. At present, some time in mid or late 1601 is the best that can be offered for the whole composition.

The other member of the duo under consideration is an undated map of the same area (but without the inset fort plans) bearing the name of Baptista Boazio, a well-known copyist, editor and, some would say, plagiarist.[24] Boazio is not recorded in Ireland at this period, though he evidently managed to keep in touch with developments there. One map historian has described his Ulster as a 'straight copy' of the *Tremontane* version, but this is going too far — as witness Boazio's correct name of 'Drogheda Haven' for Griffin-Cocket's erroneous 'Dundalk Haven'.[25] In truth each map includes a number of places absent from the other. Inscriptions peculiar to Griffin-Cocket are Causey (already mentioned), 'chief salmon fishing' on the Foyle, Lisnadell, Grange, Artamon (all north of Sligo), The Knee (Island Magee) and the Blackwater tributary of the Boyne. Boazio for his part was alone in choosing White Castle (Inishowen), Dungiven, Urkelloes, Coneballagh contrey, Glenarm, and an unnamed castle west of Lough Conn. He also includes more lords of countries in Tyrone than any other cartographer; they are roughly the same as those said by Sir Henry Docwra to have submitted to the crown in March 1601, perhaps suggesting that Boazio's information originated with the English army's north-western command.[26]

Other names individual to Boazio have more definite chronological implications, notably 'Fort Mounioye', which as we have seen was not built until July 1602. On the other hand, the standards flying at a number of Boazio's castles and forts prove nothing: his predilection for meaningless flags was already evident in the general map of Ireland he published in 1599. All the same, this feature does help to give the impression of a conquered province, and on balance Boazio's map would seem to be the later of the two. The exact relationship between Boazio and Griffin-Cocket is too complicated to be pursued much further. Both write 'Longford' as 'Langford' and 'O'Rourke' as 'Orras', and both spell the second syllable of 'Monaghan' with an 'i'. These elementary but unusual errors were presumably derived from a common ancestor, but behind that ancestor there may well have been an archetype that was more correct.

The only important date at present, however, is that of the earlier map, which with luck could help determine whether some member of the Boazio family is old enough to have influenced Bartlett. The answer to this question would appear to be a cautious affirmative. The area in which this influence appears most convincingly is Donegal. Here Bartlett's coastal outline and territorial boundaries particularly resemble the Boazio-*Tremontane* version in the countries of Inishowen, MacSweeny Fanad, MacSweeny na Doe, Hugh McHugh Duffe, Tomelagh, The Ross, O'Boyle, and MacSweeny Banagh. But even within this zone of similarity Bartlett omits O'Ferrolls country, while further east, in O'Donnell's country and beyond, his resemblance to Boazio completely disappears.

THE MISSING SOURCES

Elsewhere in northern and western Ulster there is, frustratingly, no proof either of Bartlett's presence as a surveyor or of his dependence on any identifiable earlier map at any time before his last fatal journey. The 'Generalle description' gives hints of compilation from more than one source in occasional duplicative errors. An example is on the north coast, where 'Portrush' appears as the name of an island in the Bann estuary (perhaps originally a representation of the harbour bar) and also as part of the name 'Skerries Portrush' several miles to the east. Another may be the repetition of 'Black abbie' in the Ards peninsula. However, such cases of accidental 'dittography' can also occur in copying from a single model. (The proximity of the name Blackstaff may have added to the confusion in the Ards.) A similar anomaly is the juxtaposition of 'Tor baie', 'Tor Ile' and 'Can Torbaie' just south of Fair Head, where there is actually no island and where the same place could not have been a headland as well as a bay.[27]

Another area of uncertainty is Docwra's sphere of influence in the neighbourhood of Lough Foyle. Maps of the River Foyle, of Derry and of the isthmus between Loughs Foyle and Swilly were produced for transmission to London at various times in 1600 and 1601 by a cartographer named Robert Ashby working under the command of Captain Humphrey Covert.[28] Surviving examples are line drawings with a style and content quite unlike Bartlett's.[29] Docwra also mentioned a map extending from Inishowen to MacSweeny na Doe's country which does not survive but which may have been available to Bartlett by the time he started on a comprehensive provincial map.[30]

Two regions of Ulster remain for consideration. The first is the drainage basin of the River Foyle and its tributaries upstream from Docwra's principal theatre of operations. The best surviving Elizabethan portrayal of this area is in Jobson's Ulster. At first sight Jobson differs significantly from Bartlett. For one thing his treatment is considerably more detailed, with fourteen separate tributary streams as against Bartlett's seven. And Jobson's alignment of the Foyle-Mourne-Strule waterway is markedly more correct, avoiding Bartlett's erroneous westward loop in the vicinity of Strabane and Lifford. It is still possible however that Bartlett selected only what he wanted from a Jobsonian original and that he himself twisted some of the rivers in an effort to harmonise his different sources.

Finally, Ireland's worst cartographic nightmare. Early Elizabethan maps of Lough Erne had been wrong in three major respects. (a) They made it stretch directly from east to west instead of diagonally north-westwards. (b) Its western end was sometimes placed too near the sea. (c) There was no clear separation of the upper and lower lakes. The first error seems to have been more or less accidentally corrected, or over-corrected, as the encroachment of new map-detail in central Ulster pushed the inner end of the lake in a clockwise direction towards Connacht. It was probably for similar reasons that the image of Lough Erne tended to shrink in width during the 1580s and 1590s. Jobson went further than most contemporaries in these respects, his uppermost lake even pointing slightly east of north. Bartlett took much the same course near the western edge of his campaign map. Perhaps his object was to bring as much of the lake as possible within its frame to reveal the complexity of the Erne archipelago even in defiance of the locational facts; a more creditable explanation is that he was simply following contemporary practice. Most late Elizabethan map-makers, including Bartlett in his 'Generalle description', gave a reasonably good impression of the River Erne between Belleek and Ballyshannon, but no one followed John Thomas in narrowing the waterway to a river between the upper and lower lakes, despite the publicity that must have attended the siege of Enniskillen in 1594.[31] Bartlett's final verdict was for a slight constriction of the lake at Enniskillen, shown as a named castle on its island. His other coasts and islands for Lough Erne were schematised, though less extravagantly than by some of his predecessors. It is impossible to detect the influence of any particular map in all this.

The same must be said of the north Connacht coastlands in Bartlett's Bays map. It is surprising how many cartographers had already been attracted to this remote and unnewsworthy area: in Mayo and Sligo, John Browne and others employed by Sir Richard Bingham;[32] within similar limits to Bartlett's Bays map, John Baxter;[33] in northern Ireland generally, Griffin-Cocket and Boazio. Most of the settlement names on the Bays map had been recorded by one or more of these authors (Derilighan is an exception) but there is no single earlier map that shows them all, and many of Bartlett's spellings are peculiar to himself. Also, as often elsewhere, he has numerous physical names ignored by everyone else. Planimetrically and topologically, only Browne is as good as Bartlett, though not in a way that suggests a 'family' relationship. One odd resemblance must be noticed within this group, however. Near the head of the river flowing into Drumcliff Bay, above 'Lo: Carre' (the Ordnance Survey's Glencar Lake), Bartlett marks a second lake named 'Lo: Whittagh' containing a small island that appears to be wholly occupied by a fort. This lake is unknown to modern geography, but it appears on the same river, with the same name, and occupied by a similar fort, in John Baxter's map of *c.*1600. In other respects Baxter's map is very different — not least in its representation further upstream of a third lake, 'Logh Naiule', also with its own fort. Could Loughs Whittagh and Naiule be garbled versions of Upper and Lower Lough Macnean? At any rate this error could not have been committed by two cartographers totally independent of each other.

All in all, it appears that in working on Ulster Bartlett had access to a sufficiency of earlier maps — enough, perhaps, to absolve him from making any original surveys outside a comparatively small region embracing the sites of the Bowlby plans. It would be interesting to know where he did his indoor research. Other compilers such as Boazio, Norden and Speed are known to have spent much of their time in London. In Bartlett's case this seems unlikely. It appears then that, for reasons that can only be conjectured, more maps were available in the Dublin of 1602-3 than most of his predecessors would have been able to consult. This may be combined with other evidence that ostensibly obsolete Irish maps were being copied in larger numbers around the turn of the century. Here was the 'hidden archive': it is certainly hidden from today's historians.

REFERENCES

1. J.H. Andrews, 'An Elizabethan surveyor and his cartographic progeny', typescript, [1971], National University of Ireland Library, Maynooth, abstract in *Imago Mundi*, xxvi (1972), p. 45.
2. J.H. Andrews, *Shapes of Ireland: maps and their makers 1564-1839* (Dublin, 1997), chs 2, 3; J.H. Andrews, 'The Irish surveys of Robert Lythe', *Imago Mundi*, xix (1965), pp 22-31.
3. PRO, MPF 1/90. There are of course many other surviving maps with annotations by Burghley, but since MPF 1/90 is the only example discussed in this book the name seems justified in the present context.
4. SP 63/10/38, 18/21 (Cusack); SP 63/20/11 (Denton and White); SP 63/28/10 (White); SP 63/202iv/83 (Dawtrey).
5. Harold O'Sullivan, 'A 1575 rent-roll, with contemporaneous maps, of the Bagenal estate in the Carlingford district', *County Louth Archaeological and Historical Journal*, xxi (1985), pp 31-47.
6. BL, Printed books, Harleian 5938, no. 129 [1571].
7. One such map, of the Ards peninsula, has been attributed to Bartlett himself (without any obvious justification) as his 'Map of Military Installations, *c.*1602'. This is NLI, MS 2656/21, reproduced in G.A. Hayes-McCoy, *Ulster and other Irish maps,* c.*1600* (Dublin, 1964), pl. xx. See Thomas McErlean, Rosemary McConkey and Wes Forsythe, *Strangford Lough, an archaeological survey of the maritime cultural landscape* (Belfast, 2002), pp 214, 289.
8. NMM, MS P.49/5.
9. NMM, MS P.49/5; also, 'A descrieption of Ulster the northe parte of Irelande', Lambeth, MS 635, f. 140, a small map inset in a genealogy of the O'Neill family, probably from the mid-1590s.
10. TCD, MS 1209/15.
11. For Jobson's merits, and his neglect by other scholars, see Séamus Ó Ceallaigh, 'Old lights on place-names: new lights on maps', *Journal of the Royal Society of Antiquaries of Ireland*, lxxx (1950), p. 186; Séamus Ó Ceallaigh, 'A preliminary note on some of the nomenclature on the map of S.E. Ulster bound up with the maps of the escheated counties, 1610', *Journal of the Royal Society of Antiquaries of Ireland*, lxxxi (1951), p. 4.
12. Lane to Robert Cecil, 5 May 1595, SP 63/179/69; Lane to Burghley, 5 May 1595, SP 63/179/72; Lane to Queen Elizabeth, 6 May 1595, SP 63/179/72.
13. Lane to Robert Cecil, 5 March 1602, SP 63/210/52A; 24 March 1602, SP 63/210/72.
14. NMM, MS P.49/25.
15. Hayes-McCoy, *Ulster maps*, p. xiv. In a later article ('The making of an O'Neill: a view of the ceremony at Tullaghoge, Co. Tyrone', *Ulster Journal of Archaeology*, xxxiii (1970), p. 90) Hayes-McCoy acknowledged the present author's opinion without disputing it.
16. The bridge that gave its name to the town of Banbridge was not built until the eighteenth century.
17. Passes appear as 'difficult-to-understand map signs' in Catherine Delano-Smith's 'Signs on printed topographical maps, *ca.*1470-*ca.*1640' (David Woodward (ed.), *The history of cartography, volume three: cartography in the European renaissance* (Chicago, 2007), p. 570).
18. Fiachra Mac Gabhann, *Place-names of Northern Ireland, volume seven: County Antrim II Ballycastle and north-east Antrim* (Belfast, 1997), p. 286.
19. *CSPI, 1586-8*, p. 467. The fort appears in Jobson's map of 1591.
20. *CSPI, 1600*, pp 205, 227. These sources do not mention the nearby bridge. Both fort and bridge are shown in Bartlett's Trinity map of August 1601.
21. For the opinion that Lane's map was based on Bartlett see Kay Muhr, 'Territories, people and place-names in Co. Armagh' in A.J. Hughes and William Nolan (eds), *Armagh: history and society* (Dublin, 2001), p. 314; Patrick McKay and Kay Muhr, *Lough Neagh places: their names and origins* (Belfast, 2007), pp 5, 98.
22. Charles Plessington to Robert Cecil, 17 July 1601, *CSPI, 1600-1*, pp 436-7.
23. TCD, MS 1209/14.
24. BL, Cotton MS Aug. I, ii, 30.
25. Edward Lynam, 'English maps and map-makers of the sixteenth century', *Geographical Journal*, cxvi (1950), p. 25.
26. *CSPI, 1600-1*, p. 246. This reference appears in Séamus Ó Ceallaigh ('Old lights on place-names: new lights on maps', p. 184), who is however mistaken in saying that Boazio shows all the names in question.
27. Mac Gabhann, *Place-names of Northern Ireland ... , Ballycastle and north-east Antrim*, pp 206-7.
28. NLI, MS 2656/23, reproduced Hayes-McCoy, *Ulster maps*, pl. xvi.
29. Above, ch. 3, note 5.
30. Sir H. Docwra to privy council, 23 April 1601, *CSPI, 1600-1*, p. 292.
31. NMM, MS P.49/21.
32. TCD, MS 1209/68.
33. NMM, MS P.49/7.

Chapter 6

Signs and Symbols

Explanatory map-keys were introduced in the early sixteenth century and became familiar on the European continent through the published atlases of Abraham Ortelius and Gerard Mercator. The English tradition, however, was that cartographic symbolism should as far as possible be self-explanatory, an aim achieved partly by coupling symbols with descriptive placenames and partly by drawing landscape features from the angle at which they were usually seen on the ground. Except in one of the Bowlby maps (VIII), none of Bartlett's symbols are captioned, but it is usually possible to decide what he thought he was drawing.

MARGINALIA

Bartlett was not a great innovator in matters of map-embellishment. One habit that he shared with many contemporaries was to vary the form of his marginal features, perhaps in reaction against the ever more rigid discipline imposed by cartographic custom within the body of a renaissance map. This makes him a difficult subject for generalisation. Two of his earlier productions — the Cotton and Lough Neagh maps — are completely undecorated, with only single lines bordering both the title and the map itself. Such austerity was appropriate to active service conditions, but for presentation to the lord deputy it was in danger of seeming disrespectful. Not that Bartlett ever went to the other extreme. On the contrary, compared with the work of contemporary map-engravers his decoration has at times a somewhat perfunctory look.

Most of the borders in the maps under review are coloured bands less than half an inch wide, sparsely furnished with simple flourishes or leaf patterns in ink. The cartouche designs are by Elizabethan standards unobtrusive, rectangles with comparatively narrow margins from which the ornamental projections are shorter and neater than those for example on Saxton's county maps. Instead of standing alone in characteristic Saxton mode, these panels are nearly always bonded into the margin of the map, often in one of the corners. Some of them appear to show only half a design, the other half being as it were left invisible outside the frame, evidently with the object of saving space for more important matters. The principal motif is a modest version of the familiar Elizabethan strapwork style, featuring scrolls, tabs, flaps or wings of simulated wood or leather. These may be mixed with the kind of acanthus-leaf pattern which became increasingly popular in the seventeenth century and which doubtless appealed to Bartlett as taking up less room than 'straps'. Except for an occasional grotesque human head, none of these devices can be described as representational, unless we apply that term to Bartlett's dedicatory coats of arms, already mentioned, some of which are incorporated within cartouches. As if in mitigation of their smallness the cartouches are boldly coloured, with red, pink, yellow and blue predominating.

More original was Bartlett's method of incorporating different subjects in the same composition. On four pages of the Bowlby atlas, a map appears to be drawn on an irregularly torn sheet of paper or parchment with curled-up edges, in three cases displaying a rather unnecessary decorative leaf pattern on the reverse. Each scroll is shown as attached to another sheet containing another map (characteristically, Bartlett takes care to join them by realistic-looking pins) with the scroll sometimes partly overlapping the border of the lower map in a gesture of calculated untidiness. Such overlaps were not a new idea — just rare enough to demonstrate the author's cartographic scholarship. Possible sources of inspiration, admittedly lacking Bartlett's boldness and creativity, were the 'scrolled' maps of Lake Como and Salzburg published by Abraham Ortelius in 1570.[1]

Several kinds of cultural and political symbolism have been read into this device. In each example of it the different sheets are on different scales, the smaller representing the native countryside, the larger the imprint of English militarism in the forefront of the cartographer's vision. The distinction between upper and lower layers is not so clear. One scholar records 'the strange impression that enormous maps are being unscrolled over the Ulster landscape and pinned to the conquered soil itself'. This certainly fits the representation of Monaghan (IX). Alternatively, at Armagh (III) the prewar Irish scene seems about to be rolled up and removed, with Mountjoy's fortification emerging to dominate the page. (In the parallel case of Cooley (Ia), Anglo-Norman foundations such as Carlingford must evidently count as 'Irish'.) At Tullaghoge (Vd), less straightforwardly, O'Neill's chair is said to have 'erupted through the fabric' of the upper sheet, almost pushing the nearby English encampment out of sight and thus exposing, to one reader at least, the author's half-conscious sympathy with native traditions and aspirations.[2]

Coming back to earth: apart from what are obviously views rather than maps (Armagh, Dungannon, Tullaghoge), ten out of thirteen Bowlby depictions carry a graphic scale statement. The three omissions — at Moyry Castle (Ib), Mullin fort (IIIb), and an unidentified lake (IXb) — are either oversights or hints that these sites were sketched and not surveyed. Some scale-lines are placed horizontally, others at an oblique angle chosen to fit the space available. Inscriptions specify units of measurement but not the actual scale ratio between map and ground. The scale itself is always a rectangle with checkered subdivisions; sometimes there is a separate bar for each unit, sometimes the same bar carries two sets of divisions. Many cartographers of this period drew a pair of dividers immediately above such rectangles, open as if a distance was being transferred from the body of the map on to the scale as part of the measuring process. Unusually, some of Bartlett's dividers stand as if behind the bar, others hold it in a scissors-like grip — arrangements no doubt intended to prevent these marginalia from encroaching too far into the adjacent landscape. (Here too we may detect the influence of Ortelius's maps.)[3] As we have seen, nearly all Bartlett's scale bars are shown as solid blocks of rectangular or hexagonal cross-section, sometimes inscribed on two or three sides. The blocks had been anticipated in earlier maps of Ireland, but not the multiple inscriptions.[4]

NORTH POINTS

In naming both compass points and units of linear distance, Bartlett vacillated between Latin and English. His earliest map shows the four cardinal points verbally, each in the middle of the appropriate margin, but he seems to have soon decided against this common if approximate method of orientation. At any rate his eight-point compass star in the corner of the same map looks rather like an afterthought, and he never used the marginal captions again. Next he experimented with a simple cross in which north appeared rather confusingly as a fish tail or the flights of an arrow rather than as a sharpened point. Later he adopted the popular device of an imitation eight-point compass dial or, in one corner where space was limited, a quarter-section of such a dial, with north as the now-traditional fleur de lys in both cases. More often there was room to put the whole compass on an otherwise empty water surface, and then the divisions might be continued outwards from its circular rim as rhumb lines, ending where they met the nearest seacoast or lake shore. Since rhumb lines were more characteristic of marine charts than land maps, this practice helped to advertise the breadth of Bartlett's cartographic experience.

Four out of twelve Bowlby plans have north points (IV, VII, X, XII). Each of the four includes part of a large water-body — two major rivers (IV, XII) and two lakes — as if with the intention of helping readers locate the site in question on the kind of smaller-scale regional map that was likely to include these features. At small scales north is usually at or near the top. The Lough Neagh map has west in this position, like many sixteenth-century English representations of Ireland and for the same reason — to bring the would-be invader's starting point as near as possible to the reader. Anticipating another common practice, Bartlett was also less particular about the alignment of large-scale local maps, adjusting each individual orientation to the available space.

The most controversial feature of Bartlett's north-indicators is his treatment of magnetic variation. In Cooley the standard north-south and east-west axes are obliquely crossed by a 'needle' whose fishtail points a few degrees east of north. It seems natural for the cross to show true north and the needle magnetic north, in which case true north, as we should expect, is parallel to the left and right margins of the map. What upsets this argument is that in the plan of Augher a similar needle appears to be deviating westwards from true north by roughly the same amount. Surely it was not simple forgetfulness that caused the symbolism of true versus magnetic to differ from one map to the other.[5] Had Bartlett given Augher a compass dial as it might look at a randomly chosen moment before the needle stopped swinging? We must also remember that whereas, off the map, the needle always stabilises at magnetic north (subject to local attraction), the rest of the compass may point in any direction, depending on how it happens to have been set down. Was Bartlett saying in the last resort that the compass varied from true north without wishing to commit himself between east and west? In this connection we may note that two of John Speed's British inset plans have compass roses in the style of Bartlett's Augher, in both cases with a seemingly westward variation.[6]

HILLS AND WATER

On all the maps relief is depicted in side-view by a combination of profile lines and shading, with right-hand slopes shown darker in accord with long-established custom. Mountains could be drawn rugged or smooth to match their real shape, though only within very broad limits. Thus although Bartlett singled out Ben Bulben, in Co. Sligo, for naming, he made no attempt to simulate its distinctive cliffed façade. Like the artists who worked on Saxton's maps, he varied the colour of his hills for no apparent reason. Some are brown and some grey, but most are green, as if in tribute to Ireland's popular international image.

Profile hills are less well suited to large scales, where relief is best represented from directly above by some kind of gradient-shading or by contours. Bartlett never tried to show relief features in plan. His hills are seen as if from an elevated vantage-point about half a mile away, their rear slopes out of sight, and it was fortunate that this method worked particularly well with Ulster's characteristic drumlin topography. Shading is by a mixture of brushwork and fine pen strokes. Profile lines of generally low gradient are accentuated by darkening a narrow area immediately below the summit. Hillsides are sometimes shaded by horizontal form-lines, but more often by what can only be described by the nineteenth-century word 'hachures', though in an oblique view the hachure lines run at various angles rather than making directly for the nearest valley floor as on a modern relief map. A habit of Bartlett's at small scales was to run a band of very short 'vertical' hachures immediately inland from the coast, giving the whole land mass the appearance of a low plateau. On the map, vertical or near-vertical lines contribute to relief-representation as a way of depicting cliffs, notably in the view of Dungannon. Other such lines appear in strictly limited quantity to emphasise river banks and lake shores, where low cliff-like notches are shown if these would be visible (supposing that they existed) from a viewpoint at the bottom of the map. Even more than most cartographers, then, Bartlett was concerned at every scale to stress the importance of shorelines, whether for seas, rivers, lakes, ditches or moats.

In depicting large extents of water, Bartlett rejected contemporary 'Mediterranean' colouring, preferring a more realistic mixture of somewhat murky greys, blues and greens. Inland, where water was more likely to be overlooked, he preferred to mark its presence with an eye-catching blue. Some of the features thus noted are almost vanishingly small, like the well at Taber Mellish or the upland lake near Vicars Carn. Minor lakes were also stippled in black ink, but in the Irish Sea, North Channel and Atlantic the stipple is confined to estuaries and sea loughs. In Carlingford Lough and Dundalk Bay the Cooley map features wave-crests instead of stipple, with a double broken line to mark the navigable channel. Colour usually darkens towards the shore, especially where the coast would be in shadow if a light were shining either from the top of the map or from the left. Another way to emphasise coasts was by a band of short parallel waterlines in imitation of a continuous tone. These are usually horizontal in the contemporary manner, but sometimes vertical and occasionally cross-hatched. A Bartlett speciality of unknown significance is to break the continuity of off-shore shading with longer single vertical strokes at irregular intervals, almost as if the land mass has been mounted on stilts.[7] Individual offshore rocks are represented either by miniature profile drawings or conventionally by crosses.

LAND COVER

Bogs and areas liable to flood are coloured bluish green and demarcated by finely drawn but wavering 'coastlines'. Sometimes their flatness is indicated by thin horizontal pen strokes, but Bartlett also uses such strokes outside the bogs simply to indicate an absence of marked relief. There is nothing that could be interpreted as heath or moor. Woods are shown by deciduous trees in profile, sometimes with crowns in green and trunks in brown, sometimes in a more pervasive greyish-green. Every reader of the time — and almost any other time, no doubt — would have known without being told that these symbols on maps like Bartlett's were not meant to denote particular real-life trees but only undifferentiated portions of a wooded area; however, to heighten the reader's sense of scale the size of individual tree symbols is thoughtfully made to vary with the sizes of the other features represented. Outside the bogs and woods we face a similar problem to that confronting modern Irish historical geographers in seventeenth-century references to 'arable' land. In one small area (Bowlby VI) Bartlett shows what was obviously a field of ripe corn.[8] Does that mean that all the pale green colouring in his other maps refers to nothing but grass?

Roads are drawn in pale buff or 'natural' colour as tidy-looking strips of unvegetated ground, their widths varying with the scale of the map, edged at large scales by narrow threads of yellow colour and coincident broken pen-lines. In the Blackwater valley (Bowlby VIII) the roads are shadowed on one side. To mark a ford, the double pecked lines are carried across the river; for a bridge the double line is unbroken. Causeways are indicated by widening a road or by continuous lines enclosing a narrow rectangle, sometimes with extra shading on one side to suggest embanking. They are also identifiable contextually from the flatness or bogginess of the adjacent land. In the Blackwater valley Bartlett, receptive to Irish nomenclature, additionally denotes a causeway by the word 'cash', derived from *cobhas* or *cobhsa*. On the Trinity version of south-east Ulster a few passes through woods are coloured in the style of the much earlier anonymous Leix-Offaly map,[9] but later examples are less conspicuous — perhaps in the hope that these features would soon be losing their military significance.

SETTLEMENTS AND BOUNDARIES

The Bowlby plans are large enough for a settlement to be represented by drawing its constituent buildings, usually in profile or bird's eye view. House-symbols may then be presumed to resemble their referents and to stand in their true situations. (A possible exception is just outside Monaghan in Bowlby IXa, where the house-clusters have an unrealistic look quite foreign to Bartlett's usual style, each cabin standing slightly in front of the cabin to the right of it.) Roofs are usually yellow, for thatch, but occasionally blue (slate) or reddish-brown (tiles or shingles). On the regional maps the buildings naturally had to be smaller and fewer. Where space allowed, a nucleated settlement could still be shown by a cluster of symbols, as at Newry and Sligo, though the mapped houses were unlikely to be as numerous as their counterparts on the ground. More often there was room for only one symbol per settlement. Of course there was no logical necessity for this to look like any particular building provided that there were other ways of understanding what it meant. However, it would be reasonable for a cartographer to draw something approximately similar to the most conspicuous and functionally distinctive structure on any given site, typically either a church, a castle or a fort.

Some of Bartlett's earliest church-symbols seem unnecessarily elaborate. The tower at Clandaff in the Cotton map has a multiple stepped gable more suggestive of the Netherlands than of Ulster. At Kinard in the same map there is only one step but the effect remains disturbingly implausible. Later, Bartlett fell into a more conventional routine in which most churches were horizontal rectangles representing a side wall, with a gable at each end, and a cross surmounting one or both gables. On a cathedral the cross is more prominent. Armagh, nominally the seat of an archbishop, has a double cross, a map-convention at least as old as the mid sixteenth century.

Castles are often reduced to a single apparently square tower in profile, perhaps descending stepwise on one side by lower storeys to ground level. Sometimes there are smaller towers on both sides of the central tower. Battlements often had to be omitted, and windows appear in only one storey. Many towers have flagpoles, a few displaying a standard indicative of military occupation. Sometimes there is a low outer wall apparently representing a bawn. How much verisimilitude can be inferred from these schematic features is doubtful. Ideally they should be compared either with larger-scale representations of the same site or with extant structures on the ground, but unfortunately such tests are seldom possible. Most of Ulster's more complex castles are shown only on Bartlett's smallest-scale map, where there is no room for individual symbols to be much elaborated: one could hardly expect sites like Dundrum, Dunluce or either of the two Greencastles to be realistically portrayed on such a map. At Newtown[stewart] a single tower is accompanied by a much lower annexe, with no resemblance to the symmetrical 'Harry Avery's Castle' that survives today. On the Bowlby view of Dungannon (Vb), the ruined tower rises three storeys above the top of the courtyard wall. In the much smaller Dungannon of the campaign map there is no such inequality of heights, and the top storey of the tower is shown precariously overhanging the open space outside.

Artillery forts, lacking high curtain walls, are always shown in plan, highly schematised at small scales, though invariably leaving room for an uncoloured empty interior or 'parade'. A double continuous line, with pale buff or natural-coloured filling on the large-scale maps, denotes a wall, bank or trench forming part of a fortification.

As compensation for their smallness, stone buildings of all kinds on the regional maps are almost always coloured red, but there is one symbol that breaks all the rules. This is a small open circle surmounted by a plain cross of the kind used in later Ordnance Survey maps to represent a church with a spire. There are two examples on the Trinity map in Lecale (Bishops court and Audleystown) and three in the 'Generalle description' at B.Aghren, Skerie and Omagh (Mo: Omie). These oddities may be late additions to their respective maps, possibly by another hand and perhaps inserted at a time when there were no colours available.[10]

In the 'Generalle description of Ulster', minor territories are bounded by either dotted or fine continuous lines, major territories by lines of transverse pecks, truncated hachures, or ticks. Boundaries are usually further emphasised by a band of colour on one side. On the later maps most of the territories are also uniformly coloured all over, except where interrupted by woodland or water. The colours are green and yellow, strong enough to create a slightly unbalanced effect, with various shades of orange, pink and mauve not always easy to tell apart, though we may have to allow for some post-Elizabethan deterioration in judging the present state of Bartlett's colours, which nevertheless are generally remarkable for their appearance of freshness. These differences seem to have no semiotic purpose except to prevent confusion between neighbouring territories. (The rule that four colours are sufficient to fill any territorial map without adjacent cells matching is not known to have been recognised in Bartlett's time.) Where there was a risk of running a single shade across a boundary, the solid colour gives way to a border tint. Even so, Bartlett did not always manage to distinguish neighbours: in Tyrone, for instance, Lotie, Clandawell and Clanagher are all the same colour. Where a boundary coincided with a river, the pecked lines were often considered unnecessary, ambiguities being resolved simply by a change of surface colour. In one case, between Clancarney and Toagh in Co. Armagh, hill symbols are made to function as a territorial boundary.

SCRIBAL VARIATIONS

Bartlett uses several different kinds of lettering, but almost all his names and inscriptions resemble each other in being kept apart from other kinds of linework. (Exceptions are probably the sign of a late amendment, as at 'drummuller' near Lough Muckno.) Although this rule shows a well-intentioned concern for legibility, it can sometimes leave too wide a gap between a name and its referent. Tie-lines are used to bridge these gaps on the campaign map, but not consistently — another indication, perhaps, that this map was finished in some haste. The main distinction is in the use or non-use of capital letters. This depends partly on the size of the object represented, so that Lough Neagh, Lough Swilly, Lough Foyle and Lough Erne merit capitals, while miniscules are sufficient for The Bay of Knockfergus, Sheep Haven and Lough Finn. In this respect, the Bays map is more logical than its predecessors, as none of its physical names are capitalised. With hill names, it may be fair to interpret capitals as denoting a district rather than an individual summit, though the converse is not necessarily true.[11] In human geography, capitals are used for all territories and families (in name-phrases the less important words may be in miniscule) except for a variety of church land known as 'termon'. Where capitals are used for both superordinate and subordinate territorial names, the former distinguish themselves by loops, flourishes and the use of a curly 'E' throughout the name instead of just in its initial letter. Examples are 'Tyreone', 'County of Louthe', 'Part of Leynster' and 'Part of Connachte', though Tyrconnell has only plain capitals. Decorative script is also used as a space-filler for maritime and other marginal names. To judge from the Bays map, flourishes were a habit that grew on Bartlett, a not wholly fortunate development as in truth his ornamental lettering is rather ugly.

Another sign of Bartlett's concern for legibility is his fondness for hyphenation, single and double forms being intermixed for no apparent reason. Like other writers he uses hyphens to reunite a word divided between two lines. They also serve to mark some other kinds of interruption, for instance by another name or by a geographical feature, and in a few cases they are applied rather unnecessarily to the constituent words of a phrase, as in 'chief of his name and - this country' and 'Head of the - /- Banne'.

Until the 1570s many cartographers had lettered their maps in the same kind of joined-up script that they would use for correspondence or any other prose communication. With the growing familiarity of printed maps, it became customary for handwritten characters to be kept separate in the manner of contemporary engravers, thus enabling the names of large linear or areal features to be 'mimetically' spaced out. Some artists also aspired to follow the engravers in the extreme neatness and regularity of their scripts: Boazio's map of north-west Ireland is a good example of this fastidiousness.[12] Since few habitual field workers had time to cultivate such calligraphic refinement there also developed an alternative method, which was to shape the letters more or less as in ordinary script but without connecting them — and without attempting to distinguish italic from roman. These informal scripts are illustrated in the manuscript maps of Laurence Nowell, John Norden and Timothy Pont as well as those of Richard Bartlett. The result is a pleasing combination of rigour and flexibility, though some styles, including Bartlett's, are open to criticism for using too much space.

SUMMARY

Bartlett's talents are not easily summarised. Like Leonardo da Vinci, Albrecht Dürer and Wenceslas Hollar, he combined the roles of artist and map-maker, distinguishing himself especially by a sustained effort to strike an even balance between these two activities. In this he was undoubtedly successful, one authority describing him as 'the greatest artist/cartographer ever to work in Ireland'.[13] Like most cartographers he valued the approval of his peer-group, adopting contemporary professional mannerisms even when they did not altogether suit his personal style. For all its uninspiring cartouches and compass roses, that style remained his own: he probably knew that posterity would one day recognise the work he had left unsigned. Within the body of each map a major concern was user-friendliness (perhaps in reaction to Francis Jobson's rather chaotic maps of Ulster), achieved both by rationing the total quantity of topographical detail and by not allowing nearby features to touch or overlap. The most effective aid to legibility was verisimilitude. Like most contemporary cartographers, Bartlett aimed to show the world as travellers were accustomed to seeing it, sideways — rather than downwards as in a modern map. At large scales the trick was to draw individual objects in bird's eye view and to arrange these images in their correct horizontal relations while cleverly avoiding any suggestion of discontinuity. For some sites, as we have seen, there would be a simple picture with no obvious planiform content: here the cartographic virtues were less directly represented, by a uniform sharpness of definition, with light and shadow strongly contrasted but with no details thrown into obscurity. It may be this sudden clarity, applied to a landscape clouded for so long in mystery and ignorance, that gives Bartlett's work its quality of 'eeriness'.[14]

Outside the Bowlby atlas the artist's vision was harder to express. All sixteenth-century cartographers represented hills, trees and buildings in profile, but the results were usually too dispersed to make a small-scale map look like any kind of picture. One way of attempting pictorialisation was to carpet the paper with absurdly oversized schematic landscape features. Bartlett had no time for such crudities. His own remedy was a combination of three methods: first, a quasi-realistic emphasis on the junction of land and water; second, an extremely subtle and delicate hill shading, or perhaps one should rather say ground shading, which only a sophisticated artist could hope to carry off; and third, a carefully balanced distribution of major geographical detail, including names, so that the reader's eye is easily led across the paper without ever wishing to disengage itself. Each Bartlett map is an aesthetic whole, though not the mirror of political unity that his employers would have liked.

REFERENCES

1. Abraham Ortelius, *Theatrum orbis terrarum* (Antwerp, 1570): *Larii Lacus vulgo Comensis descriptio*; *Salisburgensis jurisdictionis.* This parallel has also been noticed by Thomas Herron ('Orpheus in Ulster: Richard Bartlett's colonial art' in Thomas Herron and Michael Potterton (eds), *Ireland in the renaissance* (Dublin, 2007), p. 295, n. 19).
2. Michael Neill, *Putting history to the question: power, politics, and society in English renaissance drama* (New York, 2000), pp 393-6. In a more conventional reading, the chair is about to be hidden by the scroll depicting the English camp (Bernhard Klein, *Maps and the writing of space in early modern England and Ireland* (Basingstoke, 2001), pp 126-7).
3. Ortelius, *Theatrum*: *Galliae regni potentiss: nova descriptio*; *Thusciae descriptio.*
4. Map of lands in Kenry, Co. Limerick [*c.*1586], NMM, MS P.49/23; Maps of the manor of Tralee [*c.*1587], PRO, MPF 1/309; NMM, MS P.49/6a.
5. In preparing *Ulster and other Irish maps* Hayes-McCoy discussed this matter with officers of the Ordnance Survey of Ireland, who seem to have confined their attention to the plan of Augher. (Niall MacNeill to Hayes-McCoy, 3 February, 27 February 1956, National Archives, Dublin, Irish MSS Commission, file 97/41-286). Colonel MacNeill, the Survey's assistant director, believed that there was historical warrant for interpreting the Augher 'needle' as true rather than magnetic north.
6. John Speed, *The theatre of the empire of Great Britaine* (London, 1612): Norwich (Norfolk) and Harlech (Merioneth).
7. There is no mention of this device in Catherine Delano-Smith's wide-ranging 'Signs on printed topographical maps, *ca.*1470-*ca.*1640' in David Woodward (ed.), *The history of cartography, volume three: cartography in the European renaissance* (Chicago, 2007), pp 528-80.
8. Bartlett's only other example of what looks like agriculture is in Bowlby XI, where English soldiers occupy an embanked enclosure containing about one tenth of a statute acre of corn.
9. J.H. Andrews and Rolf Loeber, 'An Elizabethan map of Leix and Offaly: cartography, topography and architecture' in William Nolan and Timothy P. O'Neill (eds), *Offaly: history and society: interdisciplinary essays on the history of an Irish county* (Dublin, 1998), pp 244-7.

10. For a parallel case see Andrews and Loeber, 'An Elizabethan map of Leix and Offaly', p. 251.
11. Kay Muhr, 'The early place-names of County Armagh', *Seanchas Ard Mhacha*, xix, 1 (2002), p. 21.
12. NMM, MS P.49/7.
13. William J. Smyth, *Map-making, landscapes and memory: a geography of colonial and early modern Ireland* c.*1530-1750* (Cork, 2006), pp 44, 49-50.
14. Smyth, *Map-making, landscapes and memory*, p. 49.

Chapter 7

The Art of the Close-Up

Before reviewing the topographical content of Bartlett's large-scale surveys, let us try to set an appropriate standard for distances and areas, taking at their face value the scale lines that appear on nine of the Bowlby plans. For students of cartography the most meaningful basis for comparison is probably the scales of modern Ordnance Survey maps. All nine plans under review have ratios exceeding 1:25,000; eight are larger than 1:10,000; seven are larger than 1:2500; and five are larger than 1:1000. As an example, consider the middle-ranking map in the scale-sequence, which is that of Mountnorris. A typical Irish house at this scale (1:896) would be about half an inch long and in no danger of getting lost. On the other hand, with so much map-space available a single field might be so large as to swallow up a whole page of the Bowlby atlas. To test this last possibility, assume a network of square five-acre enclosures. On the Mountnorris map each field would be six by six inches and three such fields could fill the sheet. In fact, of course, most of this map is occupied not by fields but by a fort, but we might still expect to see one or two fences round the edge, and at smaller scales the number of fields per sheet would be correspondingly larger. In short, Bartlett's plans were fully capable of showing all the houses, roads and fences of an ordinary rural landscape in their correct proportions.

BARTLETT THE WAR ARTIST

Many aspects of late Elizabethan warfare are illustrated in the *Pacata Hibernia* engraving of Kinsale. Like so much contemporary battlefield art, the picture is dominated by infantry squares or 'quadrants', each containing one, two or three St. George's flags protected by a dense cluster of eighteen-foot pikes. We also see horsemen armed with lances or swords, advancing, charging, retreating and in one case just standing and watching. Muskets, calivers or arquebuses are being aimed and discharged, some from the shoulder, some supported on parapets. A number of casualties lie dead or wounded. Some twenty-five artillery pieces are distributed around the landscape, at one point accompanied by barrels of gunpowder and a pile of cannon balls. Unlike John Thomas at Enniskillen, Bartlett does not identify his guns with verbal descriptions.[1] The besiegers' encampments consist of banked enclosures containing large bell tents and ridge tents along with numerous smaller shelters of less determinate character. These images pose many difficulties of interpretation. The worst problem from our present standpoint has already been left unresolved in an earlier chapter: was the Kinsale engraver copying a Bartlett original?

In Bartlett's Ulster maps, whose authorship is in no doubt, there was less opportunity for depicting soldiers engaged in battle. By the time he caught up with Mountjoy's field headquarters in 1602, most of the enemy were out of reach among the woodlands of north Tyrone or Fermanagh. Even Dungannon castle was deserted before the English got there, and if O'Neill abandoned a place of such 'high name',[2] where was he likely to stand and fight? A few of his supporters were still ready for action, however, to judge from the later Bowlby maps.

Encampments similar to those at Kinsale are depicted near Tullaghoge and Inisloughan, the latter including quantities of neatly stacked pikes and two kinds of tent besides numerous semi-cylindrical huts with turves covering a framework of bent wooden rods.[3] Two cannon are aimed in the general direction of Inisloughan fort, but there is no trace of any attackers or defenders. The best picture of active service in the Bowlby series is Map Va, showing the attack on an anonymous crannog. Here the English troops are musketeers and a cannoneer firing on the island, with a square of pikemen in support. Advancing on the lake are two more bodies of pikemen, one apparently with a cavalry escort, led by a mounted officer with drawn sword and followed by a halberdier whom Hayes-McCoy describes as a sergeant, perhaps detailed to round up stragglers. Across the lake are three horsemen identified by Hayes-McCoy as Irish from their conical headgear, stirrupless riding kit, and staves carried above their heads.[4] Heavily outnumbered, they nevertheless seem willing to attack the attackers. It is a pity that Bartlett's maps are so sparsely populated: even his smallest and simplest human figures are full of animation.

Otherwise the most obvious signs of a military presence in the Bowlby maps are the permanent or semi-permanent fortifications. In those built by the English the ramparts are vertical or slightly battered 'curtains', their upper surfaces neatly squared off. Walkways run along the inside, with the top of the curtain serving as a protective parapet. In plan, each rampart is laid out in straight lines that usually meet in angular corners, most of which are protected by bastions comprising four straight sides — two faces and two shorter flanks. In detail, every fort is different, and no military historian has yet related these differences to the natural slope of the land. At Moyry the bastions are exceptional in being rounded instead of angular. In the original Mountnorris layout the only bastion was a simple two-sided salient. Charlemont has four half-bastions in which one face continues the alignment of the curtain, as well as a smaller bastion of more conventional design with gunports in both face and flank. The only other visible openings for guns are embrasures in the bastion-parapet at Mountjoy. Ramparts are interrupted at appropriate points by gates, some of their pillars and lintels being topped by modestly decorative finials. The gates are evidently of wood, with individual brown-painted boards clearly visible. (Any sort of wooden construction seems to have aroused Bartlett's interest.)

The ramparts themselves are harder to interpret. Although they must surely have been made of earth, the impression here is of stone walls faced with plaster. As Hayes-McCoy remarked of the Mullin fort, 'The trim and formal appearance of the fort, and in particular the well built solidity of its walls, may no doubt be attributed rather to Bartlett's pencil than to the entrenching tools of Mountjoy's pioneers.'[5] Outside the main rampart of a typical fort there runs a ditch, always full of water, beyond which is usually a narrow strip of grass and then another barrier, this time unmistakably of earth. In the more complicated layouts, where there are junctions between two lines of moat, wooden dams or sluices were built to separate the different watercourses.

Only two forts, Moyry and Augher, are shown as empty. The others all contain a number of small buildings, most of which in different circumstances would be confidently described as Irish cabins. Bartlett gave more attention to these humble dwellings than any other contemporary artist. One historian, in a refreshingly original interpretation, sees them as a symbolic device designed to emphasise the 'tyrannical' character of Irish society by contrasting with well-built structures like O'Neill's castle.[6] Most cabins have plastered or whitewashed walls one storey high, capped by roofs of yellow thatch. Otherwise, some roofs are hipped, others gabled; some houses have a chimney, more often centrally placed (presumably indicating an internal cross-wall or partition) than in the gable. Others evidently consumed their own smoke. The form most familiar to modern folklife students, a central doorway between two single windows, seems not to have made much impression on Bartlett. His windows are often grouped in pairs; some asymmetrical side-views show a sequence of two windows, an off-centre door and then a single window. Many end-walls contain a window or even a door, an arrangement hardly ever seen in modern Irish houses of this type. Larger buildings are thatched and roofed in the same style but with simple rectangular units combined into terraces, courtyards, crosses or T-junctions. A few such composite structures appear to have two storeys. Some of the larger houses are roofed with tiles, slates or shingles; one of them, at Charlemont, has a tall external chimney perhaps betokening industrial activity of some kind, a rare phenomenon in Elizabethan Ulster. Bartlett shows none of the beehive huts depicted by other Elizabethan cartographers.[7] Some of his buildings have almost defied identification, among them an 'unusual rectangular wooden framework structure' in Bowlby XI that has been interpreted in various ways, most plausibly perhaps as a defensive wooden tower in course of construction.[8] There are no purpose-built military structures such as gatehouses, prisons or barrack-blocks: presumably the English garrisons made do with the style of building that came most naturally to the available workmen, whether these were local residents or camp-followers recruited in other parts of Ireland. In the matter of vernacular building Bartlett can be said to have made his point, but we may doubt whether all his minor architectural details were meant to be taken seriously.

Places like the Mullin or Monaghan are usually called 'artillery forts', but in all Bartlett's examples there are only seven guns (including one at Dungannon castle), five of them in either Mountjoy or Mountnorris. This gives an average of only one gun for every four bastions; perhaps it was lucky the war was nearly over when the drawings were made. The size of these pieces is hard to estimate. They all have carriages with spoked or solid wheels, sometimes four, sometimes two. The four guns recorded outside the forts appear to be of similar design.

LANDSCAPES BEYOND THE PARAPET

A fort plan is not much use to tacticians without some knowledge of what lay outside the ramparts. Most of the Bowlby plans purport to cover areas that vary with the scale and size of the map from less than 3 acres in Monaghan to more than 600 acres in and around Lough Bofin. Each frame is filled to its edges with what purports to be topographical detail. All streams appear to have been mapped with care. Otherwise the features of most military significance outside the forts are hills, woods and bogs.

Once Mountjoy's troops had got beyond the Cooley mountains (dramatically portrayed overlooking the Moyry fort), the local relief of his campaign trail was generally unspectacular. Its most striking features were what look like rocky cliffs surrounding the site of the castle at Dungannon.[9] Otherwise the impression is of drumlin or 'basket of eggs' topography, best illustrated in the Blackwater valley, where many of Bartlett's hills are individually recognisable. Elsewhere justice is done to all hill-tops of special significance, among them Armagh cathedral, the rath at Tullaghoge and, on a more localised scale, the site of the guns outside Inisloughan.

Woods occur in nearly all the plans, generally forming small patches of irregular shape. On the largest scales trees sometimes stand alone, but there is little sign of scrubland or parkland: mostly the trunks appear in solid masses, like contemporary pikemen in close formation. Only once does a clear pattern emerge, where woods parallel the course of a river at Inisloughan. Bogs and flood plains are shown as flat areas of more or less foliate appearance, sometimes with indeterminate drainage marked by streams that lead nowhere. However, in evaluating such details we must remember the case in chapter 4 where the same lake was thought by Hayes-McCoy to have been mapped twice (Bowlby Va and XI) in surroundings of incompatibly different lay-out. If this highly permissive interpretation of landscape detail is accepted, a large amount of Bartlett's other background information must be treated with considerable reserve. Here we may note that two of his landscape images have been recently interpreted not as realistic outlines but as visual puns — one (a wood) a satyr representing the native Irish, the other (an enclosure) a St. George's flag representing the English conquest.[10] If nothing else, these judgements show that Bartlett's landscapes are capable of being taken less than seriously.

At very large scales an Elizabethan cartographer would usually manage to overcome his profession's strange distaste for roads. At first sight Bartlett is no exception. He shows numerous tracks and paths leading to the forts, without necessarily including every road within each rectangle: even when furnishing the Blackwater valley with one of the closest local road networks in contemporary Irish cartography, he still provides no means of access to the important castle site of Benburb. None of his routeways exhibit the straightness that has sometimes been attributed to early Irish roads.[11]

Houses outside the English forts are potentially more significant from an ethnographic point of view than those inside, being presumably free from foreign architectural influence. However, in essentials they resemble the buildings already considered, rectangular in layout, without rounded corners (as far as can be seen) but with hip roofs. In some ways the most interesting examples are the three roofless structures in Bowlby Va, which the English soldiers were probably dismantling to use the timbers for their own purposes. Here the roof had been supported by three slightly curved wooden couples resting directly on low thick walls of mud or stone.[12] Only one house outside the forts has a chimney and that is centrally placed. None of this gives much of a basis for generalisation, but Caoimhín Ó Danachair concludes from the Bowlby maps that hip-roofs and centrally placed chimneys were once common in parts of Ireland from which they were later to disappear.[13]

By the same token there is little to be learned from the Bowlby maps about peacetime rural settlement patterns. They show no buildings beside the roads, for example, or in the immediate neighbourhood of the churches near Armagh and Tullaghoge. In most maps the only houses are those with at least a semblance of protection, as in the city of Armagh, in the outer enclosure at Dungannon, and in the rath of Tullaghoge. The chief exceptions are the thirteen cabins near Monaghan, and even those were within easy reach of a fort. The truth is that we cannot expect to find a normal agricultural landscape flourishing under a conqueror's guns. With the English army just over the horizon, many inhabitants would simply have moved away. Living or dead, the only people Bartlett notices apart from soldiers are two boatmen on the Blackwater, and the only animals are a few ducks — as if water was the one place where a living creature could feel safe in the Ulster of 1602.

Much the same applies to the traditional subject-matter of economic geography. In one view after another there are neither farmyards, fences, hedges nor walls. We know that the soldiers spent much of their time killing people, driving away cattle, burning houses and destroying crops. Mountjoy admitted that it saddened him to behave so brutally.[14] Chichester admitted the brutality but not the sadness. Outside the bogs and woods, Bartlett bowdlerised the results of this policy by bathing whole landscapes in a uniform lush green. Occasionally he hints at a harsher reality. One such case was a solitary house on the shores of Lough Bofin that somebody had considered to be worth torching, evidence of the thoroughness with which the English troops could do their work. Another example, near Inisloughan, was an acre or so of ripe corn in 'lazy-beds', not being burnt, it is true, but with a road arbitrarily driven through the middle of it, presumably by the occupants of the nearby English encampment who no doubt intended to cut the corn for their own use.

MARKING THE EARTH WITH RUIN

But at least Bartlett's self-censorship was confined to recent wartime experience. He knew that the abandonment of earthworks and the collapse of medieval buildings had long been part of the Irish scene and he evidently took some pleasure in the portrayal of ancient ruins, perhaps as a way of finding historical precedents for Mountjoy's conduct. He makes a point of showing one major deserted settlement-enclosure at Emain Macha not far from Armagh. (Since drawing the Cotton and Trinity maps he had learned that there were no stone buildings on this site.) Near Monaghan the rath has no gates; at Tullaghoge it has gates but parts of its bank are badly degraded. Other raths appear to have left some traces near the upper left corner of the Blackwater valley map. Bartlett also enjoyed depicting slighted castles: there is a large one at Dungannon and a small one at Benburb, both reminiscent of another example in the Kinsale engraving. Roofless churches are not peculiar to Bartlett: they occur in most contemporary Irish maps. His speciality is to emphasise the melancholy of ruination, where the scale allows, by homing in on tokens of architectural sophistication that had somehow survived intact — lancet and rose windows, belfries, Romanesque arches, flights of steps. Such details are especially evident at Armagh, a portrait uniquely comprehensive in early Irish iconography of a ruined town, in which only parts of the cathedral and half a dozen thatched and wattled cabins still have their roofs. The nearby streets are defined only by the edges of earthen enclosures, some empty, others occupied by surprisingly well-ordered heaps of rubble — perhaps a sign that the city had been systematically demolished rather than bombarded into destruction or simply left to decay.

CONCLUSION

The Bowlby graphics, it has been suggested, 'employ a hybrid convention, halfway between landscape painting and cartography'. Attractive at first sight, this judgement might nevertheless be adversarially interpreted as one step towards a denial that maps are maps. Another straw in the same wind is to claim that in Bowlby IX (Monaghan) the marginal scale and compasses 'appear to function less as a practical adjunct to map reading than as a triumphant symbol of ... technology'. In the same vein and more generally, Bartlett's object in the whole series is described as 'more illustrative than practical'.[15] Here it would seem captious to disagree: after all, the war was effectively over when most of the drawings were made. But we may still argue that the best way to illustrate the English achievement in Ulster was by a series of realistic images; and it so happens that realism is more 'practical' than fantasy. To accommodate the 'half-way' classification we may add that some of these images (very roughly speaking, those with scales) are maps and that some of them are pictures.

In detail, the overall impression left by Bartlett's large-scale views is of a conflict between two pressures: on the one hand, shortage of time and want of security, giving much of his work a broad, impressionistic character; on the other, his keen interest in a wide range of local phenomena, manifested by unexpectedly pouncing on small features drawn with as much precision as the scale allows. Such details are by no means exclusively warlike. However, it was soldiering that had brought Bartlett to Ulster, with the landscape of military occupation as his principal subject. And of course his loyalty is never in doubt. For Hayes-McCoy the view of Dungannon castle is a 'propaganda piece' in which Bartlett's 'paean of Mountjoy' reaches a crescendo.[16] Admittedly the English flag flying over the castle is rather large; but one wonders if Hayes-McCoy may have been influenced here by having mistakenly credited Mountjoy's cartographer with the 'Lane' map of east Ulster and its provocative image of John de Courcy in the guise of a Roman general. Certainly Hayes-McCoy's 'braggadocio' hardly seems the right word for Bartlett. If anything his maps show a certain restraint, even a certain sympathy with the victims of conquest.[17] In subsequent chapters the same may prove true of his work at smaller scales.

REFERENCES

1. BL, Cotton MS, Aug. I, ii, 39 (1594).
2. Sir Arthur Chichester to earl of Northampton, 7 February 1608, *CSPI, 1606-8*, p. 405.
3. Caoimhín Ó Danachair, 'Representations of houses on some Irish maps of *c.*1600' in Geraint Jenkins (ed.), *Studies in folk life: essays in honour of Iowerth C. Peate* (London, 1969), p. 93.
4. G.A. Hayes-McCoy, *Ulster and other Irish maps* c.*1600* (Dublin, 1964), p. 10.
5. Hayes-McCoy, *Ulster maps*, p. 5.
6. Swen Voekel, 'From Irish countries to English counties: state sovereignty and territorial reorganization in early modern Ireland' in Philip Schwyzer and Simon Mealor (eds), *Archipelagic identities: literature and identity in the Atlantic archipelago, 1550-1800* (Aldershot, 2004), p. 103.
7. Examples are Carrickfergus: BL, Cott. MS Aug. I, ii, 42; TCD, MS 1209/26; PRO, MPF 1/98; Blackwater fort, Co. Tyrone: PRO, MPF 1/311; Valentia Island: Lambeth Palace, MS 625/27; South-west Cork: *Pacata Hibernia; or, a history of the wars in Ireland* ... (Dublin, 1810), iii, pp 526, 558.
8. Aidan O'Sullivan, 'Crannogs in late medieval Gaelic Ireland, *c.*1350-*c.*1650' in Patrick J. Duffy, David Edwards and Elizabeth Fitzpatrick (eds), *Gaelic Ireland* c.*1250-*c.*1650: land, lordship and settlement* (Dublin, 2001), p. 410; Colm Donnelly, Paul Logue, Jim O'Neill and John O'Neill, 'Timber castles and towers in sixteenth-century Ireland: some evidence from Ulster', *Archaeology Ireland*, summer 2007, p. 25.
9. It is uncertain whether modern research will succeed in identifying this feature, which does not exist at ground level today. A recent archaeological television programme on Dungannon, 'The fort of the earls', U.K., Channel 4, 2 March 2008, threw no conclusive light on the subject.
10. Thomas Herron, 'Orpheus in Ulster: Richard Bartlett's colonial art' in Thomas Herron and Michael Potterton (eds), *Ireland in the renaissance* (Dublin, 2007), pp 196, 299.
11. J.H. Andrews, 'Road planning in Ireland before the railway age', *Irish Geography*, v, 1 (1964), pp 17-41.
12. Audrey J. Horning, '"Dwelling houses in the old Irish barbarous manner". Archaeological evidence for Gaelic architecture in an Ulster plantation village' in Duffy, Edwards and Fitzpatrick, *Gaelic Ireland*, p. 379.
13. Ó Danachair, 'Representations of houses on some Irish maps of *c.*1600', p. 102.
14. Vincent Carey, '"What pen can paint or tears atone?" Mountjoy's scorched earth campaign' in Hiram Morgan (ed.), *The battle of Kinsale* (Dublin, 2004), p. 211.
15. For all these quotations see Michael Neill, *Putting history to the question: power, politics, and society in English renaissance drama* (New York, 2000), p. 393.
16. Hayes-McCoy, *Ulster maps*, p. 8. Reviewers of Hayes McCoy's book who took a similar view of Bartlett as a propagandist were 'B. McE.' (*Journal of the County Louth Archaeological Society*, xv, 3 (1965), pp 292-3) and E.F.D. Roberts (*Scottish Historical Review*, xliv (1965), p. 158). On this subject see also Herron, 'Orpheus in Ulster', *passim*.
17. Mercedes Camino, '(Un)folding the map of early modern Ireland: Spenser, Moryson, Bartlett, and Ortelius', *Cartographica*, xxxiv, 4 (1997), pp 14-15.

Chapter 8

More Distant Prospects: The Land

Except for the Bays map, which included an arbitrarily chosen segment of northern Connacht, Bartlett's work on smaller scales was almost exclusively concerned with Ulster. His outline of the province did not quite match the nine counties of modern reckoning — or, for that matter, the definitions chosen by some of his contemporaries. The only part of Co. Cavan he includes in Ulster is East Breifni north-east of the River Erne (a boundary unrecognised by later territorial geographers), the rest of Cavan being classified with Connacht under the name West Breifni. Jobson, more logically, had left the whole county out of Ulster. Further east there were many maps, including Bartlett's 'Generalle description', that carried Ulster as far south as Drogheda. For Jobson, however, the northern province ended in the vicinity of the River Glyde, and in Bartlett's other maps the boundary is at Dundalk. This at least conforms with strategic realities: central and southern County Louth were reasonably quiet in 1600-1, but English troops did not yet feel completely safe in the Carlingford peninsula.

Before the various subject-categories are discussed there is one general issue that affects almost every kind of information. This is the difference between thematic and general maps, the latter including the sub-class usually labelled topographical. In modern geography, a thematic map purports to record every occurrence of some particular phenomenon within a prescribed area: an example would be an economic geographer's distribution map of power stations. A general map, like those of the Ordnance Survey or the *Times atlas of the world*, attempts to characterise a tract of country for the benefit of non-specialists. Its aim is to help readers find their way about — either literally or in an imaginative sense, depending on the scale of the map. Bartlett's maps, it will already be clear, are general rather than thematic. It is sometimes thought that generality in the present sense can be achieved by superimposing numerous thematic outlines to form a kind of multi-layered cartographic sandwich, but most maps made by this method would be confusingly overcrowded in some places and unsatisfyingly empty in others. In practice the compiler's selection or rejection of detail must be governed by its local importance; also by the demands of legibility and visual composition. In this last respect we must remember that Bartlett was as much artist as cartographer: the incompleteness of his 'Generalle description of Ulster', in particular, may well owe something to aesthetic sensitivity.

THE COASTLINE

Bartlett's maps of Ulster and north Connacht cover some 900 miles of coast from Killala Bay to Dundalk Bay. Taken as a whole they seem more correct than anything attempted earlier. Most of their named bays, headlands and islands are identifiable on the Ordnance Survey map from similarities of either shape, nomenclature or both (table 1, fig. 4).[1] That does not make Bartlett's outline a model of detailed accuracy or comprehensiveness from end to end. Where he or his informants took a short cut, several miles of coastline might have to be inserted by guesswork. Like other early cartographers, he also had his own 'personal curvature'. This included many fictitious but plausible-looking capes and inlets, mostly rounded rather than angular, while many features with a real existence were less prominently mapped than they should have been. In short, we are looking at a mixture of detail, surveyed and unsurveyed; rare skill was needed to combine these two elements into a convincing whole.

TABLE 1: Named coastal features in the north of Ireland.

Bartlett	Modern maps
Negui	Benwee or Kilcummin
Rosse	Ross Point
Baye of the Moye	Killala Bay
Point Roslie	Bunowna Point
Enish omoclough or the Conie Ile	Coney Island
Enish Roins	Oyster Island
Point of the Rosses	Rosses Point
Enishe Humno or Murrie	Inishmurray
Rosboe	Shaddan or Bomore
Derinishe	Dernish Island
Point mullogh-moore	Mullaghmore
Po: Sandhills	Tullan Strand
The Bar	Bar
Bun	Bunlin Barr
Bul point	
Baye of Donnegall, Baie of Donegale	Donegal Bay
barre	The Long Ridge
Fox rock	Blind Rock
Po: St. Patricke	Doorin Point
Whitleye baye	Inver Bay
Corran Callebeg, The Rosse point	St. John's Point
Rosbaie	McSwyne's Bay
The 2 Goates	Gore Beg, Gore More
The Candle	Connellagh
The Haven of Calbeg, Harborough of Calebeg	Killybegs Harbour
White-sande baye	Fintragh Bay
The Litle Raghlins	Rathlin O'Birne Island
Haven of Telen, Baye & Harborough of Tellen	Tawny Bay
Can Telen, Tellen head	Rossan Point
The north Iles of Arran	Aran Island
Torre Insu:	Tory Island
Horre head	Horn Head
Sheep haven	Sheep Haven
Redhaven	Mulroy Bay
LOUGH SUILLIE	Lough Swilly
Inish	Inch
Haven coldagh	Culdaff Bay
LO FOYLLE	Lough Foyle
Portrush	
Skeries Portrush	Portrush; The Skerries
Ship Ins	Sheep Island
Raghlins	Rathlin Island
Whithead	Kinbane or White Head
Markenton baie	Ballycastle Bay
Faire foreland	Fair Head
Tor baie	
Tor Ile	
Can Torbaie	Torr Head
Bunondune	Cushendun Bay
Red baie	Red Bay
Baie Glanarme	Glenarm Bay
The maides	Maidens
Olderfleet	Larne Lough
Kna Ins	Isle of Muck
Baiy of Knockfergus	Belfast Lough
Carick duff	
Copland Iles	Copeland Island
Briell	Burial Island
North rock	North Rocks
South rock	South Rock
LO: CONE	Strangford Lough
Makie Ins, Maqui Ins	Mahee Island
Inshe moore, Enis moore	Islandmore
Dunanelle	Dunnyneill Island
Craggan cowes, Cragancows	Angus Rock
St. Patricks rock	St. Patrick's Rocks
Bay of Strongford, Strongford Haven	Strangford Bay
Pointe St. John, St. Johns point	St. John's Point
Baye Dundrum, Baie of Dundrum	Dundrum Bay
P. Crainfeild, Point of Crainfeld called the North Point, Point Crainfielde	Cranfield Point
Rheincullen	Soldier's Point
Reinmore	Point Barry
Black rock	
Bulpoint	
Chappel P:	
Baye of Carlingforde, Carlingforde Haven	Carlingford Lough
Point Grenore	Greenore Point
Enis moore	Block House Island
Point Ballaghan, Point Balaghan	Ballagan Point
Rhein Corweie	
Corwaie road	
Baie of Dundalk	Dundalk Bay
Rheine, or Point Dunanane	Dunany Point
Pointe Clogher	Clogher Head

Fig. 4: (a) and (b): North Connacht and west Ulster: coastal features mapped by Bartlett.

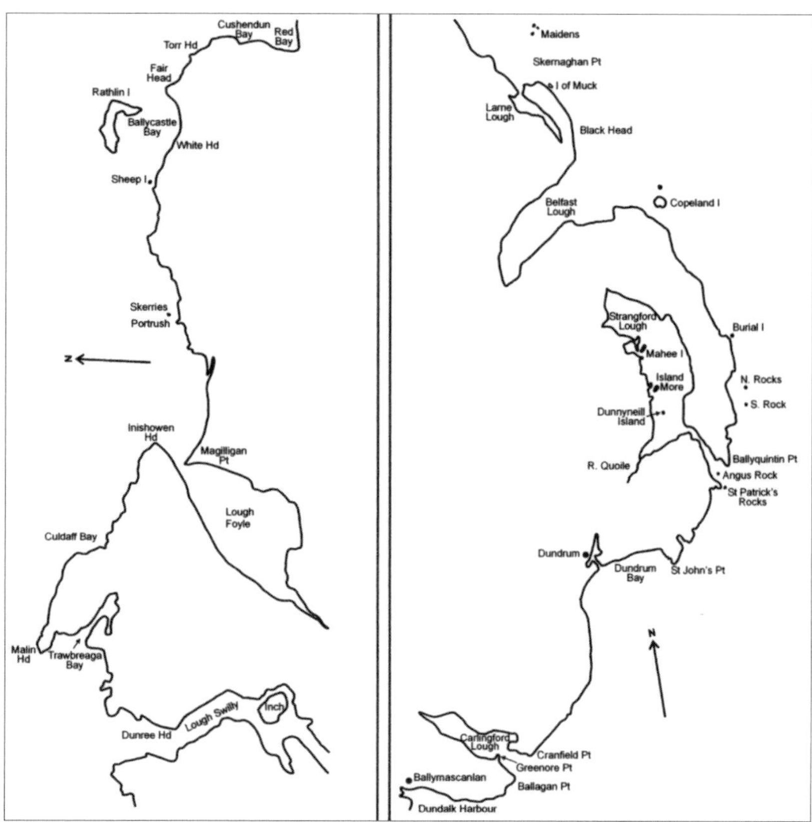

Fig. 4: (c) and (d): North and east Ulster: coastal features mapped by Bartlett.

Bartlett's interest in islands is perhaps another sign of his having been exposed to marine cartography at some stage of his career. At any rate they seemed more likely to attract his attention than mainland features of comparable extent, a few of them later being rejected by the Ordnance Survey as unworthy of inclusion in a modern half-inch map. Some of Bartlett's islands are exaggerated in size; most have their own rudimentary capes and bays, only the smallest being necessarily reduced to simple blobs. Many are badly misplaced in relation to the nearby mainland. This is understandable: on a continuous coastline, there is a sense in which sketched features can hold each other in position, whereas an object surrounded by sea is free to wander across the map, unless a surveyor has taken the trouble to intersect it with angular measurements.

One test of an early map is to ask how many of its anonymous coastal features can be matched with their modern equivalents. Leaving table 1 to speak for itself, we may now try this experiment on the north Irish coast, proceeding again in a clockwise direction from Killala Bay. On the Bays map there is no mistaking Bartragh Island, Aughris Head, or the mouths of the rivers Easky, Dunneill and Dunmoran. Nor are there any serious problems in the Bays of Sligo and Ballysadare, although the north side of Drumcliff Bay was evidently one of those peninsulas where land-based surveyors preferred to save time by cutting off a corner. Next come the inlets of Grange, Mill Haven and the Duff River, distinguishable if not particularly accurate. At the head of Donegal Bay, after a satisfactory run of coastal names, there are three anonymous islands identifiable with a slight effort, while on the north side of the bay the names of St. Ernans Point, Drumancoo Head and Inishduff can be interpolated without much hesitation. After that Bartlett's knowledge rapidly deteriorates, with nothing to distinguish either Muckros Head or the bifurcation of Tawny Bay.

So much for the basic outline of the Bays map. In the 'Generalle description' the Donegal coast is further simplified and the number of names reduced, a process even more drastically applied in the far west than the smaller scale of the 'Description' demands. Glen Bay may be recognisable, and perhaps Port Bay, while another three of Bartlett's islands are at least numerically comparable with Toralaydan, Tormore and Gull. What might be Loughros Beg and Loughros More Bays are combined into a single inlet, opening south-south-westwards instead of due west, but this feature is so approximately rendered that it could just as well be taken for the Ordnance Survey's Trawenagh Bay a good eight miles away. Among Bartlett's fifteen islands between this bay and Bloody Foreland, only Aran is individually convincing. Bloody Foreland itself seems beyond doubt, its identification to some extent confirmed by the proximity of Tory Island and the three unnamed islands to the south of it, which can only be Inishbeg, Inishdoory and Inishbofin. Perhaps these came from an unknown sea chart, especially as the large but not easily accessible inlet of Ballyness Bay on the nearby mainland is ignored. Such omissions are typical of Bartlett's work in the north-west; and some of the features that he does show are highly suspicious, among them several of his islands in Sheep Haven. Another island outside the mouth of Redhaven (Mulroy Bay) may be Island Roy, but the representation of this bay is so flagrantly inaccurate that nothing thereabouts can be identified with confidence.

Approaching the theatre of Sir Henry Docwra's recent military operations we meet a higher standard of verisimilitude with the inclusion of Dunree Head, Trawbreaga Bay, Malin Head, Inishowen Head and Magilligan Point, after which the coast becomes comparatively simple and, thanks to Francis Jobson and other precursors of Bartlett, comparatively familiar. Indeed the worst mistakes, referred to in an earlier chapter, may well have arisen from the conflation of two or more cartographic records rather than from faulty observation. From Belfast Lough to Carlingford Lough, the earlier maps are more numerous and to some extent better known, so Bartlett's readers may not have expected him to give names for places like Skernaghan Point, Blackhead, the 'Points' east of Bangor, or Ballyquintin Point. The only source of confusion is where he writes an unaccompanied letter 'N' against an otherwise nameless offshore rock: perhaps he started to write 'North Rock' and then realised that he was doing this on the wrong side of South Rock.

Another key to merit in an early map is whether it would satisfy modern geomorphologists as reliable evidence for later coastal change. Bartlett usually fails this test (sometimes by a narrow margin), but in one place he leaves no room for doubt. This is at the mouth of the River Quoile near Downpatrick, where the irregular shallow bay shown on two of his maps was not reclaimed until the eighteenth century, though even here the islands are best treated as schematic. The island south of Dundrum on the Trinity map, unknown to other cartographers, is too large to be dismissed so offhandedly; it may have been a sand bank connected to the mainland at low tide, which is apparently how Bartlett decided to explain it away in the 'Generalle description'.

In Carlingford Lough the small inlet west of Greenore Point gives further evidence of post-seventeenth-century reclamation. The Cooley map improves the shape and alignment of the Carlingford peninsula, as we have seen, but like Bartlett's other versions of this area it places two surprisingly large islands in the mouth of the lough, one of them named (also surprisingly) Enis moore. The Cooley map stands alone, however, in its neat if simplified portrayal of the inlet at Ballymascanlan north of Dundalk Harbour.

RIVERS AND LAKES

Since Bartlett seems to have plotted his rivers before fitting in the associated hills, it will be appropriate to consider drainage before relief (fig. 5). Assuming as they so often do a familiar pattern of trunks, branches and twigs, Ulster's rivers were easier subjects for cartographic speculation than most of its other physical features. Fragmentary sightings of a river system can be connected on paper by interpolation — with some risk of error, it is true, though not so much as with roads, coastlines or territorial boundaries. This process is assisted by the existence of widely known river names, an advantage not available in the case of hills. For this reason it seems unlikely that field workers in Tudor Ireland would have taken the time and trouble to follow a long river mile by mile from mouth to source.

Convention plays a relatively small part in the actual drawing of a river, which can be symbolised more or less realistically by a double line tapering

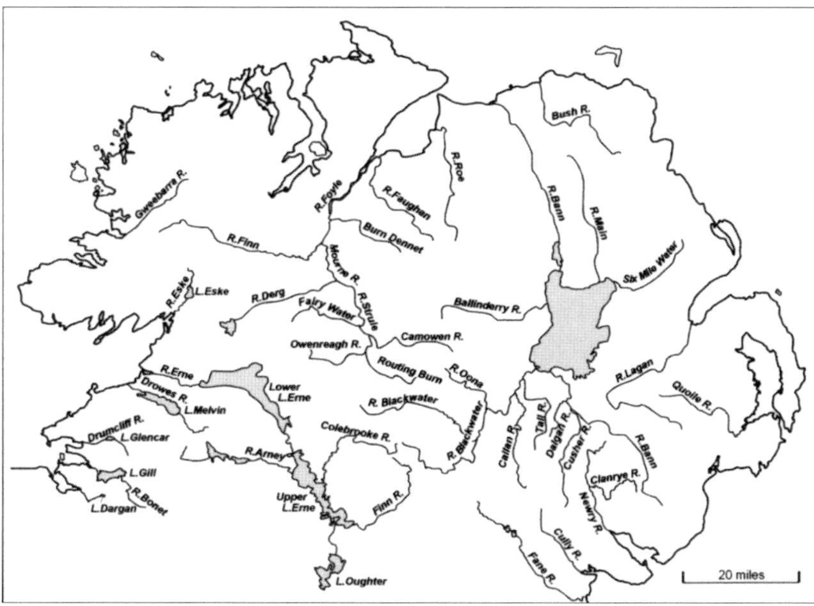

Fig. 5: Northern Ireland: major rivers. From Ordnance Survey of Ireland, *Rivers and their catchment basins* (Dublin, 1958).

upstream. Of course at small scales the only way to double a line is by making the river excessively wide. Medieval cartographers' rivers had often exceeded the necessary minimum by a wide margin, and this fault was still evident in the Ulster cartography of Bartlett's time, his own earliest maps being guilty of it in representing the Bann and Blackwater. Conventionalisation also appears in mapping the smaller curves of a river, which were often likely-looking fakes rather than products of actual observation. Bartlett managed this process with commendable discretion. Only in the River Eske do his meanders seem conspicuously exaggerated.

Selectiveness is also subject to convention at scales too small for every river to be shown. The campaign map shows some twenty-five streams not represented on the 'Generalle description', where they would have averaged just over half an inch in length. The only one of these omissions large enough to count as an editorial misjudgement is the Oona Water (1.8 inches), the first Blackwater tributary above Benburb, and even this might be considered unnecessary by virtue of not passing near any important non-hydrological features. Other things being equal, a river's chances of selection might seem to depend upon its size, but short rivers flowing directly to the sea were more likely to be chosen than rivers of similar or greater length forming the upper tributaries of larger streams. One of Bartlett's ploys was to generalise headwaters into a single fork, the identities of the two feeders being left uncertain. The mixture of realism and convention that may result is illustrated in the uppermost basin of the Blackwater, where the campaign map has a southern and the 'Generalle description' a northern tributary. The former solution seems better, if only because it respects the watershed function of the Slew Ashe hills.

The process of river interpolation was sometimes distorted by false hydrological theorising. Many medieval cartographers believed that all rivers must take their rise in some kind of natural reservoir. If anything Bartlett illustrates a contrary fault, that of showing lakes with no river entrance or exit, a practice that has created difficult problems of identification in a country with as many lakes as Ulster. He certainly showed a keen interest in water bodies of every size, partly no doubt as a result of having recently been observing crannogs under military attack. He correctly placed many small lakes at the heads of rivers, and his only obvious example of an invented Ulster lake is in the Trinity map, at the head of the Cully river flowing into Dundalk Harbour, a mistake he was later to correct. In two cases, the Bann and the Blackwater, he contradicts the reservoir theory by explicitly naming the head of a river that tapers to a point. (Coincidentally, several other cartographers have thought it worth annotating the source of the Bann, including William Petty and the Ordnance Survey.) The seemingly landlocked river south of Tempel Tallogh Carbett on the campaign map is a freakish anomaly.

A more serious aberration was the habit of joining different river systems by imaginary inland waterways. Near the coast such junctions may be rationalised as arms of the sea; elsewhere they may represent strips of boggy ground where the direction of drainage was indeterminate. Bartlett's examples occur near the southern end of the Ards peninsula and in the division of Inishowen into three islands — Malin, Inishowen proper, and a strip of country between Derry and Bert. Further inland such interconnections are less plausible, but they are common in contemporary Irish maps of other regions, especially Connacht. The copying process is most likely to go astray when two streams flow in opposite directions with a short stretch of dry territorial boundary forming a 'portage' between them on the same alignment. In this respect Bartlett overcame a temptation that even Petty failed to resist, for instance between the Newry and Bann river basins at Moineyine and between the Tall River and Dalgan River drainage along the southern boundary of Terlough Brasillough.

Regionally, as would be expected, Bartlett's drainage systems deteriorate from east to west. In the Glens of Antrim it was hard to go far wrong. The streams entering Belfast Lough, Carlingford Lough and Dundalk Bay are accurately shown, including the unexpected bends of the Rivers Lagan and Clanrye. The worst omission among east-flowing rivers is the Quoile. Further west, the Bush, the Braid and the Six Mile Water are well proportioned, and the whole Lough Neagh basin is free from serious error, though there should be more rivers approaching the lower Bann from the west and the Lough from the east. To the south, Bartlett naturally did a good job in the area of Mountjoy's recent campaigns drained by the Blackwater and the upper Bann. Not surprisingly, the Sperrin Mountains are an area of weakness, extending almost to the Foyle, which lacks its tributary the Burn Dennet. The Faughan and the Roe, however, are reasonably correct, perhaps because of their proximity to important castles at Enagh and Limavady respectively, and in the Burngibbagh Bartlett even notices a tributary not named on the Ordnance Survey's ten-mile map of Ireland's rivers. Otherwise his treatment of the middle Foyle basin is satisfactory, at least in a topological sense, with the Finn, Derg, Mourne, Strule and Camowen all more or less in position, though Bartlett differs from modern usage in the exact application of their names. Towards the Mourne headwaters his coverage becomes less comprehensive, with no sign of the Fairy Water, Owenreagh or Routing Burn.

Among the mountains of Donegal Bartlett plays safe by giving each inlet its own somewhat non-committal river, but except in the immediate hinterland of Killybegs he knows nothing of what geologists would later call the 'Caledonian' (northeast-southwest) physiographical alignment typified in real space by the Gweebarra River and Lough Finn. His hydrological interpretation of Fermanagh is perhaps best described as a moderately good guess: a single Lough Erne trends in more or less the right direction, i.e. south-eastwards, narrowing at Enniskillen in a distant approximation to the truth, after which the same alignment is continued with little deviation upstream to the modern Lough Oughter, known to Bartlett as 'Lough Cane'. Only the relation of this lake to the town of Cavan is clearly wrong. But the Erne has only one mapped tributary of any size and that is Bartlett's most erroneous river, the westward flowing Cumbre, apparently a conflation of the Finn and Colebrooke streams as recorded on later maps.

The 'inlets' theme is further pursued in the Bays map, without serious mishap except that two of the three large streams converging on the Ballysadare River are missing. Otherwise the main point of interest here is the relation of the rivers to the lakes. Lough Dargan, Lough Gill, Glencar Lough, Lough Melvin, Lough Erne and Lough Eske are all correctly shown in this respect, though some of their shapes and sizes are badly distorted, especially in the case of Lough Melvin. The mystery lakes of the Glencar River have already been mentioned.

HILLS

Bartlett's relief features hardly ever get close to reality (fig. 6), seldom exploiting even the limited amount of variation allowed by contemporary drawing styles. Few of his profile symbols can be identified as particular hills, and the words 'Slewe' and 'Knock' refer to tracts of upland rather than individual summits, a reasonable policy in an age when surveyors had not yet started recording numerical altitudes. The main exceptions, topographically interesting but of small territorial extent, are hills crowned

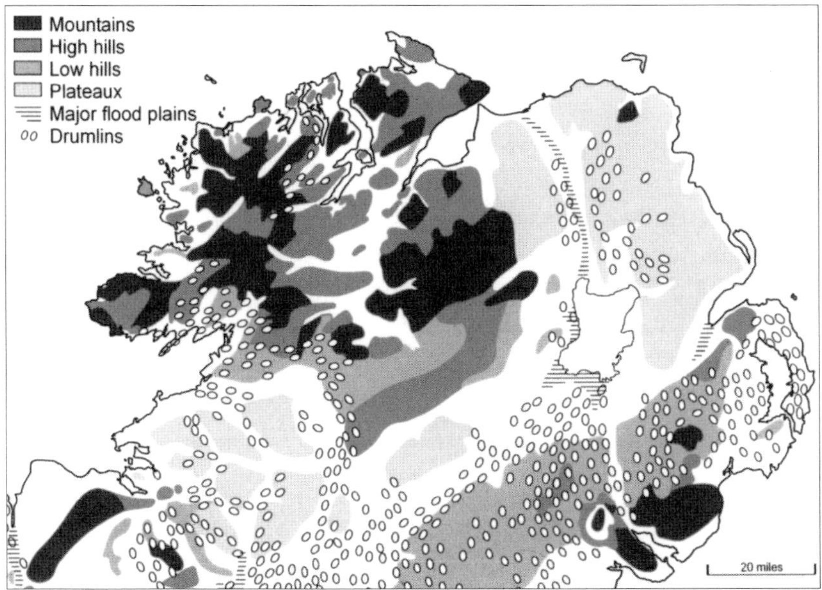

Fig. 6: Northern Ireland: major landforms. Adapted from G.L. Herries Davies in J.P. Haughton (ed.), *Atlas of Ireland* (Dublin, 1979), p. 21.

by important buildings as at Dungannon, Castlereagh, Faughart, Corway and Rathfriland. Generally, upland regions appear as groups of two or more overlapping hill profiles. To a modern eye, most of these groupings have a random look, though few of Bartlett's symbols are altogether unjustified. (A possible example lies north of Lough Melvin, an area that he had obviously never studied in detail.) Occasionally there are hints of a regional pattern. A broad swathe of country through southernmost Tyrone, mid-Armagh and across to Strangford Lough is correctly treated as lowland. In north-west Ulster, the uplands are in the interfluves and along the interiors of the peninsulas. In the north-east the eye of faith may recognise the Antrim plateau. The most common aggregate form, however, as in so many early maps, is the linear range, perhaps a dozen or so symbols in length and one or two in width. Slieve Beagh and the Mountains of Mourne are the best examples. Slieve Anierin fails to qualify because it has been imported as a space-filler from outside the limits of the map, the kind of temptation that Bartlett should have avoided. A more complex case is the Carlingford peninsula on the campaign map, where Glenmore and the Jonesborough lowland each form spaces within an M-shaped range. Sometimes the process of range-formation went too far. On the Cotton and Trinity maps, Bartlett's north-south alignment near Slieve Croob is plainly unrealistic: in the 'Generalle description' he decided not to retain this feature.

The most impressive range at first sight is a discontinuous line of hills from the border of Fermanagh near Lisnaskea almost to the north-west corner of Lough Neagh. This is too far south to be equated with the Sperrin Mountains (a name unknown to Elizabethan cartographers) and in fact Bartlett had selected two watersheds: in the west, between the Foyle-Mourne system and the upper Blackwater, hydrologically perhaps the most significant drainage divide in central Ulster; and in the east, between the Moyola and Ballinderry rivers, both flowing eastwards into Lough Neagh. Having missed so many of the Mourne headwaters he ignored the main Sperrin watershed between the upper Mourne basin and the more northerly Foyle tributaries. Another area of weakness in the 'Generalle description' is south Donegal where all the relief is omitted, even the formidable hills between Slieve League and the Blue Stack Mountains. It is especially disappointing, for instance, that Bartlett overlooks the easy English names Silver Hill and Hawk's Rock, both familiar to less knowledgeable cartographers like Robert Lythe and the author of the Burghley map.[2]

The campaign map does little better with hills than the 'Generalle description'. In the Bays map, however, the previous neglect of south Donegal is redeemed with large bold mountain symbols stretching from Teelin Head to Barnesmore, and with lesser hills, also new, forming spines to St. John's Point and the other southern peninsulas. Other hills in the same map are the Dartry mountains, Knocknarea, and the Ox Mountains where Bartlett's name Slewe Gamphe has been preserved by the Ordnance Survey as an alias.

WOODS

Unlike hills and rivers, vegetation is poorly shown on many European maps of Bartlett's time, so it is hard to generalise about how cartographers were expected to treat the subject. In this respect Ireland is perhaps unusual, the number of maps depicting woods in Ulster being almost uncomfortably large.[3] Some cartographers placed their trees in twos and threes or even singly, rather like contemporary hill symbols. Others massed them together in larger blocks. On the kind of scale now under consideration, it is most unlikely that every such cluster could be represented, any more than every lake or every village. Where trees were abundant, the interesting question for the map-reader is: could the individual symbols be replaced by drawing a quasi-regional boundary around a recognisable wood or forest? Off the map, woods obviously differed in form and content. Trees may be of any size from dwarfs to giants, and any distance apart. The distinction between woodland and parkland may therefore be arbitrary; the same with parkland as opposed to open fields or 'champion'.[4] Francis Jobson explicitly distinguished timber wood from thick underwood — sparse underwood apparently being omitted — and Boazio in *c.*1602 alternated separate tree symbols with solid blocks of green. For most map-makers, however, a wood was a wood and nothing more. Tree species were cartographically indistinguishable at most scales, unless one switched from drawing to writing like Lythe in south Co. Down (hazel, holly, alder, elder, thorn, crabtree, birch and 'such like')[5] and Jobson in other parts of the same county (beech, hazel, willow, thorn).[6]

Under all these headings, Bartlett was content to follow established custom. In detail, however, his policy for woodland varied from one map to another. The Cotton trees were tightly packed; on the Trinity map by contrast there was open parkland covering a broad strip of country (seven English miles wide) from Strangford Lough westwards to Dungannon. The Lough Neagh map shows more scattered groupings, including improbable 'ranges' one symbol wide and up to ten symbols long, with little resemblance to the woods on the 'Fugos' map of the same area. But it is by his later maps that Bartlett deserves to be judged. Here he reprises a 'block' approach with spacing uniformly close. What most distinguishes his woods from those of other cartographers is their sheer plurality and consequent smallness. Boazio for instance in *c.*1602 showed spreads of woodland covering some 20,000 statute acres near Lough Neagh. Bartlett's largest woods are about 1,000 acres. Nevertheless the proportion of Ulster that he shows to have been wooded has been estimated at approximately one-sixth.[7]

The shapes of these woods vary in a way that is superficially plausible, but on closer inspection less than reassuring. The smaller patches are usually ovals or rectangles with rounded corners, their long axis more often running from east to west than from north to south. Some larger woods are shaped like a pair of open jaws, as if exposing an intruder to ambush from the trees on either side. There has to be a strongly conventional element in these outlines: it is plain to common sense that neither Bartlett nor any other Elizabethan cartographer in Ulster ever traced the boundaries of a wood with a chain and compass.

Convention, or perhaps rather the exigencies of cartographic design, can also be seen to have influenced the geographical positioning of Bartlett's woods. For instance, it was difficult at small scales for hills and trees to be combined. To some extent this was no cause for regret, because Ireland had little woodland above 500 feet, but many lower hill slopes were quite well timbered, and to represent this relationship a large or medium scale was needed: it was successfully done, for instance, in the Cooley map for the hills around Carlingford. In general, however, tree symbols are largely confined to the lowlands.

For some earlier cartographers, Ireland's woods had been an essentially waterside phenomenon. A good example is Ortelius's map of 1573.[8] Another is the Burghley map of Ulster, which shows thick forests almost all around Lough Neagh, in the Lagan valley, on both sides of Lough Erne and along its only tributary river, beside the lower Newry River and adjoining Loughs Derg and Finn in Donegal, the only major exception being the woods of the Dufferin, inland from Strangford Lough. Bartlett's woods by contrast are almost all set back by at least a mile from the nearest river or coastline. This policy left no room for any tree symbols in the glens of Antrim,[9] and for the same reason all the islands are bare of trees, even those of Lough Erne. A similar principle of non-contiguity was applied to the relation between tree symbols and territorial boundaries, which on the ground seem often to have passed through woodland.[10] The main purpose of these rules was apparently to avoid visual confusion.

Amid all this evidence of stylisation, one proof that Bartlett's woods are not entirely conventional is the presence of supplementary script. Twice in Kilultagh and Kilwarlin a local lord is described as 'chief of these woods'. On the Bays map 'Drombegh wo[od]' is named in south Donegal. In the territorial names just quoted, and often elsewhere, the prefix 'Kil' represents the Irish 'coill' (a wood) rather than the usual 'cill' (a church),[11] a distinction supposedly observable on the map by the proximity of tree symbols and the absence of church symbols, as at Kilbrakie, Kilbronie, Kilcorway, Kildorrie, Kille-Emars, Kilfaddie, Killeslew bremtree, Killocane and Killurnie, most of them on the campaign map, where there was more space for writing. Other names refer to a pass between two woods, in either English (Pace Alaslagh, Pace Donalee, Pace Genagh) or anglicised Irish (Ballaghnebegh, Ballelurgan, Ballaghegh, Ballagh Kilfaddie, Balaghglitte, Ballemckilloura, from *Bealach*, a way) or both (Pace Balaghuirte). Interesting enough in their own right, these names still leave nearly all Bartlett's patches of woodland unaccounted for.

One ulterior motive for spreading out the woods may have been an unconscious desire to emphasise the uniformity of Ulster. They certainly show less regional variation than in earlier maps: one recent estimate gives the same proportion of woodland in the area of the campaign map as in Bartlett's Ulster as a whole.[12] On a closer view, however, some definite tendencies emerge. Like nearly everyone else Bartlett keeps his trees away from the coastal lowlands of Cooley, Mourne, Lecale and the Ards. Allowing for the tendency towards fragmentation already noted, he also follows precedent in distributing abundant woodlands through the Dufferin, Kinelarty, Kilultagh, Clanbrassil, Terlough Brassil and along the west side of Lough Neagh, though it is odd that he gives so little emphasis to Glenconkeyne, still the 'greatest fastness of Tyrone' in 1609:[13] evidently Bartlett was reluctant to admit that a notorious forest refuge might be available to the next generation of rebels. Further west, the facts are much less certain. First comes a large crescent-shaped region almost devoid of woodland, running from Inishowen across west and central Co. Tyrone towards Monaghan and thence through central Co. Armagh into Co. Louth. Beyond this open area, woods reassert their dominance — predictably in

Counties Fermanagh and Cavan, more problematically in Donegal, where the 'Generalle description' is much more liberal with forest than for instance the Boazio map of *c.*1602. Further research is needed in these western fastnesses, where a precedent for improbably thick woodlands had been set some thirty years earlier by Lythe.[14] We are on safer if barer ground in north Connacht, where Bartlett's frugal provision of wood is generally consistent with John Browne's provincial map of 1591.[15]

REFERENCES

1. The modern (i.e. eighteenth-century and later) maps referred to in Table 1 are mainly those of the Ordnance Survey. I am especially indebted to Beatrice Coughlan for help in compiling this list.
2. BL, Cotton Ch. XIII, 42; PRO, MPF 1/90. Silver Hill or Errigal Mountain was recognisable by the appearance of its quartz rock (Kay Muhr, 'Place-names of German origin in Ireland' in Heinrich Beck *et al.* (eds), *Reallexikon der Germanischen Altertumskunde*, xxii (Berlin, 2002), p. 304).
3. Eileen McCracken, 'The woods of Ireland *circa* 1600', *Irish Historical Studies*, xi (1959), pp 273-6, 286.
4. For the relevance of this fact to the interpretation of historical sources, see Kenneth Nicholls, 'Woodland cover in pre-modern Ireland' in Patrick J. Duffy, David Edwards and Elizabeth Fitzpatrick (eds), *Gaelic Ireland* c.*1250*-c.*1650: land, lordship and settlement* (Dublin, 2001), pp 186-9.
5. PRO, MPF 1/89.
6. TCD, MS 1209/17. 'Beech' was presumably a mistake.
7. William J. Smyth, *Map-making, landscapes and memory: a geography of colonial and early modern Ireland* c.*1530-1750* (Cork, 2006), p. 50.
8. Ortelius's Irish woods (unlike the rest of his map) seem to derive not from Mercator's map of 1564 but from the more authoritative Laurence Nowell.
9. McCracken, 'Woods of Ireland', p. 274.
10. Nicholls, 'Woodland cover', p. 203; Smyth, *Map-making, landscapes and memory*, p. 65.
11. Patrick J. O'Connor, *Atlas of Irish place-names* (Newcastle West, 2001), pp 44-7.
12. Smyth, *Map-making, landscapes and memory*, pp 50, 91.
13. *CSPI, 1608-10*, p. 294.
14. BL, Cotton Ch. XIII, 42.
15. J.H. Andrews, 'Sir Richard Bingham and the mapping of western Ireland', *Proceedings of the Royal Irish Academy*, ciii C, 3 (2004), pp 61-95.

Chapter 9

More Distant Prospects: The People

TERRITORIES

As a matter of logic, Irish landholding arrangements would not necessarily create a network of compact and mutually exclusive territories. Suppose in a modern (but not too modern) industrial and commercial society we pinpointed, by place of residence, the descendants of a given individual X over several generations. The resulting map might well reveal some kind of cluster, dense in the middle, sparser towards the outside, and such a pattern could be generalised cartographically by writing the family name in an appropriate position; yet we could hardly delimit 'X's country' by a single boundary that all impartial observers would agree upon. In most Irish lordships, however, definite boundaries were evidently thought to exist (fig. 7), but as with several other kinds of line featured in this essay it is most unlikely that anyone had ever walked along them with a surveying instrument. When modern Irish historical geographers reconstruct a pre-modern territorial division its limits nearly always turn out to coincide with those of one or more nineteenth-century baronies or parishes as recorded by the Ordnance Survey. For geographers of Bartlett's day this convenient source of assistance was unavailable. Probably all they knew was which other territories adjoined the territory in question, which well-known settlements belonged inside it, and (if they were lucky) which rivers, coasts or uplands marked parts of its frontier. In these circumstances it would hardly be surprising for different map-compilers to arrive at somewhat different territorial patterns.

As to the existence of recognised boundaries, in the Bays map there are five rivers separating different colours, but most of the interfluvial areas thus demarcated are made to share a number of territorial and family names. In clockwise order round the coast the six regions thus defined are:

Fig. 7: Northern Ireland: sixteenth-century Gaelic territories. From K.W.Nicholls in T.W.Moody, F.X.Martin and F.J.Byrne (eds), *A new history of Ireland*, iii (Oxford, 1976), map 1.

(1) part of Co. Mayo, Mac William; (2) Terera, Oconer Sligo, O Dowde; (3) Aurorke (astride the Garvogue river); (4) Carbie, Dertrie, MacGlanagh, McGuire, O-Flanigan, O-Harte; (5) McGuire, O-Donnelle; (6) Hugh Buoye, Mac Swine Bannah, O-Boil, The Rosse, Tyrconnelle. Perhaps native territories were perceived as having already lost some of their significance when Bartlett drew this map.

His provincial map of Ulster is more generous with boundaries and the exceptions are rare enough to be enumerated. In Armagh the border between Orier and Clancarney is only partly defined, and there are no boundaries at all between Newry and Iveagh, between McGuillin's country and the Route, or between O'Cahan's country and Coran McGilligan. In Tyrone, Clanagher adjoining Mountjoy fort is not delimited from the rest of the Lotie, and the same applies to O'Hagan's country in the campaign map. These may have been oversights or confessions of ignorance; they may conceivably have been denials that any precise boundary existed.

Irish lordships had their own hierarchy. Chiefs were subservient to other chiefs, right down to the level of the townlands, many of which were named after an occupying family past or present. In Tyrone and Monaghan for example the system had three levels: lordship, ballybetagh and ballybo or tate. In general only the larger units in these territorial structures could be mapped at Bartlett's chosen scales, and what he did manage to include was inevitably subject to a degree of generalisation in which certain territories might be considered to lie outside the regular framework. 'Termon' for instance referred to sanctuary lands associated with a particular church and supervised by a hereditary warden. 'Lotie' (*lucht-tighe*) meant land dedicated to maintaining the household troops of a king or chief. Ballene Moyerie (town of the keeper, rendered by both Jobson and Bartlett as Sergeantstown) was held by the custodian of the Book of Armagh.[1] Such cases raise a difficult issue. To generalise a map usually means making it less correct; the resulting errors, by convention, may legitimately be planimetric but not topological. This principle creates a problem in the generalisation of areas as opposed to points and lines: individual boundaries can be straightened or simplified but territories at the same taxonomic level cannot be generalised by the obvious method of leaving out the smaller ones, because this will create inadmissible errors of topology when non-contiguous territories appear as contiguous.

The hierarchical relationship has also proved difficult to generalise — even in purely verbal terms. Thus in modern historical writing the relation of one sixteenth-century Irish territory to another might include possessing 'some sort of authority' over it; being subject to it, 'at least nominally'; being 'virtually' one of its subdivisions or 'virtually' independent of it; or imposing a 'vague overlordship' upon it.[2] Such nuances do not lend themselves to cartographic expression.

Sometimes different levels of a hierarchy appear to be represented in different parts of the same map. In these circumstances, the 'rump' of a high-level territory might be left unusually large and irregular in shape after some but not all of its constituent subdivisions had been excluded. An example is Monaghan, where Owenagh, Farney, Dartree, Otranie and Trough McKernan have evidently been carved out of Uriel or MacMahon, a situation that Bartlett recognises by allowing part of the name 'McMaghon' to encroach into Dartree. The alternative, no more satisfactory, was for names to be repeated as in 'Slut Gorre of the O-Kahans' bordering on O'Cahan's country.

All this makes it impossible to say what a 'correct' small-scale map of Elizabethan Ulster lordships would look like. A further complication was introduced by the English government's policy of replacing the Irish territorial system with a network of counties similar in size and function to the shires of England, each county being divided into baronies comparable with the English hundreds. The new units were generally formed from groups of one or more complete lordships, but most of them were renamed after a pre-existing settlement that was expected to develop as an administrative centre. On paper, this process was completed for Ulster in the period 1570-91 with the creation of Counties Antrim, Armagh, Cavan, Donegal, Down, Fermanagh, Monaghan and Tyrone (fig. 8), but at first the new divisions had little or no practical significance. Some writers who recommended the 'shiring' of the province in the 1590s were unaware that their proposals had already been carried out.[3]

It is not surprising that the counties were generally under-represented by late sixteenth-century cartographers (Francis Jobson was a notable exception) and that baronies were totally disregarded. However, once the rebellion had been suppressed the situation was surely different. It now became remarkable that Bartlett's 'Generalle description' did so little to drive home the fact of conquest by highlighting the new territorial system. Like many survivors of a war he seems almost to have envisaged a return to the *status quo*, though if he had expected the lesser Irish lords to wield very much power he might have spent more time researching their boundaries. At all events it is only in Fermanagh that his map of Ulster uses the word 'county' for one of the eight divisions entitled to it, which at least shows that the idea of shiring had reached the western margins of the province. Terminology aside, the actual form of the new units seems to be represented by the more prominent of Bartlett's two kinds of territorial

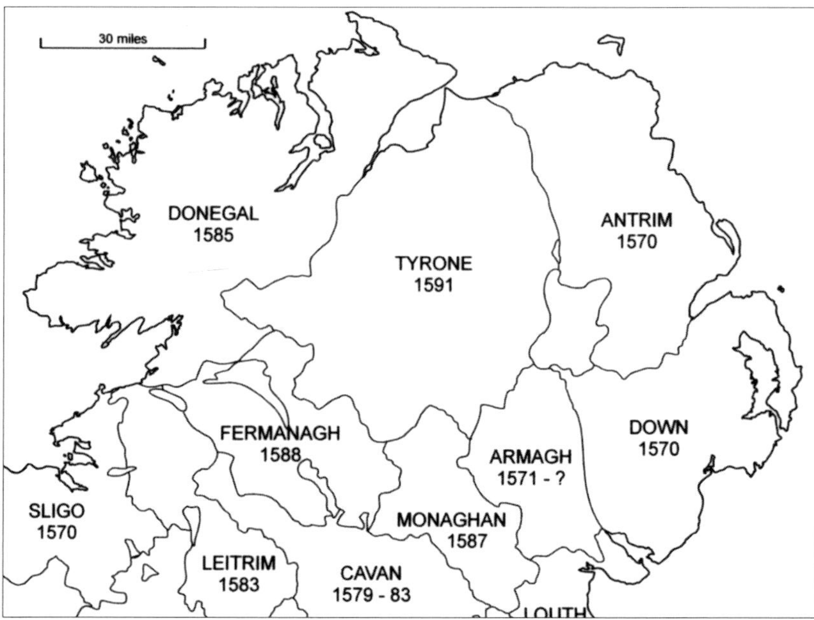

Fig. 8: Northern Ireland: counties, c. 1602. Adapted from K.W.Nicholls in T.W.Moody, F.X.Martin and F.J.Byrne (eds), *A new history of Ireland*, ix (Oxford, 1984), map 45.

boundary line. West of Lough Neagh this appearance may be deceptive, because in Tyrconnell and Tyrone (both named in large, widely-spaced capitals) as well as in Maguire's country and East Breifni there was a close coincidence between the old native territories and the new shires.

Elsewhere Bartlett's major boundaries often fail to replicate the pattern of the lordships. In one place the disharmony was of long standing and not necessarily connected with the shire system: this was the division between North and South Clandeboye on either side of Belfast Lough, as shown for instance on the Greenwich map of Ulster.[4] Other such partitions are less familiar. North of Lough Neagh, Brian Carrogh's country straddles the major boundary of the River Bann between Counties Tyrone and Antrim. Another such line, bisecting the lordship of Kilultagh, is apparently intended to separate the counties of Antrim and Down. Further south the same thing happens in the Fews, divided between the presumptive counties of Armagh and Monaghan. Within the counties (if that is what they were) Bartlett resembled earlier cartographers in disregarding the concept of the barony. Of the 54 seventeenth-century baronies in the nine counties of Ulster, 37 were given names that had never been used for any native lordship. None of these new names is applied to any territorial division in any of the maps now under consideration.

Before reviewing the territorial patterns depicted on different maps we must notice two more characteristics common to all of them. Everywhere in Ulster, map-makers can be found alternating regional names such as Tomelagh, Killeetra and South Clandeboye with nearby family names such as MacSweeny na Doe, Brian Carrogh and Kellies, a cause of confusion that modern historical geographers have generally managed to avoid. In addition, many names of both categories known to modern scholarship simply failed to achieve cartographic expression. In the territory of Iveagh, Co. Down, for example, a recent study has recognised twenty-two historic district names other than names of baronies or parishes, almost all of them recorded in early seventeenth-century documents.[5] Only three of these have been noticed on contemporary maps, two as territories (Clanbrassil and Kilwarlin) and one as a settlement. A less extreme case is the barony of Loughinsholin, which until 1613 formed part of Co. Tyrone. Here there had been four earlier territories of which two — Clandonnell and Tomlagh — were unrecorded even by the best cartographers.[6]

The difficulties of Irish territorial geography can be further illustrated by comparing Bartlett's maps with those of his chief rival Francis Jobson. In Antrim Bartlett's lordships are North Clandeboye, the Glens, part of Kilultagh, the Route (including McQuillan's country) and part of Brian Carrogh's country. He differs from Jobson in putting most of the north shore of Lough Neagh in Brian Carrogh's country and in extending Clandeboye as far north as Glenarm Bay.

In Down Bartlett's selection comprises the Great and Little Ards, Dufferin, Eriets, Iveagh (including Newry), Kells, Kilwarlin, Kinelarty, Lecale, Mourne and Slut Oneale. He substitutes Eriets for Jobson's south Kinelarty and omits Jobson's McAghle along the northwest edge of Iveagh. A minor difference is that Jobson, unlike Bartlett, makes Kells abut on to North Clandeboye.

In Armagh the divergencies begin to widen. Bartlett's lordships are Armagh, Clanbrassil, Clanconogher, Clandawell, Clancarney, Oneilland, Orier and Toagh. Unusually, the 'Generalle description' names Clancarney twice: the southern of its two occurrences, on the Monaghan border, may be a mistake for Everbuye, the campaign map's name for the area concerned. Bartlett's Clanconogher overlaps the north-eastern part of the lordship named by Jobson as Armagh. More seriously, his Clancarney is completely ignored by Jobson, who substitutes parts of Toagh, Clanconogher and Fews together with the small territory of Sergeantstown. Also anomalous is Bartlett's treatment of Fews: Jobson has it abutting on to Toagh, whereas Bartlett separates these territories by a considerable distance.

In Donegal a more recent map by Boazio can take over from Jobson as the most appropriate standard for assessing Bartlett's work. Here both authors distinguish Hugh McHugh Duffe, Inishowen, Malin, MacSweeny Banagh, MacSweeny na Doe, MacSweeny Fanad, O'Boyle, O'Donnell, Ross, Slut Art and Tomelagh. The chief irregularity is that Boazio's solid yellow for Malin is the same colour as his boundary tint for the rest of Inishowen, whereas Bartlett deliberately marks off Malin by switching from yellow to green. East of Lough Finn Bartlett has an unnamed strip of land which looks like a projection of MacSweeny Fanad, but which Boazio colours and names separately as 'Oferroll'. In the same area Boazio carries Hugh McHugh Duffe's country all the way from Lough Swilly to the upper Finn, while in Bartlett this territory stops short a few miles to the east. Finally Boazio treats the vicinity of Derry as a distinct unit while Bartlett places it within Inishowen.

After this it is a relief to find that no Elizabethan provincial cartographer attempted to subdivide either Fermanagh or Cavan. In Monaghan, however, where Jobson's first-hand county survey of 1591[7] was apparently unknown to Bartlett, the planimetric and topological variations are almost irreconcilable. Both authors show Dartree and Farney, while Bartlett's Trough McKernan is recognisable in Jobson as Trougheughter and Troughoughter. Otherwise there is little relation, in either names or boundaries, between The Lotte, Cremorne and Clancarroll (Jobson) and Otranie, Uriel, Owenagh and Clangalie (Bartlett).

In the outsize county of Tyrone we may first dispose of the area that later became Coleraine and after that Londonderry. This was territorially quite straightforward, comprising just three bounded units — Krine (O'Cahan's country), Slut Gorre and part of Brian Carrogh's country. Jobson differs only by recognising two contiguous Sluts — Gorre and, to the south of it, Donogh. Otherwise Bartlett colours the Faughan river as if for a territorial boundary, an unexpected decision that appears to leave O'Cahan's principal castle of Enagh in someone else's lordship.

Unlike earlier authorities, including Jobson, Bartlett made no distinction between upper and lower Tyrone, from which at one time it had been proposed to create two separate counties. In Jobson's Ulster, Glanconkyne (Bartlett's Clanconan) is north of Kileetra; Bartlett moves it to the west. Lottie is a large rump-like area west of Lough Neagh on both maps, with Jobson ignoring Bartlett's separate territories of Cloninish and McCahel. They agree broadly about Monterborn, Carrowmore, Portlargie and Termon McGuirk, although Jobson's Termon includes an area (containing the important hill name Mullagh Agorrie) that Bartlett leaves anonymous. Further west, in Jobson's Upper Tyrone, both authors become less explicit. Bartlett has an irregularly sprawling area from Clones to near Strabane in which the only modern name, apart from 'Tyron', is Fentenagh. North of this the narrow strip of O'Gormeley's country follows the east bank of the River Foyle, while to the west is the large but relatively compact territory of Slut-Art occupying most of the Derg valley and separated from Fentenagh by an unusually long and uncomplicated frontier. Jobson takes a different view. Of his four large territories in this region, only Slut Art has much resemblance to Bartlett, and even there Jobson marks off the area north-west of the River Derg under the rather desperate pseudonym 'Between the waters'. East of the Foyle-Mourne-Strule axis Jobson divides what is left of Upper Tyrone by an east-west boundary: in the southern compartment his only territorial name is 'Neale', in the northern it is 'Strabane'.[8] He makes no reference to O'Gormeley's country.

Although Bartlett and Boazio are closely similar in Donegal, in Tyrone they differ profoundly. Boazio repeats the names of Slut Art and Fentenagh, albeit with very different shapes and alignments, but most of his other territories in this county are named from their chiefs, the only exceptions being Munster Lyn and 'Glins Tyrone', the latter idiosyncratically applied to the woods north-west of Lough Neagh. Otherwise, with the single exception of O'Gormeley, Boazio's family names in Tyrone — Cormac McBaron, McBrien, McHugh, McGillakoon and Harry Og, O'Quin, Sir Arthur O'Neill — have no identifiable counterparts in Bartlett.[9]

SETTLEMENT

What most distinguished Ulster from Bartlett's English homeland was its paucity of urban settlement. He mapped the towns of Carrickfergus and Drogheda at too small a scale to merit more than a single building-symbol. On the campaign map Dundalk and Carlingford appear unambiguously as walled towns, and Newry has fifteen houses, two towers and a church, but Sligo in the Bays map with only half a dozen houses might just as well have been a village. There may be other reasons for regarding Ardglas, Armagh, Cavan and Downpatrick as towns, but Bartlett's small-scale maps do nothing to reinforce this belief. Otherwise the most striking feature of these maps as a record of settlement is the relative scarcity of town names familiar to the modern reader. Thus throughout the post-Bartlett era the basic geography of Ulster, compared with that of Great Britain, has been almost untouched by anything that could be called an industrial revolution; yet of the sixty or so largest towns in present-day Northern Ireland, well over half make no appearance even as single castles or churches on Bartlett's maps. There is no sign, for instance, of Ballymena, Banbridge, Cookstown, Craigavon, Larne, Lisburn or Lurgan.

The theme of rural settlement can best be introduced by resuming our comparison between Bartlett and Christopher Saxton. In England, a major preoccupation of Elizabethan county cartography was with parish churches, but in the whole of Ulster and north Connacht Bartlett records less than half as many churches as Saxton would map in an average English county, an emphatic repudiation of any claim to qualify as an ecclesiastical geographer. Apart from bishops' seats, which are carefully captioned, his churches seem to have been included for mainly non-devotional reasons. About a quarter of them can be recognised from their names as former monasteries, which since the reign of Henry VIII had no legitimate part to play in the country's religious life. Many of their symbols are surprisingly prominent, though the only features to show much architectural differentiation are the early Christian round towers at Killala and Clones. The fact is that in Ulster any stone building was worth mapping simply as a landmark for the guidance of travellers, or perhaps as a possible barrack, storehouse or stable. The same is true of non-monastic churches, where worship would have been discouraged in more than forty cases by the absence of a roof — a deficiency recognisable even in small and roughly drawn church symbols from their upward-projecting end-gables.[10] This makes it hardly surprising that the issue of parochial status was seldom if ever confronted by cartographers in Elizabethan Ireland. Bartlett certainly seems to have known even less about parishes than about lordships, and modern historians have been in much the same position, the nearest accessible data-base on this subject being the unsatisfactorily late maps of William Petty's mid-seventeenth-century Down Survey. Among a random sample of fifty Down Survey parishes in Antrim, Armagh, Down and Tyrone, there are only seventeen for which Bartlett records a church.

On a rough estimate Bartlett's maps show 133 castles as opposed to 87 churches. At first sight the castles make an interesting and significant geographical distribution. They are relatively most numerous in the maritime counties of Louth and Sligo bordering on modern Ulster. They also make a fair showing in east Co. Down, along the north coast of Co. Antrim, round the heads of Loughs Foyle and Swilly and among the bays and headlands of south Donegal. By contrast the heart of Ulster — Tyrone, Fermanagh, Monaghan, Cavan and Armagh — is notably deficient in castles, on the face of it a surprising fact, though supported by modern historical inquiry.

Secular buildings are harder to evaluate than churches, because we cannot assume a one-one or many-one correspondence between castles and lordships as we can between churches (ruined or otherwise) and parishes. The 'Generalle description' makes this clear by leaving Trough McKernan, Clanconkan, Carrowmore and Slut Gorre completely empty of buildings. This is not the only evidence of selectivity in Bartlett's treatment of castles. One obvious cause of bias was that some of his maps, by virtue of their larger scales, could accommodate a higher density of sites than others and were probably based on more comprehensive field work. This may help to explain the proliferation of castles in north Connacht and south-east Ulster. Thus the Bays map includes an island castle in Lough Eske omitted from the 'Generalle description', while sites in central Ulster appearing on the campaign map but not the general map are 'The new castle' in Otranie, Castletown west of Dundalk and Bally Rone on the upper Bann. Not that the campaign map is fully comprehensive. In Louth, for instance, it omits both Roche and Ballylogh, shown on the Cotton and the Trinity maps respectively.[11] Despite these differences it seems likely that Bartlett had begun by hoping to include as many castles on his maps as possible.

We must next consider the free-standing unfortified structures (classifiable for all practical purposes as cabins) that would probably be regarded at most historical periods as by far the commonest buildings in the Irish landscape. In the large-scale Bowlby plans there are more than twenty cabins for every operational fort or castle. In Bartlett's small-scale maps, omitting the settlements previously classed as urban, there are fewer cabins than castles. The reason for this disproportion is obvious: there was not enough time to survey and not enough space to map more than a very small fraction of the cabins that existed.

In the regional maps under review more than 95 per cent of sites with cabins contained from two to six separate buildings, with three as the commonest group-size. At three-quarters of the sites the cabins adjoined a castle, the best examples, again at least partly for reasons of scale, being those of the Cooley map at Ballymascanlan, Castletown, Dowdallstown, Greencastle, Segeriestown and Whitestown. Such 'castle clusters' are a well-known early settlement type in many parts of Ireland, the cabin-dwellers being generally interpreted as labourers or tenants subservient to the owner of the castle.[12]

Finally, a small but interesting category: cabins with no other buildings nearby. In Ulster Bartlett shows ten such sites, of which eight comprised either two or three houses. It may be more than coincidence that eight of the ten had names beginning in 'Ba:' or 'Balle'. Perhaps these were some of the 'clachans' later made famous by the geographer Estyn Evans.[13] He is not the only scholar to have associated the word 'bally' with the phenomenon of clustered rural settlement. In central Ulster, however, where 'Bally' names are comparatively rare in maps of any period, this prefix has been associated not so much with farm villages as with 'centres of local importance'.[14] In either case the settlements in question were probably of little military account, and doubtless often hard for a surveyor to see from a distance. Their inclusion in Bartlett's maps was probably a matter of luck.

For a cartographer with Bartlett's professional background, forts were clearly an attractive subject (fig. 9). Altogether he recorded some twenty-eight such sites, almost always including 'Forte' in their name even where the map left little space for script. Eight were places that he himself had surveyed individually in 1602. The same theatre of war contained the obsolete but still mappable enclosure at Benburb together with Mountjoy's fort on the shore of Roosky Lough. Further north, four forts (Culmore, Derry, Lifford and Dunnalong) had been built by Sir Henry Docwra during the Lough Foyle campaign. Another group, around the margins of Lough Neagh, were mainly associated with Sir Arthur Chichester's advance inland from Belfast. Those of English origin in this region were Massereene (previously a monastic centre in the modern townland of Balloo) and Toome in the townland of The Creagh, apparently on the site of an earlier native fort. The Irish constructions were Clonoe (Killary Glebe townland) with one or two unnamed sites to the west of the lough, Bunvalle (at or near the present village of Bannfoot) and Bundorlin (probably in Maghery townland at the mouth of the

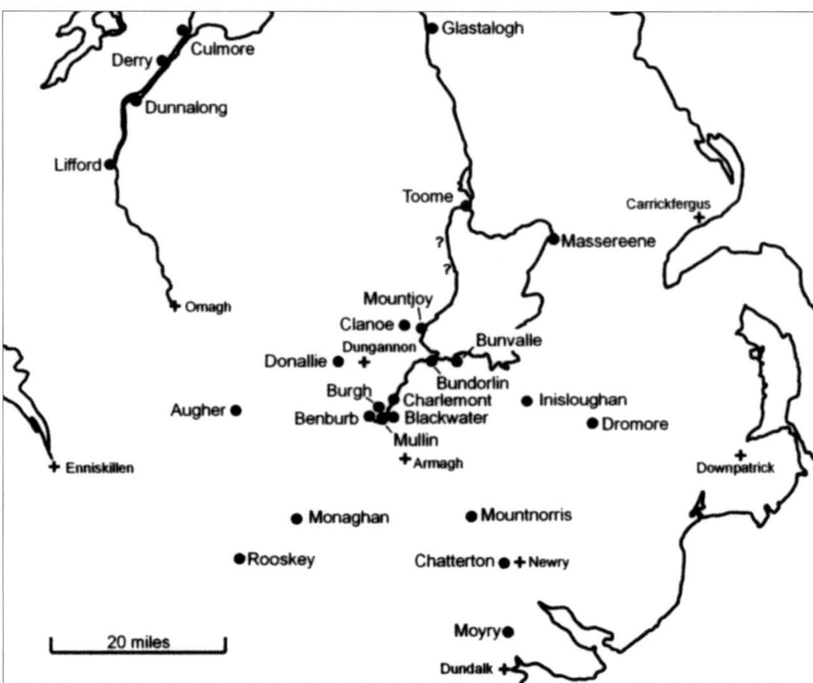

Fig. 9: Northern Ireland: forts recorded by Bartlett.

Blackwater). Bartlett shows substantial-looking earthworks at all these places, but none of them seem to have left any physical traces.[15]

Four sites difficult to classify are Fort Glastalogh on the east bank of the Bann three miles from Ballymoney; Fort Donallie at Castlecaulfield west of Dungannon; Fort Dromore (so-called in the Cotton map), perhaps near Carnew seven miles east of Banbridge; and what was left of a fort established in the 1570s by a would-be planter, Thomas Chatterton, a mile west of Newry.[16] Finally there are two fortified sites on the Bays map: one at the north-western end of Lough Gill and one on an island in Lough Whittagh south-east of Glencar Lough. The half-dozen last-mentioned locations are barely known to historians, but Bartlett was in a better position than most cartographers, contemporary or modern, to decide whether a fort was genuine or not.

COMMUNICATIONS

We have already noted how few roads appear as such in Elizabethan maps of Britain and Ireland. What the Cotton, Trinity and campaign maps show in Ulster are not roads as such but troop movements, though it is natural to assume that these followed tracks and paths that were already in use by the local population. If so, the road network in parts of Ulster must have been impressively close, to judge from the complexity of Mountjoy's journeys in the immediate vicinity of Armagh and Newry. However that may be, the only road features acknowledged as objects in their own right are causeways, passes and bridges. There are two causeways between the Moyry fort and Newry, and Bartlett's only designated ford, in the Cotton and Trinity maps, is on the same line of road. To these must be added nineteen 'passes' shown either by name or by a double broken line. A degree of approximation seems evident where these routes were mapped running beside a wood rather than through it, as happened for instance at Balla Eri Trit near Sligo. Most of the passes are quite short, although there is one of about five miles on the north side of Carlingford Lough.

Bridges were apparently unknown in Ulster outside the south-east and even there the evidence is somewhat equivocal, as we have already seen in discussing Bartlett's cartographic sources. The best chance of riding dryshod across a river was on the way from Co. Louth towards Dungannon. Bartlett is consistent in showing bridges at Newry and (predictably enough) at Sixmilebridge south of Mountnorris. The Cotton map shows a bridge at Fort Burroughs on the Blackwater, replaced on the campaign map by Mountjoy's new bridge at Charlemont. The most enigmatic of Bartlett's river crossings is at Dundalk. On the Cotton map this appears as two continuous double lines — unmistakably different from the two single broken lines that he would have used to represent a ford or ferry, and consistent with the known existence of a bridge at this site from the fifteenth century at least until Jobson's time. On the Trinity and campaign maps there is definitely no bridge, and none is visible in the 'Generalle description': here Bartlett's opinion matches the unbridged river on two larger-scale maps of the Dundalk area in the 1650s. This is a matter on which local historians have yet to give a verdict.[17] There are no bridges on the Bays map.

MISCELLANEA

Confronted with the great outdoors in all its wealth of detail, even the most conscientious field worker must occasionally be tempted to stray beyond the formal categories of cartographic language. Then he may surprise us with out-of-the way information, sometimes hardly deviating from his customary quasi-pictorial symbolism, sometimes interrupting himself with quite long verbal phrases and sentences. This practice was well established in medieval European cartography, contrasting with the simplicity of Ptolemy's earlier preference for a narrow range of names. The Ptolemaic approach was perhaps more suited to the formality of engraved maps, but in Ireland the tradition of manuscript 'asides' remained alive, notably in Robert Lythe's map of the central and southern counties and in John Baxter's 'bays' map.[18]

Bartlett made one verbal gesture towards the world of natural history: this was in 'the high Hills of Benbolbin' on his Bays map, 'where yearly limbereth a falcon esteemed the hardiest in Ireland'. Otherwise his chief extraneous interest was in political geography. In the campaign map the territories figure mainly as power bases. Thus in 24 out of 33 cases we are given the chief's name, albeit in small writing, as well as that of the territory itself. Occasionally there are supplementary details unnoticed by other cartographers. Thus the Lotie is described as 'the household or demesne land of the Oneales' and McCahel is 'one of the five farmers of the Lotie'. Everybuye was 'Madonnelle the gallowglass his country'. Clancarney was the country that 'the O-Neales have used to give unto the Captain of their Galloglass for their entertainment & bonage'. Here then was one Norfolk man who knew that gallowglasses were mercenary foot-soldiers of Scottish origin and that bonage was an Irish tenant's obligation to work on his lord's arable land.

Apart from names and boundaries the institution of lordship expressed itself geographically at two kinds of site; the chief's house and the place of inauguration or assembly. On these subjects Bartlett was disappointingly reticent without being altogether uninformative. Lough Gall, Co. Armagh, was Art McBaron's 'chief house and hold',[19] and Lough Eske in Donegal was 'where Sir Neale Garve chiefly resideth'. That was all. Then, in contemporary English terminology for a chief's inauguration, Bartlett records just three sites of 'making': the MacMahons at a place still known as McMahon's Stone;[20] the Magennises at Lisnaree south of Loughbrickland; and the O'Neills at the celebrated chair of Tullaghoge. No such explanation is given for the names of Knockmullagh (described by Jobson as a 'parley hill') or Mullagh Leac, while Ardnatitian (O'Dogherty), Sgiath Gabhra (Maguire) and Shantemon Hill (O'Reilly) are omitted altogether.[21] Other cartographers could occasionally do better: the anonymous Greenwich map of Ulster mentions three different 'chief houses'[22] and Boazio's published map of Ireland gives prominence to 'Kilmacrenan where O'Donnell is made'.[23] Once again we must remember that no topographical map can be expected to serve as a compendium of thematic maps.

Bartlett's sympathy with Irish preoccupations is also illustrated by several brief forays into historical geography. As we have seen, his Ulster map includes a number of Ptolemaic and other apparently classical names. Nor was he totally indifferent to Celtic language-history, though content to prove this point with a single example — 'Maghea-yllie' as the 'ancient name' for Evagh or MaGennis's country.[24] Despite his interest in ruins, archaeology can hardly be considered a major Bartlettian preoccupation. One monumental cross is pictured in the Cooley map near Grange, and another, named Crosse-Grenan, between Newry and Narrow Water on the campaign map. These again are obviously no more than tokens: it is neither unexpected nor reprehensible for Bartlett to have ignored the three crosses mapped in the Bays area by John Baxter.[25] Otherwise we can only speculate about the six occurrences of 'lis' (lios, fort) among the placenames of the campaign map, none of them unambiguously attached to any point-symbol; with the possible exception of Jobson in Co. Monaghan, no Irish regional cartographer took much notice of ring-forts. The same is true of Anglo-Norman mottes: Bartlett's only example, Mount Sandel near Coleraine, had already been mapped in print by Boazio and may well have been interpreted as a natural feature. The unique case among earthworks is Emain Macha, prominent on both the Cotton and Trinity maps as 'the ancient seat of the kings of Ulster'. Later the same location was chosen, perhaps as a triumphalist gesture, for one of Mountjoy's short-stay camp sites, but references to Irish kings were less appropriate now that the Tudor conquest seemed nearly over and the caption for this royal seat on the campaign map is simply 'Owenmagh'.

Finally there was the mapping of historic emergencies. One was the slaying of Shane O'Neill at B.Terain (Ballyteerim) in Co. Antrim, recorded in the 'Generalle description'. More recently there were the 'Three Spanish ships here cast away in Ano Dm 1588' near Dernish Island, Co. Sligo. This inscription on the Bays map is perhaps the latest of some half-dozen near-contemporary cartographic references to Armada wrecks on the Irish coast.[26] Less happily, at Ball McKilloura (Ballymackilmurray) beside the Blackwater the campaign map commemorates the reverse of English fortunes ten years later in the Battle of the Yellow Ford, with the note, 'Here Sir H. Bagnall the Marshall was slain'. Bartlett was as important in cartographic history as Bagenal in military history, but there was no one to put him on a map when he was slain.

REFERENCES

1. P.W. Joyce, *Irish names of places*, ii (Wakefield, 1973), pp 114, 213-15, 470-71; Kay Muhr, 'Territories, people and place-names in Co. Armagh' in A.J. Hughes and William Nolan (eds), *Armagh: history and society* (Dublin, 2001), p. 309.
2. D.B. Quinn and K.W. Nicholls, 'Ireland in 1534' in T.W. Moody, F.X. Martin and F.J. Byrne (eds), *A new history of Ireland*, iii (Oxford, 1976), pp 12, 14, 15, 16.
3. Joseph McLaughlin, 'Richard Hadsor's "Discourse" on the Irish state, 1604', *Irish Historical Studies*, xxx (1997), p. 351.
4. NMM, MS P.49/5.
5. Kay Muhr, *Place-names of Northern Ireland, volume six: County Down IV North-west Down/Iveagh* (Belfast, 1996), pp 8-15.
6. Gregory Toner, *Place-names of Northern Ireland, volume five: County Derry I The Moyola Valley* (Belfast, 1996), pp 2-3.
7. Jobson's survey of lands in Co. Monaghan was made in September and October 1591. The relevant maps are TCD, MS 1209/31; PRO, MPF 1/76; PRO, MPF 1/79 (all Co. Monaghan); PRO, MPF 1/312[I] (Farney).
8. Jobson's 'Neale' is placed near the southern border of the otherwise unnamed territory that contains it. His 'Strabane' adjoins a castle-symbol with no other name, but it is written in capital letters as if denoting a territory. (The only other town with a capitalised name in 'The provence of Ulster' is Dundalk.)
9. For praise of Boazio's territorial geography see Séamus Ó Ceallaigh, 'Old lights on place-names: new lights on maps', *Journal of the Royal Society of Antiquaries of Ireland*, lxxx (1950), p. 184.
10. J.H. Andrews, 'The mapping of Ireland's cultural landscape, 1550-1630' in Patrick J. Duffy, David Edwards and Elizabeth Fitzpatrick (eds), *Gaelic Ireland c.1250-c.1650: land, lordship and settlement* (Dublin, 2001), p. 165.
11. A parallel case in the Bays map is the omission of the castle at Teelin marked in the 'Generalle description'.
12. W.J. Smyth, 'The dynamic quality of Irish "village" life – a reassessment' in J.M. Dewailly and R. Dion (eds), *Campagnes et littoraux d'Europe (Melanges offert à Pierre Flatres)* (Lille, 1988), pp 109-13; Andrews, 'The mapping of Ireland's cultural landscape', pp 169-71.
13. E. Estyn Evans, 'Some survivals of the Irish openfield system', *Geography*, xxiv (1939), pp 24-36, the first of a long series of publications on this subject by Evans and his fellow geographers.
14. Philip Robinson, 'Irish settlement in Tyrone before the plantation', *Ulster Folklife*, xxii (1976), p. 65.
15. Sites of the Lough Neagh group may be approximately located in Patrick McKay and Kay Muhr, *Lough Neagh places: their names and origins* (Belfast, 2007), pp 14, 70, 84, 90 and 118, but the only one that these authors identify as a fort is Bunvalle.
16. These forts are not mentioned in Paul M. Kerrigan, *Castles and fortifications in Ireland, 1485-1945* (Cork, 1995). For Chatterton, see Rolf Loeber, *The geography and practice of English colonisation in Ireland from 1534 to 1609* (Athlone, 1991), pp 31, 33.
17. Harold O'Sullivan, *Irish historic towns atlas no. 16: Dundalk* (Dublin, 2006), p. 19.
18. Robert Lythe, map of central and southern Ireland [1571], West Sussex Record Office, PHA 9581; John Baxter ('finished by Baptista Boazio'), 'A true description of the Norwest partes of Ireland', NMM, MS P.49/7.
19. Jerrold Casway, 'Identifying "Arte McBaron's chief house his hould"' in David Edwards (ed.), *Regions and rulers in Ireland, 1100-1650: essays for Kenneth Nicholls* (Dublin, 2004), pp 146-59.
20. McMahon's Stone appears in the Automobile Association's *Road book of Ireland* (Dublin, 1962), map 26, but not on Ordnance Survey maps at similar scales.
21. Elizabeth Fitzpatrick, 'Parley sites of Ó Néill and Ó Domhnaill in late sixteenth-century Ireland' in Edwards, *Regions and rulers in Ireland*, pp 201-16.
22. NMM, MS P.49/5.

23. Geraldine Stout and Matthew Stout, 'Early landscapes' in F.H.A. Aalen, Kevin Whelan and Matthew Stout (eds), *Atlas of the Irish rural landscape* (Cork, 1997), p. 60, fig. 69, 'Inauguration sites'.
24. Muhr, *Place-names of Northern Ireland ... North-west Down/Iveagh,* p. 257
25. NMM, MS P.49/7. Baxter's crosses are unnamed. The nearest settlements to them are Assaroe, Castletown (Co. Mayo) and Castle Finn.
26. Armada wrecks also appear in maps of Ulster, *c.*1589, at Hatfield House (J.H. Andrews, 'Post-Armada cartography in Galway', *Journal of the Galway Archaeological and Historical Society*, lii (2000), pp 30-48); of Munster, probably by Jobson, *c.*1590 (NMM, MS P.49/27); of Ulster by Jobson, 1591 (TCD, MS 1209/15); and of north-west Ireland by Baxter and Boazio, *c.*1600-3 (NMM, MS P.49/7).

Chapter 10

Yards, Paces and Miles

Few Tudor surveyors have left any written record of how their information was collected. Bartlett is no exception. Even circumstantial evidence on this point is rather sparse. Since we have a rough idea of how little time he could devote to field work, certain particularly laborious survey techniques can be ruled out. On the other hand, the maps themselves may be judged too good to have been produced by the most approximate of available methods, the crucial question being whether any instrumental survey was involved. Such backward reasoning from product to process, though common enough in map history, is almost always dangerous. For one thing, it entangles us in the intricacies of cartographic accuracy assessment. This is controversial territory, some historians having dismissed all such 'judgemental' studies as irrelevant and anachronistic. At any rate, we should not broach the subject without trying to make sympathetic allowance for the dangers, hardships and privations of cartographic fieldwork in contemporary Ulster.

For present purposes accuracy is the degree to which a map's horizontal distances and directions are correct either in relation to each other (internal accuracy) or with reference to some independent standard such as a known unit of linear distance or a fixed point on the earth's surface like the north pole (external accuracy). The relationship between these two properties is asymmetrical. An internally near-perfect Ordnance Survey sheet could be made externally worthless by adding a few noughts to its scale-statement or by ruling a line labelled 'Equator' across the middle of it. But the implications of this argument cannot be reversed. If a map's scales of distance, latitude and longitude are all correct, then (provided the scale information is detailed enough) its internal geography must necessarily be correct as well. The inclusion of such marginal statements therefore constitutes a claim to both kinds of accuracy, and unscrupulous cartographers may be tempted to pass off poor maps as good ones by embellishing them with inappropriate scale lines, graticules and north points.

EXTERNAL ACCURACY

There are no meridians or parallels on Bartlett's maps. In this he resembled most other cartographers who worked in Ireland before the late seventeenth century.[1] His readers were unlikely to be interested in longitude and latitude, and his theatre of operations was too small to be affected by the earth's curvature.[2] However, again like other cartographers, he did generally provide distance-scales and north points, and part of this chapter will be devoted to describing them.

On the face of it, the more finely divided a scale line, the higher the level of accuracy asserted, but some cartographers weakened such claims by sloppy draughtsmanship, carelessly varying the lengths of adjacent scale divisions that purported to represent the same distance. Bartlett is sometimes guilty of this fault. Within the body of a map, pretensions to accuracy may appear in finely drawn line-work and closely articulated curves, though again such marks of precision have often turned out to be misleading. In his later maps Bartlett cultivated a free and not over-punctilious style of line-drawing and writing that warned his readers not to expect too much. Noteworthy in this respect is the sixteenth-century custom of marking the supposed exact position of a site with a small circle enclosing a dot, a practice probably copied from contemporary plane-table surveyors. This too could be deceptive, and colourists of printed maps would often give the game away by almost obliterating an engraver's dots and circles with red paint. In the Cotton map Bartlett's circled dots are so selectively distributed that it is tempting to seek some significance in them (they occur at Armagh, Ballymoyer, Benburb, the Blackwater fort, Carlingford and Narrow Water) but in his later work he hardly ever uses this kind of convention even though some of his building-symbols are a quarter of an inch long.

Next, and more consequentially, a cartographer's units of measurement may throw some light on his working practices. Metrologically, the Bowlby plans present few problems. Eight of their scale-bars refer to 'paces'; in four, the yard provides an alternative or substitute — helpfully given its modern definition in the plan of Mountjoy (VII). Three times the pace is specified as 'common', twice as 'geometrical'. At Charlemont (IV) the double scale-bar equates a geometrical pace with five feet, which is also the value quoted for paces (not otherwise characterised) in the Monaghan scales (IXa). The ratio of five feet to a pace occurs in many near-contemporary sources, including John Speed's *Theatre*:[3] it had presumably originated as the distance between successive positions of a pedestrian's right or left foot rather than as a single step. 'Common miles' was a familiar and harmless phrase in Irish map scales (few people remembering the etymology of the word 'mile'), but since walking is an individual activity 'common pace' could only be a misnomer for anyone who understood the ordinary meaning of the more straightforward word 'pace'. Was Bartlett simply recording the number of his own footsteps between the ends of each survey line? Or was 'common' an accepted alternative to 'geometrical'? Linguistically this latter suggestion may seem improbable, but at least it would illustrate the typical Tudor cartographer's habit of varying the style and form of his marginal information for no particular reason.

Bartlett's regional maps include eight scale-statements, simple or compound. The Cotton units are undefined — an irritatingly frequent practice in Tudor cartography, though here as in other English small-scale maps it is safe enough to interpret them as some kind of mile. The inset of the Cotton map showing Mountnorris fort is scaled in feet. The Lough Neagh map offers 'miles' without any qualification. On five other maps the miles are 'Irish', and in two cases (the Trinity map and the 'Generalle description') these are juxtaposed with their English counterparts to define an Irish mile as equivalent to 1.25 English miles. The Bays map strikes an original note by combining Irish miles with leagues, each league implicitly containing three English miles.

In both Ireland and England the mile had been the normal measure for long distances since medieval times, although it was not until 1593 that Queen Elizabeth's parliament fixed its value at 5280 feet, and then only for the London area. Before that, and no doubt for long afterwards, most people's conception of a mile probably came from word-of-mouth local opinion about the distances between places familiar to them. This doubtless was the kind of mile referred to in certain place-names especially characteristic of south-east Ulster — Three Mile Water, Four Mile Water, Sixmilebridge, Eight Mile Church, Eight Mile Water and Twelve Mile Church, all of them publicised by Bartlett, the miles in question perhaps being reckoned from either Armagh or Newry.[4] From such rather vague premises a traveller could easily infer, without taking measurements, that Irish miles were longer than English miles; and from the same kind of information Irish sketch-maps could be furnished with scale statements that would often specify which kind of mile was intended. There might even emerge from this unpromising background a generally-approved numerical relationship. At any rate the earliest recorded statement that one Irish mile equals 1.25 English miles appears in an otherwise unpretentious sketch map of unknown authorship — as it happens, from within Bartlett's later sphere of cartographic action.[5]

It was only towards the middle of the seventeenth century that systems of linear mensuration in both kingdoms were stabilised to yield the familiar modern Irish-English ratio of 1.2727 — or, expressed in yards per mile, 2240 to 1760. But even in Elizabethan times the rough and ready methods described above would not necessarily have satisfied a cartographer with experience of large-scale local operations. Property surveyors like Francis Jobson might wonder how many perches were contained in one mile; military cartographers would ask the same about feet or paces. In other countries this question had a long history: for Latin-speakers the very word 'mile' embodied an allusion to the number one thousand. In Ireland two cartographers had contributed to the subject. Robert Lythe cited miles of 6000 feet and 5000 feet in 1567-8, again with reference to areas subsequently mapped by Bartlett.[6] The second of these figures was happily consistent with the traditional reckoning of five feet to a pace and a thousand paces to a mile, and if this is accepted as a characteristically English conception then perhaps 6000 feet was Lythe's attempt to regularise the Irish mile. Some time afterwards, however, as a warning against facile solutions, we encounter a mile of 1500 five-foot paces (1.42 statute miles) in John Browne's map of Co. Mayo.[7]

Unfortunately Bartlett offers no such equation. One can only compare his mileages with the corresponding modern distances, and from such comparisons we may deduce the following equivalents for an Irish mile in statute miles: Cotton map 1.256, Trinity map 1.286, Cooley map 1.182, campaign map 1.107, 'Generalle description' 1.168, Bays map 1.043. The Lough Neagh map is not included in the list because its miles, at less than 0.6 statute miles each, are too short to be credible and had presumably been miscalculated in some way. (The cartographer's uneasiness on this point appears in an inscription on the same map that he found himself unable to finish: 'waye from Knockfergus to Massarina being 1[-] miles'.) Can we infer from the other ratios just quoted that in the course of his short career Bartlett had second thoughts about the length of an Irish mile? Such a judgement would require his distances to be in harmony with their own map scales. But regional maps of *c.*1600 can never quite be trusted in this sense. Suppose for the sake of argument that Bartlett placed Armagh cathedral 20 Irish miles from Dundalk bridge, and that the corresponding Ordnance Survey distance is just over 25 statute miles. Suppose also that his linear measurements or estimates were in error by up to ten per cent: his figure for an Irish mile might then vary for this reason by as much as 0.25 statute miles, a range that could comfortably embrace and explain away all the differences listed above.

This suggestion may be further illustrated with a single example. Applying the average of 1.168 quoted above for the 'Generalle description', the Irish miles on this map can first be converted to statute miles and then compared, for each sampled pair of points, with the correct distance measured in the same units. Sure enough, Bartlett's values differ from the truth by an average of 11.5 per cent. But some significance may still attach to the average ratio for all the maps of 1.184 statute miles per Irish mile. By earlier standards this was an unexpectedly low value, which yields the even lower value of 0.947 statute miles for Bartlett's English mile — startlingly different from the usual historian's estimate of about 1.3 for the 'old' miles of sixteenth-century England.[8] It might even be suggested that Bartlett had been adjusting his mileages to the 'London' legislation of 1593. But if he was rebuilding his distances from the ground up, would he have bothered to acknowledge any measure as unregenerate as an Irish mile? Perhaps his units of distance, like his place-names, could be interpreted as a gesture of respect towards Irish national identity, though more probably it showed that he or his informants chose to follow local estimates rather than take their own measurements. Until such doubts can be laid to rest, the question of accuracy must be pursued without any further reference to scale.

Bartlett's compass points are just as problematic as his distances, and for the same reason, which is the difficulty of 'factoring in' contemporary errors of measurement or estimation when drawing inferences from the lengths and angles on an early map. Magnetic variation in Ireland at the beginning of the seventeenth century appears to have been approximately eight degrees east.[9] The variation shown in the awkwardly small north-indicator of the Cooley map is not grossly different from this amount. Otherwise the most that can be said of Bartlett's regional maps is that their alignment seems closer to true north than magnetic north. The best candidate for magnetic orientation is Donegal in the Bays map, the Connacht section of the same map being evidently closer to true north.

INTERNAL ACCURACY

Turning now to questions of planimetric self-consistency, we must first dispose of Bartlett's large-scale plans a good deal more perfunctorily than they deserve. Admittedly he was not himself a designer of fortifications, but as a military cartographer he would have wished to respect the traditions of a peer-group comprising both map-makers and engineers. Unfortunately, western Europe's early seventeenth-century fort plans are far from easy to evaluate in this respect, because most of their banks and ditches have long since been obliterated by later building. Even in Ireland, hardly the most urbanised of western countries, none of Bartlett's forts survived long enough to be shown on a reliable modern map. Perhaps the best-documented of his sites is Charlemont, and that was soon to be so completely rebuilt by Sir Toby Caulfield that not one of its features can be found in Nicholas Pynnar's plan of 1624, let alone in any later map.[10]

We are left with the undeniable fact that Elizabethan survey methods were fully capable of mapping such structures by enclosing them within simple geometrical figures whose sides and angles could be measured by chain and azimuthal instrument respectively, with short perpendicular offset distances fixing the position of key points on the fort's perimeter. It is also clear that in the summer of 1602 Bartlett would have had enough time to conduct a number of such localised surveys. That is admittedly a feeble argument in favour of his having done so: what makes it worth a mention is the prevalence in map-historical discussion of a contrary practice, which is to credit early surveyors with field work that was far beyond their resources. So altogether in 1602 there were means, motive and opportunity to produce an accurate set of south Ulster fort plans. The Bowlby plans certainly look good, in this as in other respects.

At smaller scales the situation is different. Here many of Bartlett's locations are identifiable from modern maps, allowing accuracy to be tested more objectively through a comparison of new and old. The simplest kind of test is the distortion grid, where a network of squares is transferred from an old map to a modern map, or vice versa, with the original cartographer's errors revealed in the resulting deformation of the interpolated lines (fig. 10). The advantage of the grid, after transformation, is in the ease with which even the unpractised eye can detect and compare quite small deviations from straightness, from parallelism, from rectangularity, and from uniformity of spacing.[11] Thus annotated, the 'Generalle description of Ulster' falls a good deal short of perfection; but it also bears witness to Bartlett's skill as a compiler in that, despite the absence of a rigorous control survey, errors do not seem to accumulate across the map. Furthermore, the grid registers maximum accuracy in the region of Bartlett's authenticated travels, an area south of Dungannon and east of Monaghan. The worst distortions are in north Tyrone, Derry, Donegal and Fermanagh. Distortion grids have been criticised for not yielding the kind of numerical index that would allow different maps to be ranked in order of merit. In fact they can be made to produce such an index,[12] but this does not overcome another objection to the grid, which is that the usual method of interpolating lines from points is more subjective than measuring from one point to another.

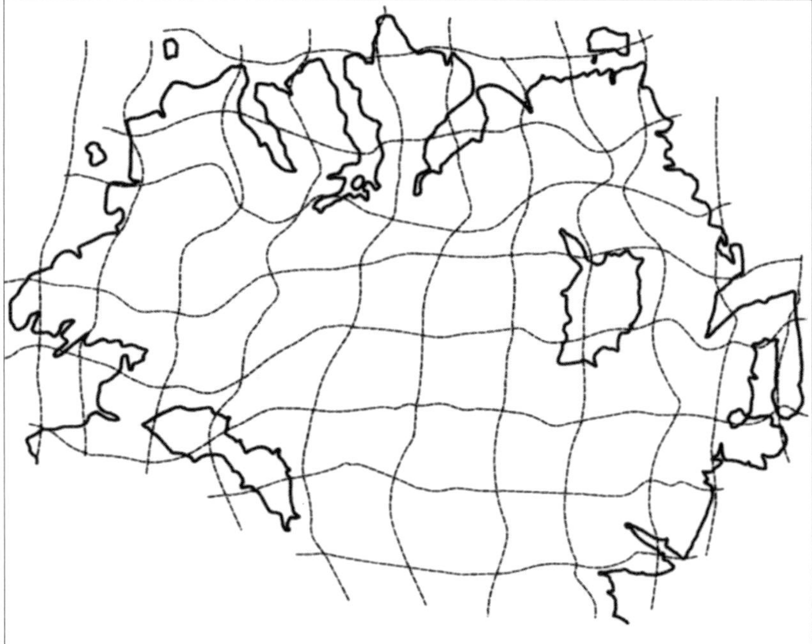

Fig. 10: Bartlett's accuracy, shown by transferring a square grid from the Ordnance Survey map to his 'Generalle description of Ulster'.

Various statistical techniques have been proposed as alternatives to the grid; in fact researchers have generally been more concerned with devising original methods of assessment than with collecting enough accuracy-values to support any general conclusions. In the present case, however, the problem has been made easier by the researches of Joan Murphy on early maps of Ulster.[13] Murphy studied Bartlett's 'Generalle description' alongside representations of the province by six other cartographers from the same period: for Ireland as a whole, parts of a printed map by Gerard Mercator (1564) and of manuscript maps by Laurence Nowell (*c.* 1564) and John Goghe (1567); for Ulster by itself, the anonymous Burghley map of *c.* 1570, and two later maps of comparable quality to Bartlett's, one by Baptista Boazio (*c.* 1602) and the other by John Speed (1610).[14] Murphy's tests were wholly concerned with internal accuracy — an important advantage in view of the difficulties with scale-statements encountered above. The first used a sample of straight-line distances between pairs of points recorded by both the early cartographer and the Ordnance Survey. If the old map were correct, the ratio between early and modern distances would always be the same, so the variability of this ratio is a measure of the inaccuracy under investigation. A second experiment grouped the test points into triangles and then compared corresponding angles in the early and modern outlines. A possible difficulty here is that since the three angles of a triangle are determined by its three sides, it may be considered unnecessary to impose separate tests upon distances and bearings; it is certainly alarming to find that Bartlett's relative distances were better, and his angles worse, than Speed's.

Such problems could be avoided by disregarding both triangles and matched distances, and by quantifying each sampled point instead as a pair of rectangular coordinates. Here Murphy chose the method of bidimensional regression pioneered by W.R.Tobler.[15] For this purpose the Ordnance map coordinates could be obtained from the Irish National Grid, the old map being divided by an arbitrary square grid of the researcher's own invention. The most striking feature of Tobler's procedure is that the scale, point of origin, and orientation of this 'manufactured' grid are immaterial: the computer programme adjusts all its variables to produce the best fit between the two maps that can be achieved without altering the shapes of the grid squares. The resemblance between early and modern coordinates is then expressed as a Pearson correlation coefficient, a perfect match being represented by a value of 100 per cent. Murphy's percentage results for Ulster in ascending order of merit are: Nowell 84.86, Goghe 85.75, Burghley 88.55, Mercator 89.82, Speed 96.49, Boazio 96.57, Bartlett 96.60.

So far, so good. But these figures are all higher than unsupported visual inspection would lead one to expect. When university undergraduates were asked to mark the same maps 'intuitively', the best average percentage scores were in the low sixties, the worst less than twenty. Murphy's results are therefore worth comparing with those of other maps measured by other researchers.[16] In one case at least, the present writer's results are reassuringly similar. Bartlett's percentages (again omitting the Lough Neagh map) emerge as largely self-consistent: campaign map 96.84, Trinity map 96.77, Bays map 96.16, Cotton map 94.58. Before *c.*1600 the majority of Irish regional maps had apparently been sketched from topological information together with reputed road distances: their scores are hardly ever above ninety per cent, and sometimes below seventy. These mediocre performances may be contrasted with the products of authenticated instrumental surveys, a typical result for Christopher Saxton's English county maps being as high as 99.3. Clearly Tobler's index may present methodological difficulties when applied to the even more exact surveys of the eighteenth and nineteenth centuries. Values for the period under review, though distractingly high, at least exhibit a reasonable spread.

FROM MERITS TO METHODS

It remains to ask whether techniques of accuracy-testing can throw any light on how a cartographer did his field work. In this respect it is a disappointment that the campaign map recording Mountjoy's routes is not considerably more accurate than Bartlett's coverage of areas that he is unlikely to have visited himself. Here we must recognise a countervailing influence, which is that (other things being equal) Tobler scores tend to be lower for large-scale than for small-scale maps. Leaving scale differences aside, one might expect mathematical methods to yield a more satisfactory diagnosis by applying separate tests not just to different areas but to different kinds of location, for instance distinguishing groups of points which, taken together, were either likely or unlikely to have been surveyed rather than estimated. In reply it can only be said that for other maps such experiments have hitherto proved inconclusive, with different subjects (for instance towns, river-confluences, hill-tops and boundary junctions) yielding unhelpfully similar results. In the present case, as a variation from Tobler's method, two sets of fifteen points each in the campaign map were tested for angular accuracy, one set situated on Mountjoy's routes, the other set at some distance from those routes. As it turned out, what should have been the 'better' points scored slightly lower than the 'worse'.

Future researchers may be more fortunate or more efficient, but one reason for this lack of differentiation is clear enough. Where numerical survey data conflict with other kinds of knowledge, apparent errors will typically be 'distributed' or smoothed out to give nearby places a plausible-looking mutual relationship; the map-maker's ability to cover his tracks in this way is one of the frustrations of cartographic history. Our final conclusion, then, must be modest. If Bartlett's test scores fall between those associated respectively with sketching and surveying, the obvious conclusion is that his own methods were probably a mixture of the two. In Hayes-McCoy's opinion, Bartlett and other contemporary regional surveyors 'probably "viewed" from a suitable height or heights the areas with which they were concerned, using the circumferentor to determine the relative positions of the noticeable features. Beyond that it is unlikely that they used instruments'.[17] In this context, 'circumferentor' can be interpreted as any instrument with sights and a magnetic compass used for measuring horizontal angles, and instruments 'beyond that' may be taken to include surveyor's chains and measuring wheels. With that proviso, this is one of many occasions where it would be hard to improve on Hayes-McCoy.

REFERENCES

1. Among Elizabethan authors of all-Ireland maps based on original data the main exceptions are Laurence Nowell (*c.*1564: BL, Cott. MS Domitian, xviii, ff 97, 101, 103; Add. MS 62540) and John Goghe (1567: PRO, MPF 1/68).
2. The text at this point needs amplifying in the light of Uta Lindgren's suggestion that one of Bartlett's Irish predecessors had measured latitudes and longitudes in the field ('Land surveys, instruments and practitioners in the renaissance' in David Woodward (ed.), *The history of cartography, volume three: cartography in the European renaissance* (Chicago, 2007), p. 506). This belief rests on the assumption, mistakenly attributed to the present writer, that Lythe travelled mainly by river boat and was therefore unable to 'get the necessary overview for terrestrial surveying'. It is more probable that Lythe travelled mainly by land, occasionally by sea or lake, and that his surveys like Bartlett's consisted for the most part of horizontal angles and distance-estimates. For the sake of completeness it should be added that what looks like an original Elizabethan Irish latitude value appears uniquely in the margin of an anonymous undated map of Carrickfergus (PRO, MPF 1/98).
3. John Speed, *The theatre of the empire of Great Britaine* (London, 1612): 'to the well-affected and favourable reader'.
4. See also Francis Jobson's earlier 'The eight mile church' (TCD, MS 1209/15).
5. Map of north Down and south Antrim, BL, Printed books, Harleian 5938, no. 129.
6. Maps of Belfast Lough [1567], PRO, MPF 1/77 (5000 feet) and Lordships of Cooley, Omeath, Mourne and Newry [1568], PRO, MPF 1/89 (6000 feet).
7. PRO, MPF 1/92.
8. C.F. Arden-Close, *Geographical by-ways* (London, 1947), pp 12-22; Philip Grierson, *English linear measures, an essay in origins* (University of Reading, 1972); I.M. Evans, 'A cartographic evaluation of the old English mile', *Geographical Journal*, cxli (1975), pp 259-64.
9. C. Hansteen, *Untersuchungen über den Magnetismus der Erde* (Christiana, 1819), part 1, p. 17; *Magnetischer Atlas gehörig zum Magnetismus der Erde, Map I. Abweichungskarte für das Jahre 1600*; J.H. Andrews, 'An Elizabethan map of Kilmallock', *North Munster Antiquarian Journal*, xi (1968), pp 27-35.
10. BL, Add. MS 24200, ff. 38-9.
11. J.H. Andrews, 'Motive and method in historical cartometry', International History of Cartography Conference, Greenwich, 1975 (National University of Ireland Library, Maynooth), pp 12-13.
12. Thomas F. McIlwraith, 'Measures of displacement and distortion in early maps' in W.P. Adams and F.M. Helleiner (eds), *International geography* (1972), pp 440-41.
13. Joan Murphy, *Quantitative methods of map accuracy assessment with reference to some early maps of Ulster*, B.A.Mod. dissertation, Trinity College, Dublin, 1977; Joan Murphy, 'Measures of map accuracy assessment and some early Ulster maps', *Irish Geography*, xi (1978), pp 88-101.
14. For Nowell and Goghe see note 1 above; for Boazio BL, Cotton MS Aug. I, ii, 30; for Speed, *Theatre of the empire of Great Britaine.*
15. W.R. Tobler, 'Medieval distortions: the projections of ancient maps', *Annals of the Association of American Geographers*, lvi (1966), pp 351-60; Waldo R. Tobler, 'Computation of the correspondence of geographical patterns', *Papers of the Regional Science Association*, xv (1965), pp 131-9. For operational reasons it has not been possible to use Tobler's original method, which has the additional merit of yielding average values for the scale and orientation of the map under investigation.
16. Percentages quoted below are derived from a version of Tobler's method explained in Rob Kitchin, *CMAP users handbook* (Swansea, n.d.).
17. G.A. Hayes-McCoy, *Ulster and other Irish maps, c.1600* (Dublin, 1964), p. xv.

Chapter 11

Englishmen's Place-Names

Altogether Bartlett collected names for approximately 650 features, most of them in Ulster. Only 46 per cent of them were names of settlements. While this apparent scarcity of human nomenclature was doubtless due in part to what his compatriots would have considered a low level of social and economic development, it also reflected the diversity of Bartlett's own geographical interests. The percentage of physical names is 35 — mainly hills, rivers, lakes, capes, bays, islands and a few woods — while 17 per cent refer to territorial divisions or their ruling families. It was a far cry from the English atlas of Christopher Saxton, where 94 per cent of the names in Bartlett's home county were those of towns, villages and other well-known habitation sites. We must not forget, however, that as toponymic sources the Irish maps now under consideration were selective to the point of ruthlessness. In particular, townland names as such, being irrelevant to Bartlett's purpose (as well as intractably numerous), are for the most part left unrecorded. As an example, consider two parishes just north of the Mourne Mountains, both within the limits of Bartlett's most detailed regional survey, the campaign map. In this area a recent investigation has collected forty-eight names of seventeenth-century or earlier date, of which just three were recorded by Bartlett.[1]

PROBLEMS OF PLACE-NAME STUDY

Before we proceed, a few matters of principle require attention. A proper name does not have to be 'in' any language. Many science-fiction writers' names, for example, are intended to be seen as alien by anyone who reads them. Of course the names of places in England do not generally seem alien to an inhabitant of that country, but the fact remains that even in the sixteenth century most of them were unintelligible in any connotative sense to the majority of Englishmen. This is still the case today: there are no dictionary definitions for 'Wigan' and 'Halifax'. It hardly needs saying that almost all the cartographers who worked in Tudor Ireland were English, most of them 'new' English with little previous experience of the Celtic world. Unless they happened to be students of linguistic science as then understood, such people would be unlikely to look for place-names that meant anything in the sense of being replaceable by synonymous words or phrases. In the cartography of his homeland, an English author's main concern with any given name would be not in correctly describing the place it denoted, but in helping his readers to find that place on the ground. This is the attitude he would have brought with him to Ireland.

It so happens, however, that for fairly obvious historical reasons Ireland and England have long been rather different in this respect. A much larger proportion of Irish names do possess a fairly obvious connotative significance, which meant that there were two senses in which any particular pronunciation or spelling of such a name could qualify as correct or incorrect. It could successfully direct attention to a particular place on the earth's surface; or it could evoke some kind of generic image in the minds of Irish speakers, regardless of their personal interest or lack of interest in the location concerned. The difference can perhaps be summarised as follows: to speak of Irish and non–Irish forms for, say, 'Ballybeg' seems perfectly reasonable, whereas any corresponding reference to the English and non-English forms of 'Stogumber' or 'Tixall' would look distinctly odd.

Since maps are a visual and not an aural medium, the obvious way for a cartographer to collect the names he needed was to get some knowledgeable person to write them down. At this point several difficulties arise. Although the Irish and English alphabets are almost the same, the functions of their constituent symbols are often different, so that even when an Irish letter or group of letters is recognisable to an English reader, the sounds it conveys may be totally unlike what he would expect. In many cases this might be a matter of small importance, because most of the Irishmen encountered by an Elizabethan English surveyor in the field would have been illiterate. He would not have time to seek out literature in the Irish language and might well be unlikely to encounter any scholars who could read that literature. For a majority of names, in any case, it seems improbable that their Irish forms had ever been committed to writing. In these circumstances a cartographer's only course would be either to copy a presumably non-Irish version of a name from whatever documents might be available, or to transcribe its spoken form in accordance with his own orthographic instincts. The result of these processes, repeated over the years, would be a set of unformulated but influential guidelines, themselves not quite English and not quite Irish, for writing Irish names in a manner acceptable to Anglo-Saxon prejudice. In Bartlett's time these rules had not yet converged to produce a common standard.

One more complication remains. Not all cartographers were as indifferent to etymology as the hypothetical Englishmen of the foregoing paragraphs. Laurence Nowell was an expert on both maps and words, with Ireland as a major field of study.[2] Even Robert Lythe, by profession a military engineer, seems to have taken more than a simple copyist's interest in Irish toponymy.[3] Such predilections have inspired various well-meant foreign attempts to devise spellings more correct than those in majority use, culminating in the efforts of the Ordnance Survey. (Often the results have pleased neither the linguistic purist nor the practical map-user.) There are limits, nevertheless, to what can be expected from scholarly endeavour. Even in the hyperactive world of modern academicism few serious students of language appear to have concentrated their attention for long on the 'corruptive' influences exercised by foreigners upon Irish toponymy in post-medieval times.[4] In some ways this neglect is understandable. For many Irish patriots, the anglicised forms of native names are wrong-headed, distasteful, demeaning and not worth wasting time on. For English commentators the inhibiting factor may be a sense of post-imperialist historical guilt. In these circumstances the uninstructed dabbler can only do the best he can.

TOPONYMIC IMPORTATIONS

On the subject of historical guilt, at least we have no evidence that Bartlett invented his own nomenclature, as English cartographers are widely believed to have done in Ireland, and as soldiers in general have often done when fighting foreign wars. Most of his names, if not already known from other sources, look typically Irish (a quality often plain to the inexpert eye) and therefore uninviting to the oppressively-minded Englishman of popular perception. Among the exceptions are three of Lord Mountjoy's celebratory fort-names (Charlemont, Mountjoy and Mountnorris), to which must be added the alias 'Lough Sydney' for Lough Neagh along with its companion name 'Ile Sydney' for modern Coney Island.[5] This last once-inspiring eponym, adopted by many late sixteenth-century map-makers, may well have had a cartographic origin, referring as it did to the lord deputy of Ireland responsible for the appointment of Bartlett's predecessor Robert Lythe.

So much for recent coinages. Next to be disposed of are names with earlier English or Scandinavian origins. In Bartlett's maps many of these denoted historic settlements in areas of Anglo-Norman occupation such as Cooley, Lecale and the Ards. There was also a tendency along the whole Ulster coastline for maritime names to be wholly or partly English, and in exceptional cases Latin. This is unremarkable for what might be called half-names (and half-descriptions) such as Baye, Foreland, Harborough, Haven, Head, Ile, Insula, Point, or Rock, but more noteworthy in the case of English-language allusions to colour — Black Abbey, Green Castle, Red Bay, Red Castle, White Abbey, White Castle, White Head — or to animal analogies involving foxes, goats and sheep.[6] Such names may be a sign that sea charts or chart-users were among Bartlett's sources of information. The names of two of his four named lake islands are also English — Coney Island and 'Sommer Iland'.[7] All in all, however, no less than eighty-five per cent of his nomenclature is unmistakably Gaelic.

VARIANT READINGS

In matters of spelling Bartlett could be surprisingly strict. For example he takes trouble to finish the compactly written territorial name 'Tyreon' by adding an awkwardly detached 'e' to it, despite the interposition of an unrelated hill-name; many cartographers would have regarded such terminal 'e's as optional. However, it cannot be pretended that Bartlett brought a fully scientific approach to Irish toponymy. On the contrary, his work bristles with apparently inexplicable orthographic variations. Where (as often happens) a name varies from the campaign map to the 'Generalle description', the motive may have been simply to reduce the number of its component letters in harmony with a smaller scale. Thus Bun-valle became Bunebal; Clonogh, Clono; Donoghmoore, Dono-moor; Killemoore, Kilemoor; Lough Corran, L: Corun; Mountioie, Montioy; and Terlogh Brasillogh, Terlo Brasilå. Elsewhere the differences often seem more capricious than rational: Bartlett was quite capable of writing 'Dondalk' and 'Baie of Dundalk' side by side on the same map. Perhaps he wished to convey that 'o' and 'u' were equally good, or bad, representations of the phoneme in question. Perhaps, more generally, he was alerting readers to the orthographic variety they would encounter if they chose to study Ireland in more detail. This motive is most evident where the variants are explicitly presented as such within a single map, for instance 'Carickfergus or Knockfergus', 'Lo: Neagh or Euagh', 'Cogier or Cuisher'.

Particularly interesting would be genuine attempts at self-correction. A possible example was Kilkeel, Co. Down, where 'Killel' in Bartlett's first two maps appears later as 'Kilcol'. Another, not far away, was the replacement of 'Kilbron' by 'Kilbronie', a name that all other authorities had agreed in rendering trisyllabically. The advantage of these last two examples lies in having undergone a recent scholarly investigation.[8] In other less fortunate cases it is more a matter of conjecture that the Bundorlin, Enislaghon and Kille-mana of the 'Generalle description' are better than the Bondounan, Enish Alaghon and Kil Banagh of the earlier campaign map. Perhaps these second thoughts of Bartlett's were inspired by 'expert' criticism of his first thoughts. Not all such changes can be seen as improvements, however: 'Narawater' seems no better than 'Narowater'. In the last analysis there is something inconsistent about the orthography of Bartlett and his contemporaries that cannot be rationalised except by saying that this is how things were done in the 1600s.

HOW TO ANGLICISE AN IRISH NAME

Amid these complexities, Bartlett's work provides a useful illustration of two themes, both related to the distinction already drawn between denoting and connoting. One is the adjustment of English spelling conventions to Irish nomenclature, the other is the realisation that most Irish names actually have a meaning. The first of these operations may for the sake of simplicity be conceived as replacing or modifying Irish characters or sequences of characters whose spoken equivalents were uncertain. Some of the Irish forms were seldom or never found in English; others occurred in contexts which in English would have given a clue to their pronunciation but which in Irish were baffling to foreigners. Examples of the first were the digraphic consonants 'bh', 'dh', 'fh' and 'mh', and the vowel-sequences 'ao', 'eai' ,'eoi', 'iui', and 'uai'. The second category included 'aim', 'ch' and 'th'; also 'c' as an isolated consonant, which writers of English could deal with by substituting the non-Irish letter 'k', as when 'Cilldara' became 'Kildare'. In this last case as in a number of others the anglicisers appeared to act in concert; an equally well-known example was the universal rendering of the Irish 'Cabhan' as 'Cavan'. At the same time Englishmen were willing to acknowledge that Ireland was a foreign country by accepting a strictly limited degree of orthographic strangeness. Note for example the frequency in anglicised names of the digraph 'gh', medial as well as terminal, and following not just 'i' and 'ou', as in normal English, but also 'a' and 'e'. An 'h' without the 'g' would sometimes serve the same purpose.

Beneath this rough and ready conformism we may sometimes detect an element of individuality. Bartlett for instance was unusual in often doubling the letter 'o', as in 'Chloonys and 'Moorne'. In a list of seventy-four versions of 'Dromore' and its variant spellings he is one of the only two writers who chose 'Dromoore'.[9] Other personal habits are best illustrated by a comparison with fellow-cartographer Francis Jobson, Bartlett's name being the first and Jobson's the second of each pair in the following lists. An example is his preference for 'u' over 'o': Clunis, Clonis; Dunan-ne(?), Donaney; Dunnamawe, Donomane; Ruskie, Roske. Here 'Dunanne' also illustrates a marked antipathy to the letter 'y' on Bartlett's part: Antrim, Antrym; Bunondune, Bunnondany; Conie, Cony; Derrie, Dirry; Fawne, Fauny; Omie, Omey. Less pronounced, and at odds with the case of 'Dunanne' just quoted, is a certain coolness towards repeated consonants: Belfast, Bellfast; Clanbrasil, Clanbrasill; Dirie, Dirrie; Dunganon, Dungannan; Scaterik, Scatterik; Tyreone, Terron.

Since Bartlett was a compiler as well as a surveyor, his spellings were not necessarily all his own. In general, as we have noted in an earlier chapter, his nomenclature shows many resemblances to the map of eastern Ulster associated with Sir Ralph Lane, sometimes extending to the kind of detail itemised above, so that both men write 'Dromore' as 'Dromoore', for instance. In other cases, however, Bartlett differs from Lane in much the same way as he differs from Jobson. A case in point is the avoidance of doubled consonants already mentioned, as in B.Dirie, B.Dirry; B.Terain, B.Terraine; Edendufcarick, Edenduffcarrick; Glastalogh, Glastallogh. (Again, Bartlett's versions are given first.)

THE IRISHNESS OF IRISH NAMES

We next pass from linguistic structure to semiotic content as manifested by recurrent place-name elements, in Ireland usually prefixes, that can be assumed to bear a constant meaning. Among map-makers a pioneer in this as in other fields was Robert Lythe, who thirty years earlier had acknowledged the validity of such generic terms by the simple method of initialising them. While Lythe's 'C' for 'castle' is not particularly remarkable, his 'M' has the interest of signalling an anglicised version of 'Mainister'. (The equivalent abbreviation in a map of England would have been 'ab' for 'abbey'.) Lythe's 'B' for 'baile' brings us deeper into Irish territory. Jobson in 1590 took the further step of listing his initialisations in a marginal note and including among them 'L' for 'Logh' and 'K' for 'Knocke or Mountain' as well as matching Lythe's 'B', 'C' and 'M'. Jobson's most original touch was 'T' (i.e. 'Temple') for a church, a somewhat eccentric gesture necessitated by having already used the initial 'C' for a castle; we cannot assume that he thought of 'Teampull' as an element in any particular settlement-name used by the local population.[10] The next stage, seen in the all-Ireland maps of Jodocus Hondius (1591) and Baptista Boazio (1599), was to tabulate the elements themselves in a separate glossary — 'Can: a Promontorie or hed Land', 'Slew a Mountaine' and so on. Bartlett did not go as far as that, but several initials and contractions occur within the body of his maps; with variants bracketed, they are B (Ba), Ca, Fl (Flu, Flum), Lo, Mo and, in the manner of Jobson, T (Te, Temp).

Otherwise the standard Irish prefixes can be recognised from being spelt out in individual names, sometimes as syllables within a more complex structure, sometimes written as separate words. Bartlett's commonest examples, with variant forms in brackets, are Ballagh, Balle, Bun, Can, Carick, Carn, Drum, Dun (Don), Enis (Inis, Inish), Kil (Kill), Knock (Nock), Lis, Mollogh (Mullogh), Ra, Rhein (Rein), Slew(e) and Tarman. Of these Rhein (a point, elsewhere more usually Rin or Ring) is interesting because Bartlett seems later to have decided that it needed a translation — 'Rheine, or Point Dunanane' in the 'Generalle description'. Others, such as Clan, Clo, Mac (Mc), Mont, O and Slut, come from the lexicon of territorial and family names. Bartlett clearly understood that these were common nouns as well as parts of proper nouns: a form like 'Lo & Ba: Carntel' invites us to accept the words 'lough' and 'bally' as grammatically (and logically) similar. A connotative vocabulary had its dangers for the student of nomenclature, one of them being false etymology. Twenty miles from salt water, Bartlett is unlikely to have believed that 'Sea St. Patrick' was ever meant as a reference to the sea. But he was certainly misled when he wrote 'Reagher insul', 'Reagher Ile' and 'Rafer-Ile' instead of 'Rathfriland', which in fact is thought to come from the personal name 'Fraoileann' and not from the site of this settlement on a hill among bogs.[11]

For non-Irish readers the best way of summarising the toponymic impact of Bartlett and his fellow countrymen may be simply to tabulate a more or less random selection of his names alongside their Irish equivalents. The Irish forms are those given by a modern scholar;[12] whether Elizabethan Irish would have been any different will be left for the experts to say.

TABLE 2: VARIANT NAME-FORMS

Bartlett	Irish form	Modern form
Agher	Eochair	Augher
Calbeg	Na Cealla Beaga	Killybegs
Clanconoher	Clann Chonchabhai	
Clan Karnye	Clann Chearnaigh	Clancarney
Cloonys	Cluain Eois	Clones
Coldagh	Cúil Dabhcha	Culdaff
Dirigh flu	Abhainn na Deirge	River Derg
Innis-owen	Inis Eoghain	Inishowen
Killalow	Cill Ala	Killala
Knock Glad	Cnoc Leithid	Knocklayd
Lemwaddie	Léim a' Mhadaidh	Limavady
Lo Foylle	Loch Feabhail	Lough Foyle
Lo: Ghille	Loch Gile	Lough Gill
Lo Neagh	Loch nEachach	Lough Neagh
Lough Mellou	Loch Meilbhe	Lough Melvin
O Gurmelie	Ó Gormlaigh	O'Gormley
Omie	An Ómaigh	Omagh
Raghlins	Reachlainn	Rathlin
Ramullen	Ráth Maoláin	Rathmullan
Slew Gullen	Sliabh gCuillinn	Slieve Gallion
Slut Gorre	Sliocht Goraidh	
Taghmore	Teamhuir	
Toaghe	Tuath Eachaidh	Toagh
Tyreone	Tír Eoghain	Tyrone

Although it may be unlikely that Bartlett ever made much progress in speaking or understanding the Gaelic language, at least he lacked the usual English cartographer's squeamishness in the face of Irish place-names. This sympathetic attitude is exemplified in his occasional citation of bilingual aliases, with 'Enish omocloigh' doubling for 'Conie Ile' (an inscription made more impressive by virtue of having apparently been inserted as an afterthought) and 'Blackwater' accompanying both 'Owen Trough' and 'Owen-mor'. At least once he gets ahead of modern scholarship, by adding the mysterious words 'Der & Nicoman Poelam' to the customary name for the River Derg. Other doubles take the form of a straightforward translation, either overtly, as in 'B:Moighrye or the sergeante towne', or implicitly where 'Ballagh' and 'Pace' are applied to the same road, and 'Fl' and 'Owen' to the same river. In one case — 'Moineynine or the strange marish' — the translation appears for its own sake without claiming to qualify as a place-name.

More daring is the monolingual use of Irish. In a collection of ten documentary and literary sources for Co. Down Bartlett is alone in describing Angus at the mouth of Strangford Lough as a 'Crag' and not a 'Rock';[13] and again in writing 'Enis moore' for what was usually called 'Great Island' just north of Ballagan Point.[14] He was also the only authority who added 'Owen' rather than 'River' or 'Fluvius' to the name 'Glen Ree', other cases of the same usage being 'Roeowen', 'Owenduff' and 'Owen ne Trough'. Equally revealing, though admittedly rare, is his insertion of an otherwise superfluous hyphen to analyse a name into its linguistic elements. Occasionally he does this with his own language, as at 'New-castle' in the Cotton map. More often it is a treatment reserved for native names. Examples like 'O-Hanlan' and 'O-Hagan' are unsurprising, but with 'Innis-owen', 'Clan-Brasil' 'Dono-moor' and 'Tollogh-oge' we are taken a step further. Sometimes a space serves instead of a hyphen, as with 'Lough ne Glin'. Like his precocious interest in native landholding customs already noticed, Bartlett's treatment of toponymy did at least show a certain feeling for Irishness.

REFERENCES

1. Mícheál B. Ó Mainnin, *Place-names of Northern Ireland, volume three: County Down III The Mournes* (Belfast, 1993), pp 74-118, parishes of Clonduff and Kilcoo.
2. J.H. Andrews and Rolf Loeber, 'An Elizabethan map of Leix and Offaly: cartography, topography and architecture' in William Nolan and Timothy P. O'Neill (eds), *Offaly: history and society: interdisciplinary essays on the history of an Irish county* (Dublin, 1998), p. 256.
3. J.H. Andrews, 'The maps of Robert Lythe as a source for Irish place-names', *Nomina*, xvi (1992-3), pp 7-22.
4. Séamus Ó Ceallaigh, an authority often cited in this book (see below, note 12) once wrote an article entitled 'Wanted, a history of anglicisation', *An Claidheamh Solais*, v (1903), p. 5.
5. Patrick McKay and Kay Muhr, *Lough Neagh places: their names and origins* (Belfast, 2007), p. 86. This identification is made explicit in Bartlett's Lough Neagh map (PRO, MPF 1/133). The Irish name for Coney island is Inis Dabhaill (Bartlett's Enish Dowel).
6. For Bartlett's 'Ship [Sheep] Island' see Fiachra Mac Gabhann, *Place-names of Northern Ireland, volume seven: County Antrim II Ballycastle and north-east Antrim* (Belfast, 1997), pp 100-1.
7. For Sommer Island ('never seen but in summer') in the south-west embayment of Lough Neagh see MPF 1/133. Neither this name nor Bartlett's Enish Garlin (presumably the modern Ram's Island) is discussed by McKay and Muhr.
8. Ó Mainnin, *Place-names of Northern Ireland, ... The Mournes*, pp 13-15; Gregory Toner and Mícheál B. Ó Mainnin, *Place-names of Northern Ireland, volume one: County Down I Newry and south-west Down* (Belfast, 1992), pp 132-4.
9. Kay Muhr, *Place-names of Northern Ireland, volume six: County Down IV North-west Down/Iveagh* (Belfast, 1996), pp 106-8.
10. Patrick J. O'Connor, *Atlas of Irish place-names* (Newcastle West, 2001), pp 138-9; Toner and Ó Mainnin, *Place-names of Northern Ireland, ... Newry and south-west Down*, p. 56. See also Pat McKay, *Place-names of Northern Ireland, volume four: County Antrim I The baronies of Toome* (Belfast, 1995), p. 133.
11. Toner and Ó Mainnin, *Place-names of ... Newry and south-west Down*, p. 127.
12. Séamus Ó Ceallaigh, 'Old lights on place-names: new lights on maps', *Journal of the Royal Society of Antiquaries of Ireland*, lxxx (1950), pp 172-86; Séamus Ó Ceallaigh, 'A preliminary note on some of the nomenclature on the map of S.E. Ulster bound up with the maps of the escheated counties, 1610', *Journal of the Royal Society of Antiquaries of Ireland*, lxxxi (1951), pp 1-7; Séamus Ó Ceallaigh, *Gleanings from Ulster history* (Oxford, 1951), *passim*.
13. A.J. Hughes and R.J. Hannan, *Place-names of Northern Ireland, volume two: County Down II The Ards* (Belfast, 1992), p. 135.
14. Ó Mainnin, *Place-names of Northern Ireland, ... The Mournes*, pp 56-7.

Chapter 12

A Bequest to the Nations

It is natural to wonder how maps drawn in the reign of the first Elizabeth can still be available for inspection four centuries later. This is not just a matter of idle curiosity. Respectable concerns for cultural history are involved in asking why people collect and preserve maps through many changing circumstances and with many different results. The chief reason in the case of Ireland is that these were records of government, worth cherishing partly because they might help future political and military decision-makers but also because no one liked to take the responsibility of throwing them away. Their custodians were immune from the vagaries of family history that so often cause private possessions to be voluntarily relinquished, though of course this did not infallibly protect official documents from damage, loss or theft.

COTTON AND CAREW

Sir Robert Cotton (1571-1631) is an exception to the foregoing rule. He was neither soldier nor administrator and had no particular connection with Ireland. Nor were his interests specifically geographical. He was primarily an English antiquarian scholar and collector whose audacity and persistence gave him privileged access to the state papers, many of which were to find a place among his personal possessions before eventually passing to the British Museum.[1] Some of his acquisitions were town and fort plans of limited appeal, but he seems also to have developed a special concern for Ireland's most able regional cartographers — Laurence Nowell, Robert Lythe, Francis Jobson, John Thomas, Baptista Boazio and the anonymous author of the Leix-Offaly map. Some of these men, it is true, are represented in Cotton's collection only by work of secondary importance, but perhaps this fact itself confirms his understanding of their stature. Bartlett and Bartlett's 'Cotton' map may be a case in point.

In George Carew (1555-1629) a similar collecting instinct was combined with an inside knowledge of contemporary Irish affairs and a passion for Irish history, particularly that of his own service as lord president of Munster in the last years of Elizabeth's reign. He was also a good judge of cartographic merit. Carew's collection of Irish maps, which was larger and richer than Cotton's, is now unequally divided between the two great scholarly libraries of Lambeth Palace in London and Trinity College in Dublin. Lambeth has one Bartlett item, a plan of Duncannon fort endorsed in Carew's handwriting. The contents of Trinity's magnificent 'Hardiman atlas' appear to have reached the college through unknown channels at some time between the late seventeenth and late eighteenth centuries but it was not until the 1950s that the keeper of the college manuscripts, William O'Sullivan, discovered where they came from.[2] This was done by recognising Carew's hand in many of their annotations and by collating the maps themselves with lists of early seventeenth-century date. One such list of Carew's holdings includes: 'A mapp of parte of Ulster from dundalke to the little Ardes Pap[er]'.[3] No such map was present when James Hardiman catalogued the Trinity maps in 1821, but he did find a list (no longer extant) of maps that had formerly belonged to the same collection, one of which was said to represent 'parts of counties of Armagh, Down, Tyrone & Antrim in Ulster'.[4] Coincidentally, what seems to be the same map reached the college by gift or purchase at some time later in the nineteenth century, with the description quoted by

Hardiman on its reverse. This is the item referred to in the present work as the Trinity map. As we have seen, Carew's arms occur within its interior alongside those of Sir Richard Wingfield.

Carew's archive is not known to have been used by any seventeenth-century map-editor working on Ireland, but we have it in John Speed's own words that the Cotton collection contributed to his *Theatre of the empire of Great Britaine*. A well-known instance is the representation of Enniskillen castle in BL, Cotton MS Aug. I, ii, 39, believed to have been the source for Speed's view of the castle in *The province Ulster described*, 1610.[5] Another possible example from the same map is the reference to Owen Maugh as 'the ancient seat of the Kinges of Ulster'.[6] This inscription seems not to have been recorded by earlier map-makers such as Jobson. Bartlett's version of it appears in both his Cotton and his Trinity maps. Circumstantially, the former is more likely to have been Speed's source, though he may have been following the text of William Camden's *Britannia*.

JOHN NORDEN'S SOURCE-MAPS

Bartlett's other regional maps of Ulster have had a more complicated history. Three of them (now PRO, MPF 1/35, MPF 1/36 and MPF 1/37) were studied by the eminent English cartographer John Norden when he was collecting information about Ireland for King James's principal secretary, Robert Cecil.[7] Two important products of Norden's Irish researches have survived: a small map of Ireland in Trinity College, Dublin, mostly copied from Boazio's *Irelande* of 1599;[8] and a large one, evidently later in date, now in the British National Archives.[9] Both are dedicated to Cecil under the title of earl of Salisbury, lord high treasurer of England, so they are unlikely to have been finished until after the earl's appointment to this high office in April 1608. The second map was accompanied by a written description that includes Norden's famous lament about his 'tedious conferring of so many disagreeing plots together'. Predictably enough for an Elizabethan map-maker, he omits to name the authors of these various plots, some of whom are now unidentifiable. Two, however, can be recognised from a simple comparison between source and derivative: they are Boazio (1599 vintage) and, more surprisingly, Bartlett.[10]

In Norden's National Archives map, his debt to Bartlett is revealed by the shape of certain physical features and, more conclusively, by the occurrence of quite elaborate inscriptions that are unlikely to have been composed independently by more than one author: examples are 'Clonduffe or the 8 mile churche' and 'Here Shane ONeale was slayne'. Most of these Bartlett-related features belong to the 'Generalle description of Ulster', but some come from the campaign map and a few from the Bays map: like many compilers Norden was reluctant to leave a source unused once he had taken the trouble to find it. It appears probable, then, that when he started work on these three maps they were all being kept in the same place.

In the earlier, Trinity College, version of Lord Salisbury's map Norden includes a number of Ulster names not recorded by Boazio in 1599, but none of these can be conclusively attributed to Bartlett. It is when we focus on the second, National Archives version that important issues of archival history begin to arise. We may assume the Bartlett originals to have been kept by Lord Mountjoy in England for several years. At any rate they are unlikely to have been available in Dublin: if Sir John Davies had seen the 'Generalle description of Ulster' he would hardly have implied that all maps of Donegal made before its author's last expedition were bad enough to be condemned as 'false and defective'. After Mountjoy's death the three Bartlett maps were presumably acquired by Salisbury, who is known to have been interested in the disposal of the former deputy's estate. It is a moot point whether they were ever enclosed within any of the (now empty) vellum covers apparently relating to early seventeenth-century maps of Ireland in the National Archives.[11] Anyway, it may have been dissatisfaction with Norden's first attempt at Ireland that caused the lord treasurer to order a search for more up-to-date sources under his own roof. And perhaps it was when Norden had finished with the Bartlett maps that Salisbury decided to transfer them from private custody to the state papers, which at this time were being reviewed and reorganised by their official keeper, Thomas Wilson.[12]

For all his labour, Norden's maps had no influence on the later cartography of Ireland. In this respect they differed radically from *The province Ulster described*, dated 1610 and published two years later in John Speed's *Theatre of the empire of Great Britaine*. Speed's map was reprinted many times, and copied by nearly all the famous European atlas-makers of the seventeenth century. It was itself another compilation, of considerable merit by the standards of the time, which differed from earlier maps mainly in its heavy dependence throughout the centre and east of the province upon Francis Jobson's model of 1591. Although Speed made a creditable effort to deploy the most recent available information, he apparently knew nothing of Bartlett's later work. He was unaware, for example, that Bartlett had recorded the destruction of O'Neill's chair at Tullaghoge. Speed is known to have been preparing his *Theatre* as early as the period 1603-5, when Bartlett's last three maps were probably still with Mountjoy and therefore out of reach.[13]

We have not yet finished with Norden, however, because his description of Ireland also contains plans of Mountnorris, the Mullin, Charlemont, Inisloughan, Mountjoy, Monaghan and Augher that were obviously copied from the originals in the Bowlby series or at least from a derivative of those originals.[14] Bartlett's fort surveys were already out of date by 1608 and in any case were hardly of major consequence from Norden's point of view. They would have made better sense if augmented with plans of more lastingly important Irish fortifications such as Cork, Haulbowline, Kinsale and Galway. The truth is that for Norden these northern maps were little more than window dressing, and it is hard to believe that resurrecting the originals could have caused him very much trouble. Which means that like Bartlett's regional maps they were probably held in *c.*1608 either by the lord treasurer or by the keeper of state papers. Later the histories of the large-scale and small-scale Bartlett maps were to diverge in a dramatic fashion.

THE BODLEY CONNECTION

Once in official custody Bartlett's three most important regional maps proved to be safe enough. The problem was how to classify them. To a contemporary archivist taking a broad view of Irish affairs, it might have seemed appropriate to store them with a different cartographic package, namely the barony maps now in course of production by Sir Josias Bodley to facilitate the forthcoming settlement in Counties Armagh, Cavan, Coleraine (later renamed Londonderry), Donegal, Fermanagh and Tyrone — though in truth Bartlett's and Bodley's maps had hardly anything in common apart from depicting aspects of Ulster and their long-running association is probably no more than a red herring.

The Bartlett-Bodley link may date from an early stage of the maps' archival history, judging by a list in the British National Archives (SP 64/1) that probably belongs to the early seventeenth century. Among the items enumerated we can recognise Bodley's barony maps for four counties,[15] Norden's copies of the seven Bartlett fort plans, and three maps described as 'A Generalle discription of Ulster', 'Tyrone' and 'Tyrconnel, O'Donnel &c', which were surely the three whose history we are now tracing. (At this early stage, it may be noted, the maps were already being cited in the order that became habitual in the nineteenth and twentieth centuries.) Later entries refer to 'The booke of forts', 'A description of Lough Eaugh or Sidney pointing oute the forts lately erected by Tyrone &c' and 'The plot of Irland with the confines'. Of these the 'Eaugh' map must be Bartlett's Lough Neagh, now MPF 1/133, while the word 'confines' probably identifies the plot of Ireland as Norden's, now MPF 1/67.[16] 'The booke of forts' remains a mystery which for the moment may be left unsolved.

The non-Bodley entries in this undated list may well commemorate the association already postulated between Norden and Bartlett: perhaps Norden had returned his source-materials to Lord Salisbury at the same time as he delivered his own 'plot'. Evidently these items had continued to stand somewhat apart from the main body of state paper maps. But it is unlikely that the anonymous Lough Neagh map was grouped with other Bartlett maps in recognition of their common authorship: there was no seventeenth-century Hayes-McCoy to make the necessary attribution. More probably it was the word 'forts' in the title that had caused this map to receive special attention. Pursuing the same line of argument, we may also wonder whether the interest in military subjects revealed by SP 64/1 was due to the outbreak of an Anglo-Spanish war in 1625, when new fortifications were planned and executed in many parts of Ireland.[17]

Nothing more is known about the Irish maps in the state paper office until well into the nineteenth century, but their archival inter-relationships appear to have remained essentially the same. A note headed 'Particulars of ancient maps relating to Ireland Nov 1833' preserved among the Irish Ordnance Survey memoirs begins by listing the three Bartlett maps of Ulster, immediately followed by Bodley's barony series individually named, and then a miscellaneous assortment of Irish maps that includes Bartlett's Lough Neagh and Norden's Ireland with its related description.[18] However, this document contains no reference to a book of forts, and the same is true of two other mid-century lists of Irish maps. The first of these is F.S. Thomas's brief reference to three volumes — one with no subject-matter specified (but probably embracing a number of now-familiar state paper maps), one evidently including the escheated counties barony maps, and one almost certainly identifiable as Norden's 'description'.[19] A second list, by the historian of County Monaghan, Evelyn Shirley, confirms this impression by specifying each individual item, again with Bartlett's three regional maps immediately preceding Bodley's.[20]

These are not the only sources that have been interpreted as evidence of a Bartlett-Bodley connection. At some stage, it is impossible to say exactly when, a belief grew up in the state paper office that Bartlett's three large regional maps had been enclosed with the plantation barony surveys in a letter of 15 March 1610 from the Irish treasurer at war, Sir Thomas Ridgeway, to Robert Cecil.[21] This idea has found expression in the official Record Office catalogue of maps relating to the British Isles (1967) and also, despite a reviewer's scepticism, on the departmental web-site of forty years later.[22] However, there is nothing to support any such assumption either in the Ridgeway letter or in the Bartlett maps themselves, which are devoid of pre-nineteenth-century endorsements or annotations. Two years earlier, admittedly, Ridgeway had helped to campaign against the rebel Cahir O Doherty in Donegal, an experience that might well have involved consulting maps of the same type as the 'Generalle description',[23] but that does not make him likely to have obtained and retained possession of Bartlett's maps. Bodley's barony surveys are a different case: as one of the Ulster plantation commissioners in 1609-10 Ridgeway is quite likely to have worked with these. But if the barony coverage had then needed augmenting on a smaller scale, the resulting maps would surely have differed from Bartlett's by including the names and boundaries of the escheated counties and their baronies — and indeed maps of just this kind are known to have existed in 1610, or at any rate to have been in preparation.[24]

BARTLETT IN PRINT

The Bartlett-Bodley conjunction was renewed in 1861 when facsimiles of both series were published by the Ordnance Survey office at Southampton. These usually occur bound as a single volume, sometimes under the brave title 'The Irish historical atlas'.[25] Editorially there was an important difference, unnoticed at the time, between the two main components of this work. Although the whole atlas was said to have been produced by the new technique of photozincography, the Bodley facsimiles appear to have been traced manually — and in some places erroneously. The Bartlett versions on the other hand are evidently true to the originals except perhaps for some of the colouring which as usual with contemporary Ordnance maps was added by hand. The juxtaposition of two facsimile sequences within the same pair of covers understandably tempted some historians to give all the originals the same date, even though the chronologies of the two groups were clearly distinguished by the Record Office calendarist Hans Hamilton, both on the reverse of MPF 1/35 and in the little-known introduction to the 'Historical atlas'.

In 1877 a further step forward was taken by the Reverend George Hill, the first modern historian of the Ulster plantation. By this time Sir John Davies's not-yet-famous reference to the beheading of 'one Barkeley' had been published in both text and preface of the *Calendar of state papers, Ireland*, disappointingly without any editorial comment. It was Hill who made the crucial connection: 'With the baronial maps of Ulster, 1609, recently published ... there is one, of an earlier date, showing the coasts of Tirconnell or Donegal, which may have been wholly, or in part, the work of the unfortunate map-maker above-named'.[26] This is an obvious reference to what we are here calling the Bays map, MPF 1/37. While he did not mention the other two Bartlett maps, Hill had scored a palpable hit, though it was many years before anyone followed up his discovery.[27]

BOWLBY BEFORE THE BOWLBYS

We now return to the large-scale plans presently in the National Library of Ireland. Note first that Bartlett accounts for only twelve of the twenty-three items in the Bowlby atlas. The remaining maps, like Bartlett's, are mostly unsigned and undated though evidently varying in authorship. Ten of them depict different parts of Ireland ranging in space from Lough Foyle to Kinsale and in time from 1587 to 1625. There is one non-Irish item, a more or less contemporaneous map of Lewis in Scotland. They are all military or political maps of the kind that one would expect to find in the state paper office, and most of them can be linked with well-documented phases of government activity, but they give no indication of when or why they should have been constituted a separate physical entity. Perhaps this was another reaction to the Spanish crisis of 1625-6. The cover enclosing the Bowlby maps was assigned by Hayes-McCoy to the eighteenth century, but it might be safer to describe it as 'probably neither seventeenth- nor twentieth-century'.

On the reverse of the first page in the Bowlby Bartlett series is an almost illegible inscription uncovered by conservation measures in 1990. It is signed by James I's record-keeper Thomas Wilson, who was apparently asking for the return of the maps to his office when they were no longer needed. There is no evidence as to who else might have seen them in the 1600s except that William Camden's published description of Armagh city in 1610, with its 'very few small wattled cottages' among the ruins, seems likely to have been based on Bartlett's view.[28] In the light of later events, the Wilson memorandum is an important revelation. Of course it may not necessarily have achieved its object, but there is other evidence that points in the right direction. For one thing, the entry 'The booke of forts' in SP 64/1 may be a reference to the maps under discussion. As a brief approximation this phrase fits the Bowlby maps well enough, both the whole series and the Bartlett maps considered in isolation.

Then there are the other inscriptions contained in the National Library volume itself. One simply reads 'P 9 T N 16'. Similar marks appear in other maps that have never left the state paper office: Bodley's maps for instance are annotated P18 B 63-66.[29] It has been suggested that P here stands for 'press', B for 'bottom' and T for 'top', and that these inscriptions date from the period 1705-1838 when the maps were stored in the Middle Temple Gallery in London.[30] Slightly apart from this press-mark is the letter 'C', which was apparently an accepted code for 'secretaries of state', one of the categories of document recognised by the keeper of state papers in *c.*1704.[31] The difference between P.9 and P.18 suggests that the two sets of Bartlett maps were no longer in close proximity. To complicate the story even further, other alphanumeric references (apparently of nineteenth- or twentieth-century date) occur on two torn labels inside the National Library volume; their archival significance has not yet been established. On arrival at the Library the volume also contained a loose handwritten sheet, watermarked 1837, listing monetary payments unconnected with the maps, some of them dated 1836, 1837 or 1838. No official archivist would have inserted this paper, which may therefore be taken as evidence that the maps were already in private hands by the later 1830s.

We reach a firm date — but no other kind of firmness — with C.W. Russell and John P. Prendergast's preface of 1872 to the *Calendar of state papers, Ireland* for 1603-6. Here the Record Office maps are once more stated to comprise three volumes. Of these the first two appear to match the first two volumes mentioned by Thomas. The third ought therefore to correspond with what we have identified in Thomas's account as the work of John Norden, but in that case Russell and Prendergast's description of it — 'Plans of many forts erected in Ireland in reign of James' — is to say the least misleading, especially in view of their claim to have 'carefully catalogued' all three volumes.

Russell and Prendergast postponed any further comment, promising to take up the subject again when their *Calendar* reached the year 1609, but the promise was never kept, and the careful catalogue has never materialised. The Record Office's next calendarist for Ireland, E.G. Atkinson, showed no particular interest in early cartography.[32] One can only hope that all these maps and references to maps will one day be the subject of long and leisurely research by a properly qualified archival historian. Meanwhile, the current state of knowledge, ignorance and conjecture may be summarised as follows. How and when the Bowlby maps were first brought together is not known. They were probably press-marked in the state paper office at some time in or after 1704. They may or may not have been the 'book of forts' referred to in SP 64/1. They probably escaped from official custody between 1704 and the accession of Queen Victoria. They surely cannot be the 'plans of many forts' mentioned by Russell and Prendergast because it seems inconceivable that such treasures could have gone astray after the Public Record Office had been properly constituted in 1838.

FROM HAMPSTEAD TO DUBLIN

The scene now shifts from the centre of London to the northern suburbs, where Bartlett's large-scale plans finally resurfaced among the possessions of the eminent architect and town-planner Sir Raymond Unwin (1863-1940). Unwin's interest in historic settlement is clear from his book *Town planning in practice* (London, 1909) and he is known to have been professionally concerned with Ireland.[33] It seems probable that he acquired this item by gift or purchase as a curiosity at a time when collectors could still buy manuscript maps for very low prices. Whether any lasting record might have been kept of such an acquisition is impossible to say. Some of Unwin's papers were destroyed during the second world war. Others eventually found their way to the University of Manchester; no one has searched them piece by piece for evidence of his collecting activities, but it appears virtually certain that no such evidence exists.

It seems to have been more than ten years after Unwin's death that his daughter-in-law began to dispose of his surviving effects. There is no truth in the rumour that the Irish maps were at one stage rescued from a dustbin, but they might still be said to have had a narrow escape: in fact they were given to Richard Bowlby, son of the Unwins' neighbour in Hampstead.

Bartlett's masterwork thus became the property of a pre-teenage child. Eventually the maps engaged the attention of Richard's father, Dr. John Bowlby, who early in 1955 presented them to the National Museum of Ireland.[34] Sir Richard Bowlby remembers feeling 'upset and rather aggrieved' that his parents had given the maps to Dublin,[35] but nobody else was heard to say that these English documents should have remained in England. In March 1956 the maps were transferred from the National Museum to the National Library of Ireland.

For reasons that it would be unprofitable to guess at, the Bowlby donation was ignored by Irish newspapers. Among academics, however, the maps may be said to have created a sensation, illuminating many features of the Ulster scene at a period for which remarkably few graphic illustrations had hitherto been available. For the first time Mountjoy's troops and their enemies could be seen in action outside Munster; and apart from the products of renaissance military architecture there were pioneering representations of raths, crannogs, thatched cabins, lazy-beds and other interesting but not always easily identifiable features of the Gaelic landscape. That the maps should be published by the Irish Manuscripts Commission was proposed in October 1955 by Ireland's leading military historian, Professor Gerard Hayes-McCoy. This suggestion was immediately accepted subject to physical confirmation of authenticity, which was duly obtained from the British Museum laboratory.[36] No one doubted that the facsimiles should be edited by Hayes-McCoy. There could not have been a better choice.

After the usual delays, *Ulster and other Irish maps,* c.*1600* was finally published in 1964 to general acclaim.[37] It included not only a separate commentary on each facsimile but an excellent introductory review of Elizabethan Anglo-Irish map-making as a whole. Apart from the Bowlby acquisition, the authorship of Bartlett maps in four major British and Irish repositories had finally been determined beyond reasonable doubt. In particular, the different strands of a talented cartographer's career — regional and political, local and military — had been brought together for the first time. This, in the long run, was Hayes McCoy's most important editorial achievement. After centuries of confusion it could now be claimed with some confidence that the queen's last map-maker had not lived in vain. The subsequent course of Bartlett historiography is illustrated in the present book.

REFERENCES

1. C.W. Russell and John P. Prendergast, preface, *CSPI, 1603-6*, pp xxxvii-xlix.
2. T.D. Hardy and J.S. Brewer, *Report to the Right Hon. the master of the rolls upon the Carte and Carew papers in the Bodleian and Lambeth libraries* (London, 1864); M.R. James, 'The Carew manuscripts', *English Historical Review*, xlii (1927), pp 261-7; William O'Sullivan, 'George Carew's Irish maps', *Long Room (Bulletin of the Friends of the Library of Trinity College, Dublin)*, xxvi-xxvii (1983), pp 15-25.
3. Lambeth Palace, MS 637/117-19.
4. James Hardiman, 'Catalogue of maps, plans &c. relating to Ireland', *Transactions of the Royal Irish Academy*, xiv (1824), pp 76-7. The original manuscript of Hardiman's catalogue, dated 1821, is TCD, LIB MUN 1/62.
5. R.A. Skelton, *County atlases of the British Isles 1579-1703* (London, 1970), p. 44.
6. This point was noticed by Kay Muhr in 'The early place-names of County Armagh', *Seanchas Ard Mhacha*, xix, 1 (2002), p. 4, n. 16. William Camden's *Britannia* also associates this site with the kings of Ulster.
7. J.H. Andrews, 'John Norden's maps of Ireland', *Proceedings of the Royal Irish Academy*, c, C, 5 (2000), pp 159-206.
8. TCD, MS 1209/1.
9. PRO, MPF 1/67.
10. For the speculation that Norden and Bartlett were personally acquainted see Andrews, 'John Norden's maps', p. 185.
11. SP 64/1, SP 64/2.
12. F.A. Thomas, *A history of the state paper office, with a view of the documents therein deposited* (London, 1849), pp 7-8.
13. Skelton, *County atlases*, p. 34. For an ideological explanation of Speed's failure to notice recent developments in Ulster see Mark Netzloff, 'Forgetting the Ulster plantation: John Speed's *The theatre of the empire of Great Britain* (1611) and the colonial archive', *Journal of Medieval and Early Modern Studies,* xxxi, 2 (2001), pp 313-48.
14. PRO, MPF 1/117. The margins of the maps copied by Norden are annotated with titles in a contemporary hand which are absent from the other Bowlby maps.
15. It is interesting that the lost barony maps for Donegal and Coleraine (Londonderry) had already been separated from the others when the list was compiled. They were probably removed when the government was investigating the state of the Londonderry plantation in the early or middle 1620s.
16. Norden's map was endorsed with the unusual phrase 'The Plott of Irelande with the confines' (Andrews, 'John Norden's maps', p. 162).
17. Paul M. Kerrigan, *Castles and fortifications in Ireland, 1485-1945* (Cork, 1995), pp 76-83.
18. Royal Irish Academy, Ordnance Survey memoirs, Box 27, Fermanagh, II.
19. Thomas, *History of the state paper office*, p. 19.
20. E.P. Shirley, 'Catalogue of maps and plans relating to Ireland, in Her Majesty's State Paper Office, Whitehall, London', *Ulster Journal of Archaeology*, iii (1855), p. 275. For the first volume Shirley lists the maps later numbered MPF 68-100, in the same order as that later given by Public Record Office, *Maps and plans in the Public Record Office, 1: British Isles,* c.*1410-1860* (London, 1967).
21. *CSPI, 1608-10,* pp 401-2; original in SP 64/2.
22. J.H. Andrews, review of Public Record Office, *Maps and plans in the Public Record Office, i British Isles* in *Irish Historical Studies*, xvi (1968-9), pp 372-5.
23. *CSPI, 1606-8*, p. 599.

24. 'A generall mapp of the six excheated Counties in Ulster, wherein is particularlie sett forth the scituation and adiacence of all the [?] precinct entended to be planted ...', Hatfield House, CPM supp. 2 (*c.*1610); 'A plott of the six escheated counties of Ulster', BL, Cotton MS, Aug. I, ii, 44 (*c.*1610).
25. J.H. Andrews, 'The maps of the escheated counties of Ulster, 1609-10', *Proceedings of the Royal Irish Academy*, lxxiv, C, 4 (1974), pp 133-70.
26. George Hill, *An historical account of the plantation in Ulster at the commencement of the seventeenth century 1608-1620* (Belfast, 1877), p. 169.
27. In *c.*1950 Séamus Ó Ceallaigh made a number of penetrating comments on the date and content of Bartlett's regional maps without identifying their author. Like Evelyn Shirley before him, he went slightly astray by mistaking the year in which Mountjoy had been created a knight of the garter; this should have been 1597 (Séamus Ó Ceallaigh, 'Old lights on place-names: new lights on maps', *Journal of the Royal Society of Antiquaries of Ireland*, lxxx (1950), p. 184; Séamus Ó Ceallaigh, 'A preliminary note on some of the nomenclature on the map of S.E. Ulster bound up with the maps of the escheated counties, 1610', *Journal of the Royal Society of Antiquaries of Ireland*, lxxxi (1951), p. 1; Shirley, 'Catalogue of maps and plans relating to Ireland', p. 275).
28. William Camden, *Britain, or a chorographicall description of the most flourishing kingdomes, England, Scotland, and Ireland* ... (London, 1610), p. 109, quoted in Caoimhín Ó Danachair, 'Representations of houses on some Irish maps of *c.*1600' in Geraint Jenkins (ed.), *Studies in folk life: essays in honour of Iowerth C. Peate* (London, 1969), p. 94.
29. Another example is P18 B 71 in an Elizabethan map of Mayo and Sligo (PRO, MPF 1/91).
30. Elizabeth M. Hallam, 'Nine centuries of keeping the public records' in G.H. Martin and Peter Spufford (eds), *The records of the nation: the Public Record Office 1838-1988, the British Record Society 1888-1988* (Woodbridge, 1990), p. 37; R.A. Skelton, personal communication, 24 June 1969.
31. Hallam, 'Nine centuries of keeping the public records', p. 37.
32. A certain naïveté appears in Atkinson's comment of 1905 that MPF 1/133 shows 'how much the contour of Lough Neagh has changed' (*CSPI, 1600-1*, p. 408). It was true that the shape of the lake had changed (Patrick McKay and Kay Muhr, *Lough Neagh places: their names and origins* (Belfast, 2007), p. 5), but the maps of *c.*1600 were too inaccurate to furnish conclusive evidence on this point.
33. Mervyn Miller, 'Raymond Unwin and the planning of Dublin' in Michael J. Bannon (ed.), *The emergence of Irish planning 1880-1920* (Dublin, 1985), pp 263-305.
34. National Library of Ireland, accessions book, no. 1763, and *Trustees annual report* for year ending 31 May 1956, p. 5. The exact chronology of the Bowlby discovery is uncertain. Caoimhín Ó Danachair, perhaps relying on contemporary word-of-mouth information, described the maps as having been 'promptly' presented by their discoverer to the National Library ('Representations of houses on some Irish maps of *c.*1600', p. 92), but Sir Richard Bowlby recalls a gap of a year or two between first seeing the maps and first realising how old they were, and then another year or two before the donation took place (Richard Bowlby, personal communication, 17 November 2006).
35. Richard Bowlby, personal communication, 16 July 2005.
36. R.A. Skelton to G.A. Hayes McCoy, 27 January 1956, National Archives, Dublin, Irish MSS Commission, file 97/41-286. There are no details of how the test for authenticity was carried out; apparently only one of the maps was involved.
37. After many vicissitudes the maps suffered their worst misfortune in *c.*1964 when one of them, Mountjoy fort (VII), was lost at the printers. Since the map had already been photographed, the published volume was not affected: here the only casualties were the colouring and a presumed annotation (not included in the photograph) identifying this as one of the seven maps copied by John Norden in *c.*1608. A new copy was drawn from the photograph and coloured (presumably by analogy with the surviving maps), perhaps on one of several loose sheets of old blank paper found in the volume, and this counterfeit version was inserted with the genuine maps in NLI, MS 2656. The Mountjoy copy shows various minor differences from the published facsimile, which remains the nearest approach to a primary source for this map and which has accordingly been used in the present volume.

Appendix

The Maps of Richard Bartlett

BL, Cotton MS Aug. I, ii, 37. South-east Ulster, with inset of Mountnorris fort, parts of Cos Armagh, Down, Louth, Monaghan. Signed, 1600. 'The Cotton map'.

Lambeth Palace, MS 635, f. 193. Duncannon fort, Co. Wexford. [1601].

PRO, MPF 1/133. 'A description of Loughe Eaugh or Sydneye poynting out the fortes latelie erected by Tyrone ... ', parts of Cos Antrim, Armagh, Derry, Down, Tyrone. [1601-2]. 'The Lough Neagh map'.

TCD, MS 2379. 'The descriptione of a parte of Ulster conteining the pticuler places of the righte Ho. the Lo Monioie now Lo Deputie of Irelande', parts of Cos Armagh, Down, Louth, Tyrone. Signed, August 1601. 'The Trinity map'.

Possible lost original of 'The army of the Kinge of Spayne comaunded by Don Iohn de Aguila besieged in the towne of Kinsale by the forces of her victorious and sacred Matie, under the command of Charles Lord Mountioy ...'. 1601. In *Pacata Hibernia. Ireland appeased and reduced* (London, 1633), third book, between pp 352-3, second book, between pp 188-9.

NLI, MS 2656, i[a]. The Carlingford peninsula and adjoining regions, parts of Cos Armagh, Down, Louth. [1602]. 'The Cooley map'.

NLI, MS 2656, i[b]. Moyry castle and fort, Co. Armagh. [1602]. 'Bowlby Ib'.

NLI, MS 2656, ii. Mountnorris fort, Co. Armagh. [1602]. 'Bowlby II'.

NLI, MS 2656, iii[a]. Armagh city. [1602]. 'Bowlby IIIa'.

NLI, MS 2656, iii[b]. 'New fort or of the Mullin', Co. Tyrone. [1602]. 'Bowlby IIIb'.

NLI, MS 2656, iv. Charlemont fort, Co. Armagh. Signed, [1602]. 'Bowlby IV'.

NLI, MS 2656, v[a]. Unidentified lake and crannog. [1602]. 'Bowlby Va'.

NLI, MS 2656, v[b]. Dungannon castle, Co. Tyrone. [1602]. 'Bowlby Vb'.

NLI, MS 2656, v[c]. Tullaghoge, rath, Co. Tyrone. [1602]. 'Bowlby Vc'.

NLI, MS 2656, v[d]. Tullaghoge, chair. Co. Tyrone. [1602]. 'Bowlby Vd'.

NLI, MS 2656, vi. Inisloughan fort, Co. Antrim. [1602]. 'Bowlby VI'.

NLI, MS 2656, vii. Mountjoy fort, Co. Tyrone. [1602]. 'Bowlby VII'.

NLI, MS 2656, viii. Blackwater valley, Cos Armagh and Tyrone. Signed, 1602. 'Bowlby VIII'.

NLI, MS 2656, ix[a]. Monaghan fort. [1602]. 'Bowlby IXa'.

NLI, MS 2656, ix[b]. Unidentified lake and crannogs. [1602]. 'Bowlby IXb'.

NLI, MS 2656, x. Augher island and fort, Co. Tyrone. [1602]. 'Bowlby X'.

NLI, MS 2656, xi. Unidentified lake and crannog. [1602]. 'Bowlby XI'.

NLI, MS 2656, xii. Lough Bofin, Cos Leitrim, Roscommon. [1602]. 'Bowlby XII'.

PRO, MPF 1/35. 'A generalle description of Ulster'. [1602-3].

PRO, MPF 1/36. South-east Ulster: Cos Antrim, Armagh, Fermanagh, Louth, Monaghan, Tyrone. [1602-3]. 'The campaign map'.

PRO, MPF 1/37. Donegal Bay and Sligo Bay, parts of Cos Donegal, Leitrim, Mayo, Sligo. [1602-3]. 'The Bays map'.

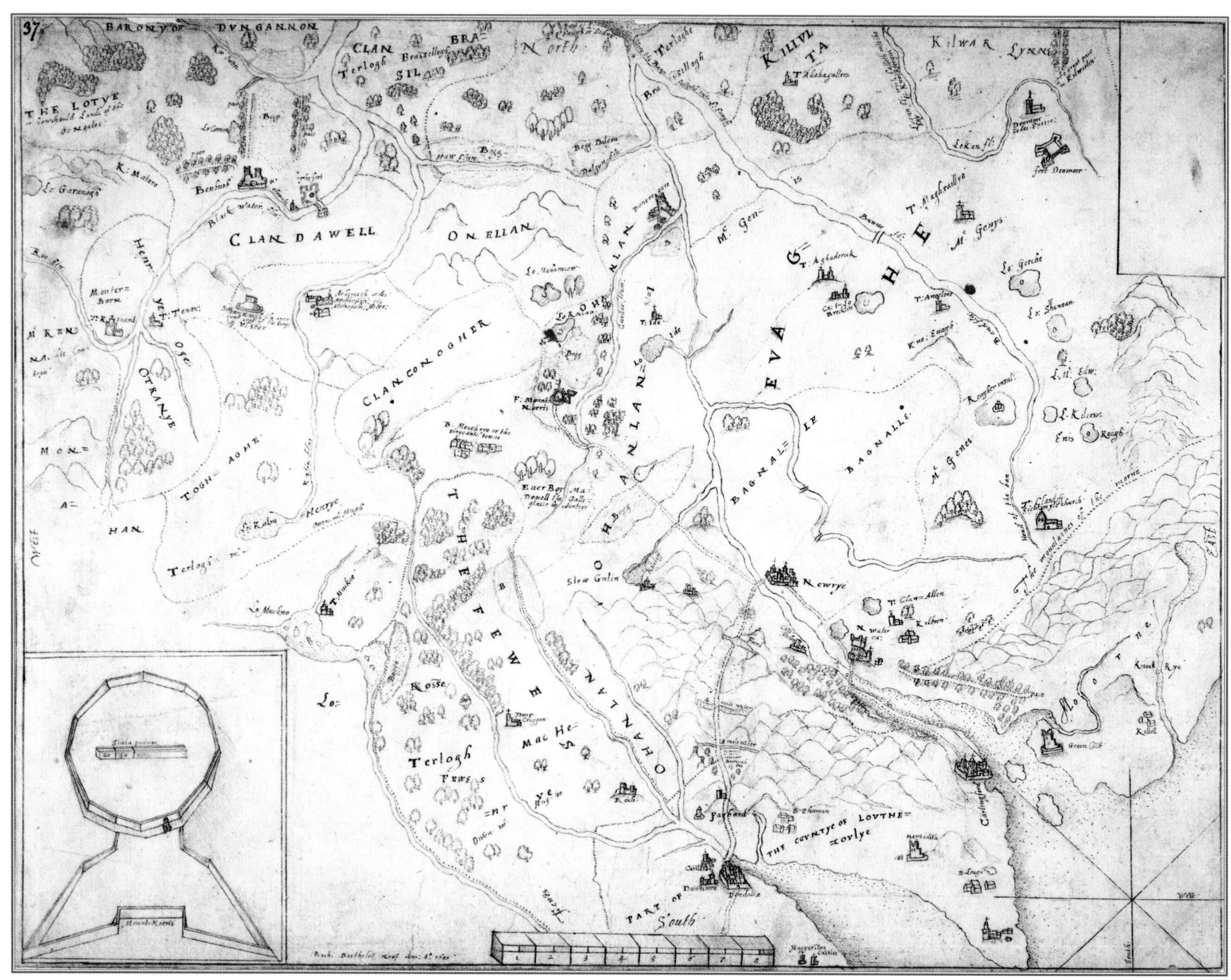

Plate 1. South-east Ulster, 1600. BL, Cotton MS Aug. I, ii, 37.

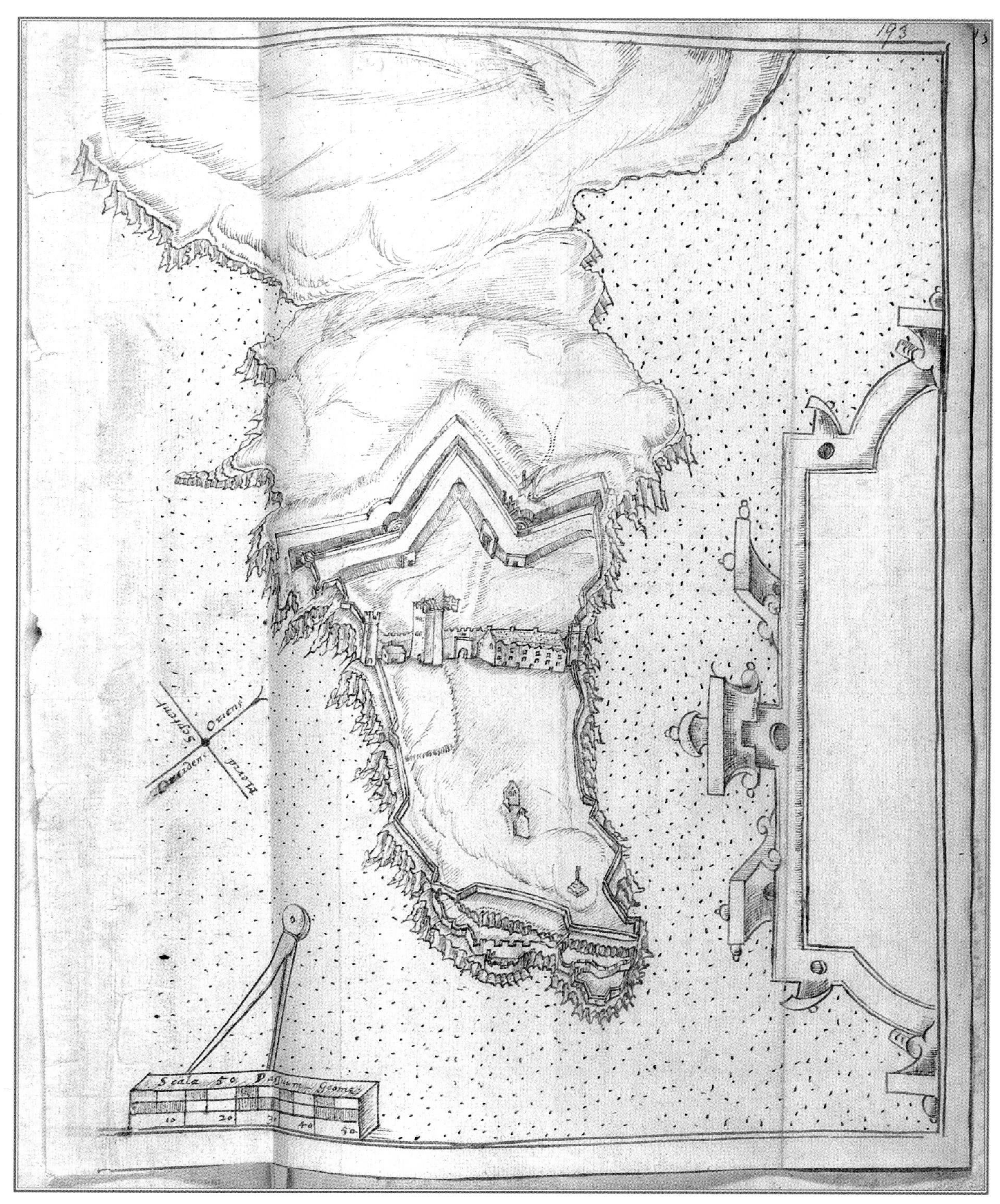

Plate 2. Duncannon fort, Co. Wexford, 1601. Lambeth Palace, MS 635/193.

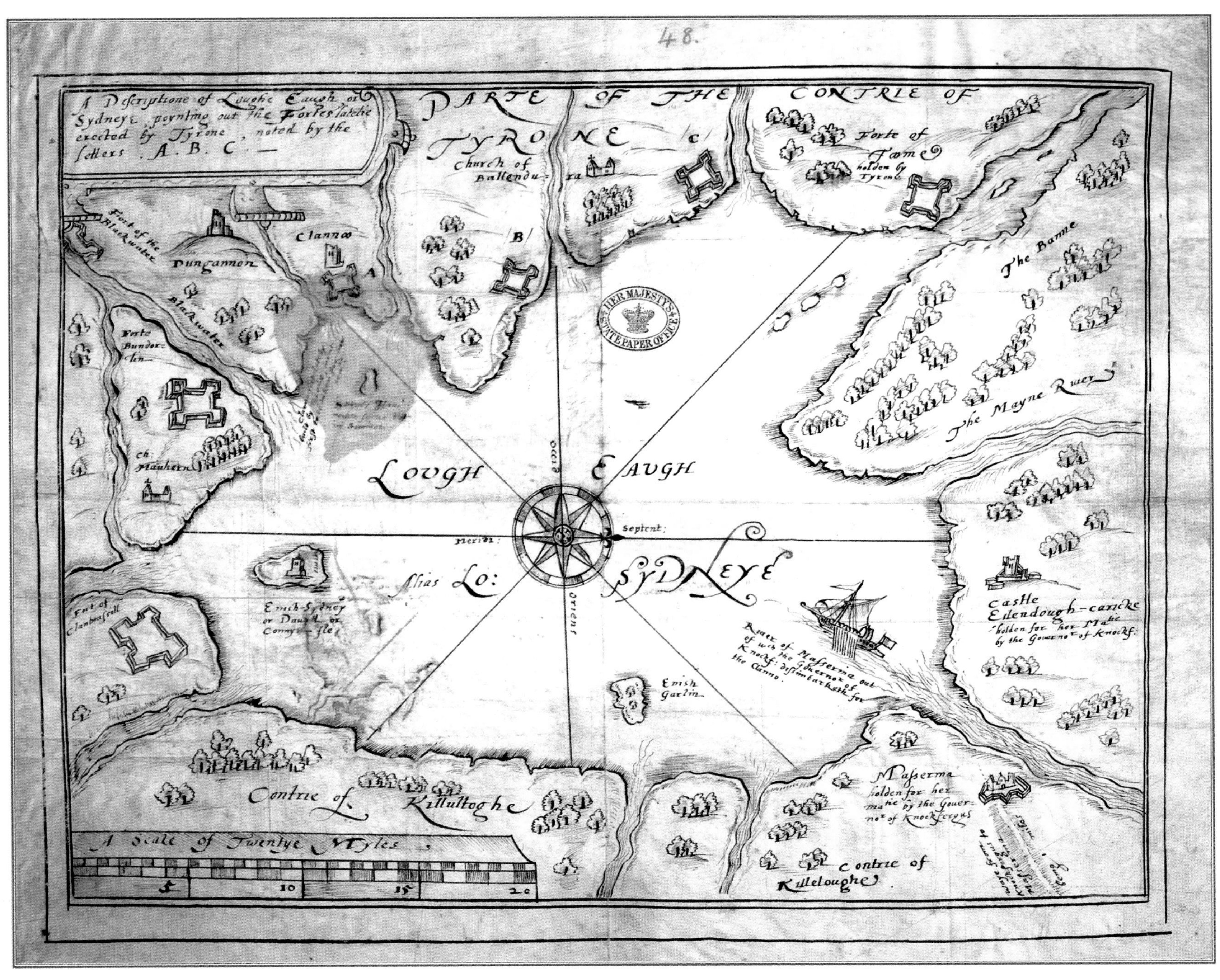

Plate 3. Lough Neagh, 1601-2. PRO, MPF 1/133.

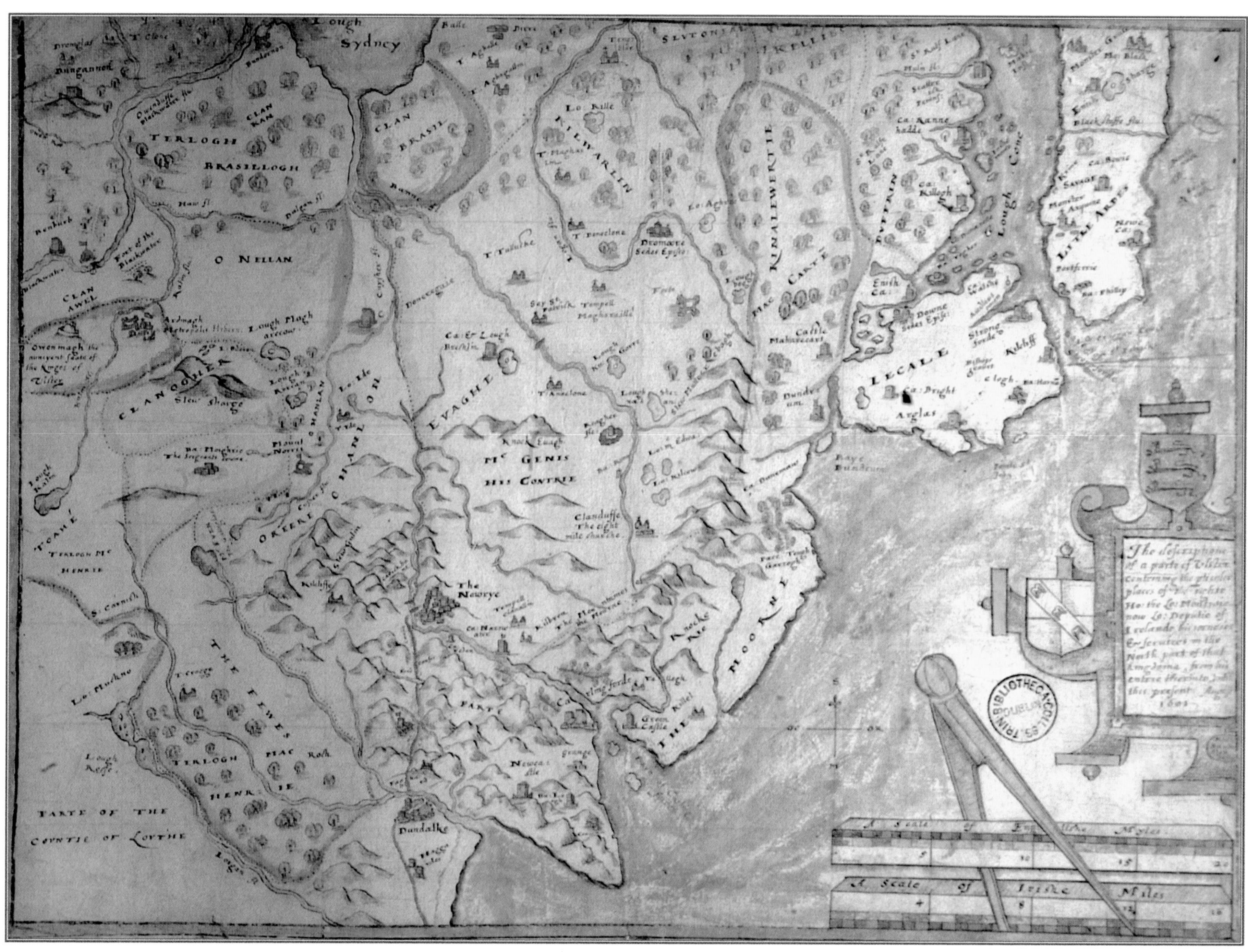

Plate 4. South-east Ulster, 1601. TCD, MS 2379.

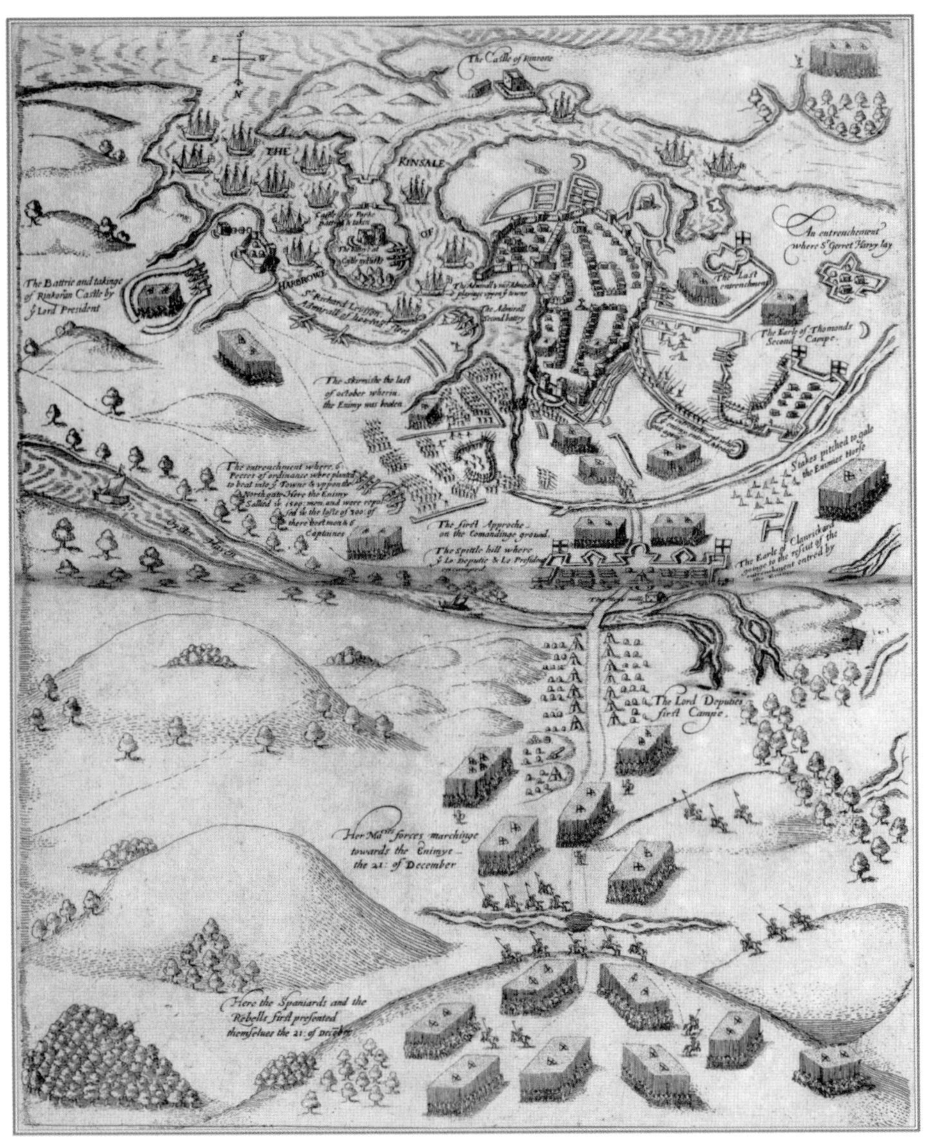

Plate 5 (a) Siege of Kinsale, 1601. *Pacata Hibernia. Ireland appeased and reduced* (London, 1633), third book, between pp 352-3.

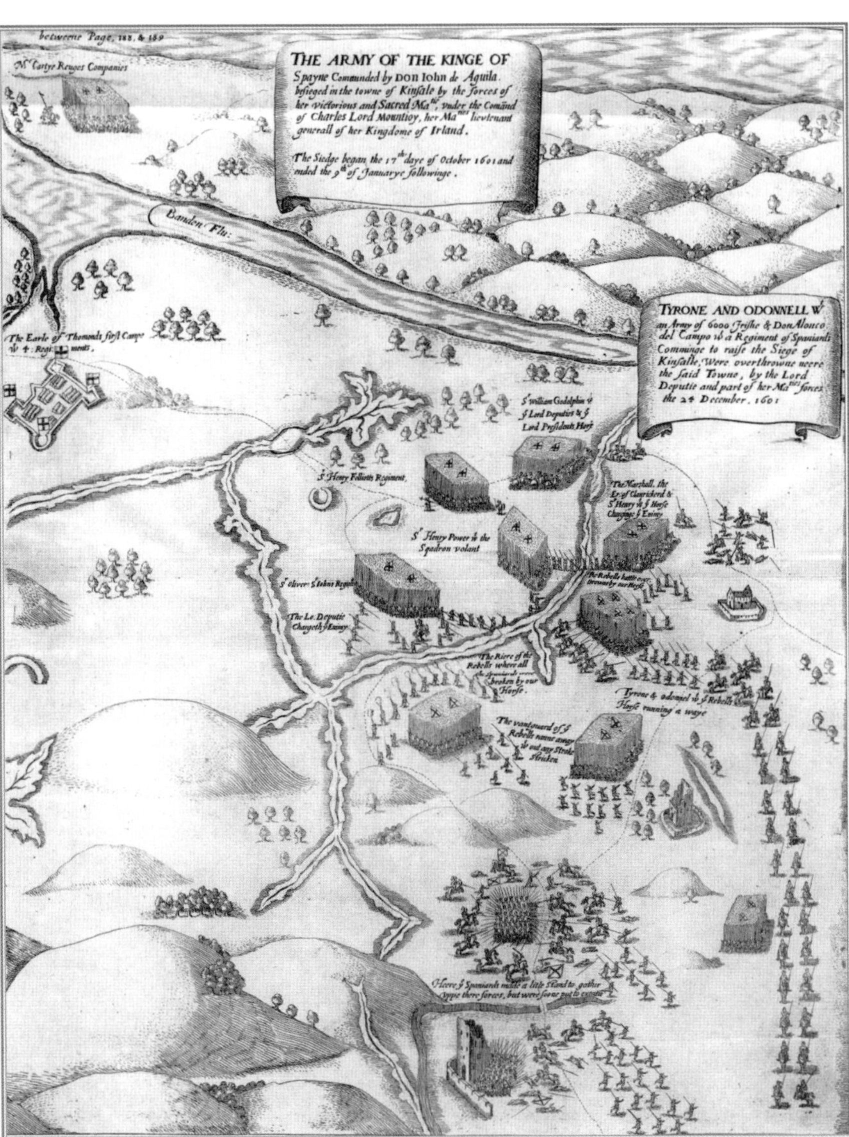

Plate 5 (b) Siege of Kinsale, 1601. *Pacata Hibernia. Ireland appeased and reduced* (London, 1633), second book, between pp 188-9.

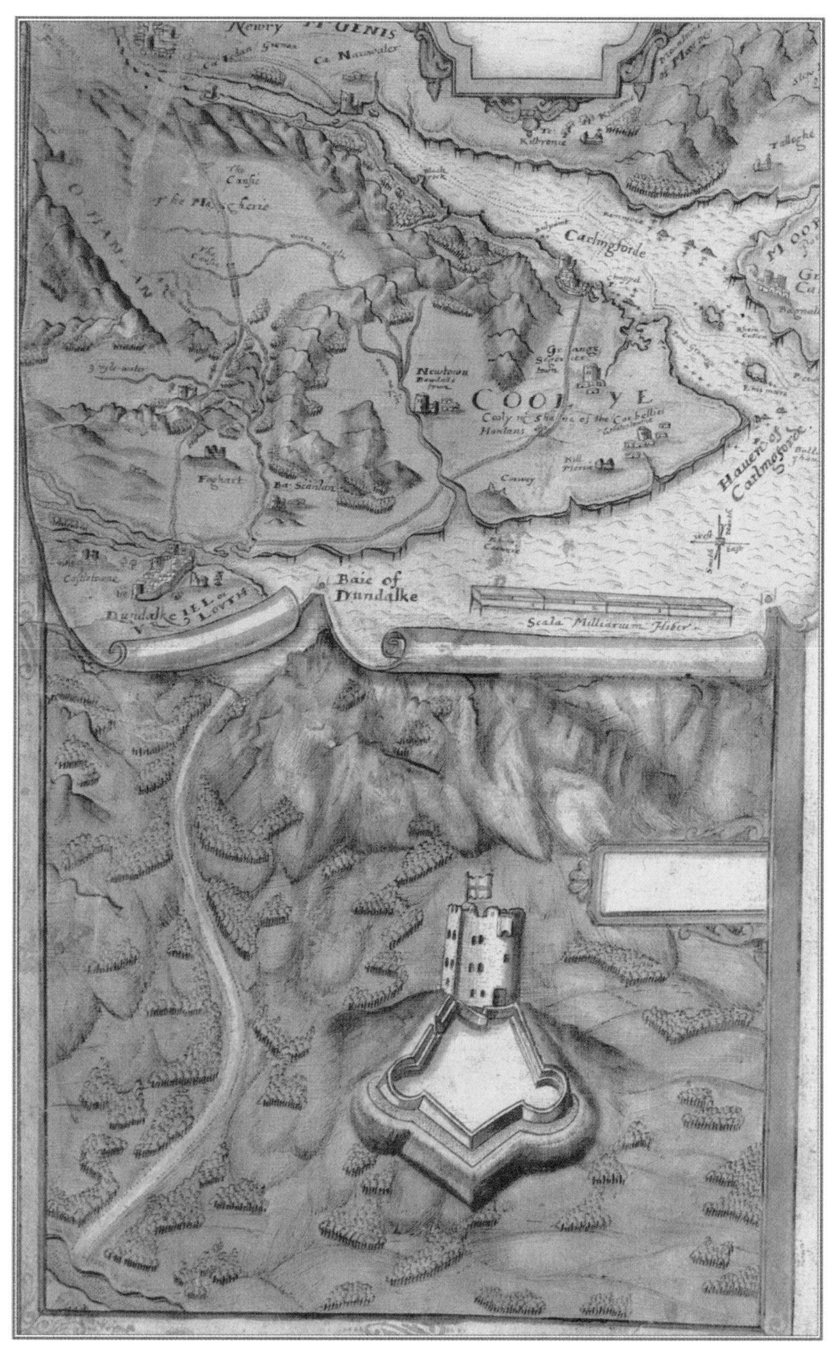

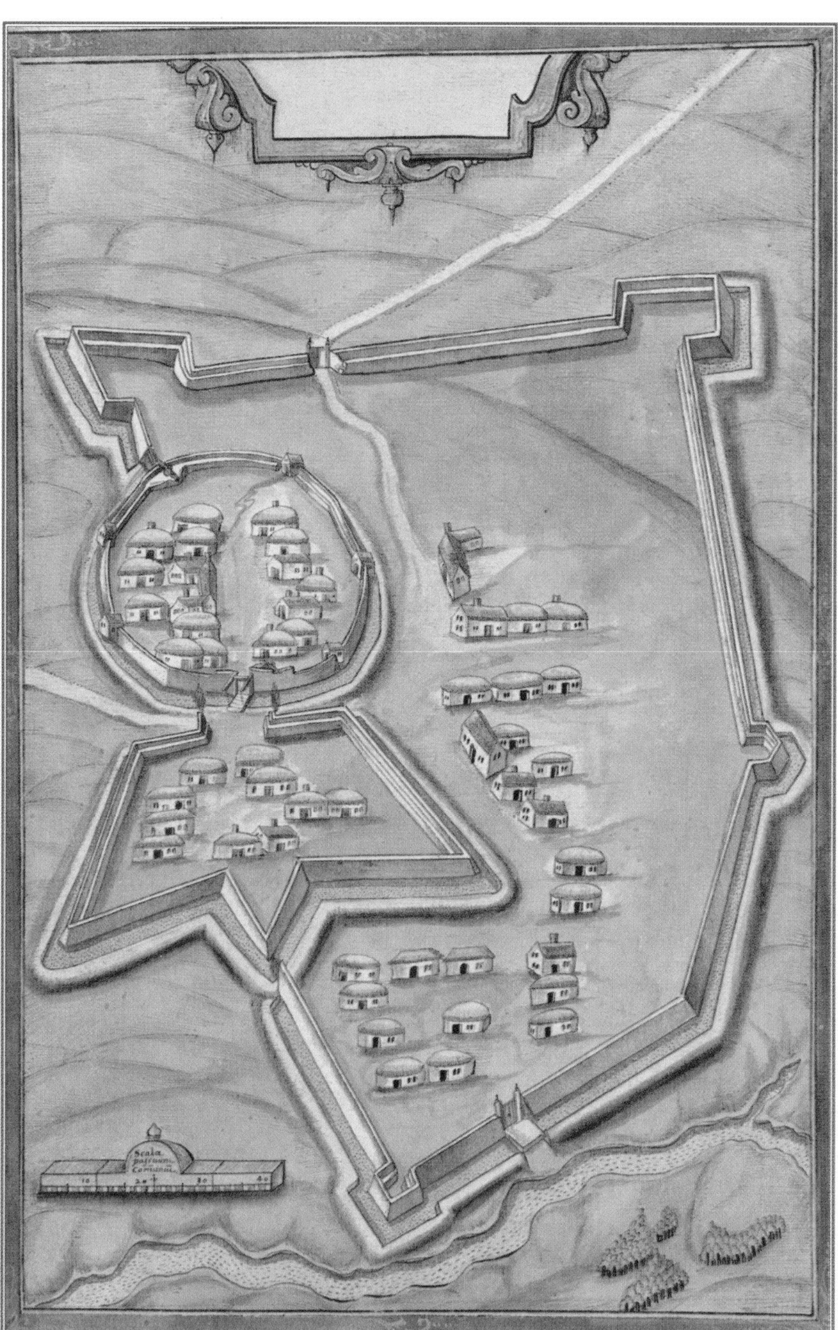

Plate 6. (a) Above: Carlingford peninsula and adjoining regions, 1602; (b) Below: Moyry castle and fort, 1602. NLI, MS 2656, i.

Plate 7. Mountnorris fort, 1602. NLI, MS 2656, ii.

Plate 8. (a) Above: Armagh city, 1602; (b) Below: Fort of the Mullin, 1602. NLI, MS 2656, iii.

Plate 9. Charlemont fort, 1602; NLI, MS 2656, iv.

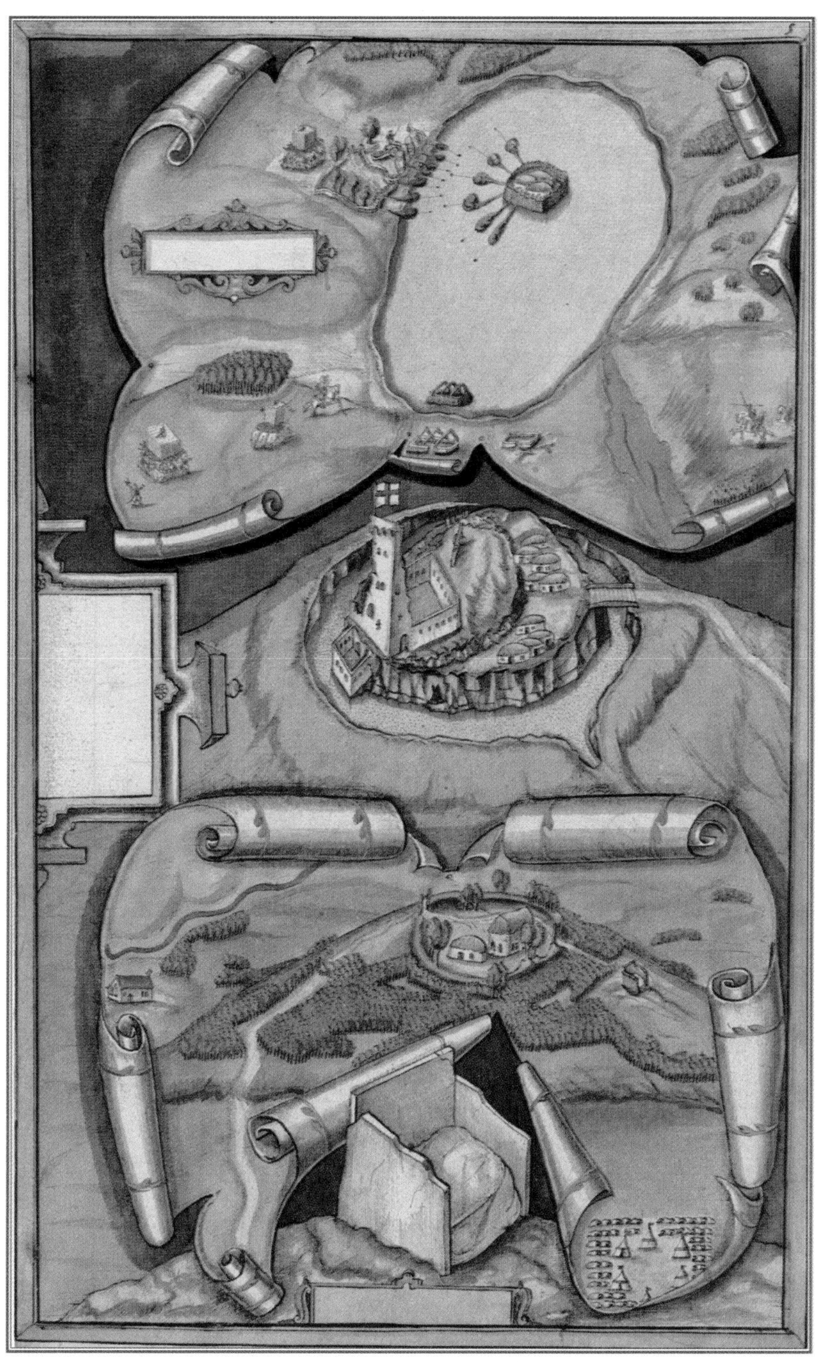

Plate 10. (a) Above: Unidentified lake and crannog, 1602; (b) Upper centre: Dungannon castle, 1602; (c) Lower centre: Rath of Tullaghoge, 1602; (d) Below: The O'Neills' chair, 1602. NLI, MS 2656, v.

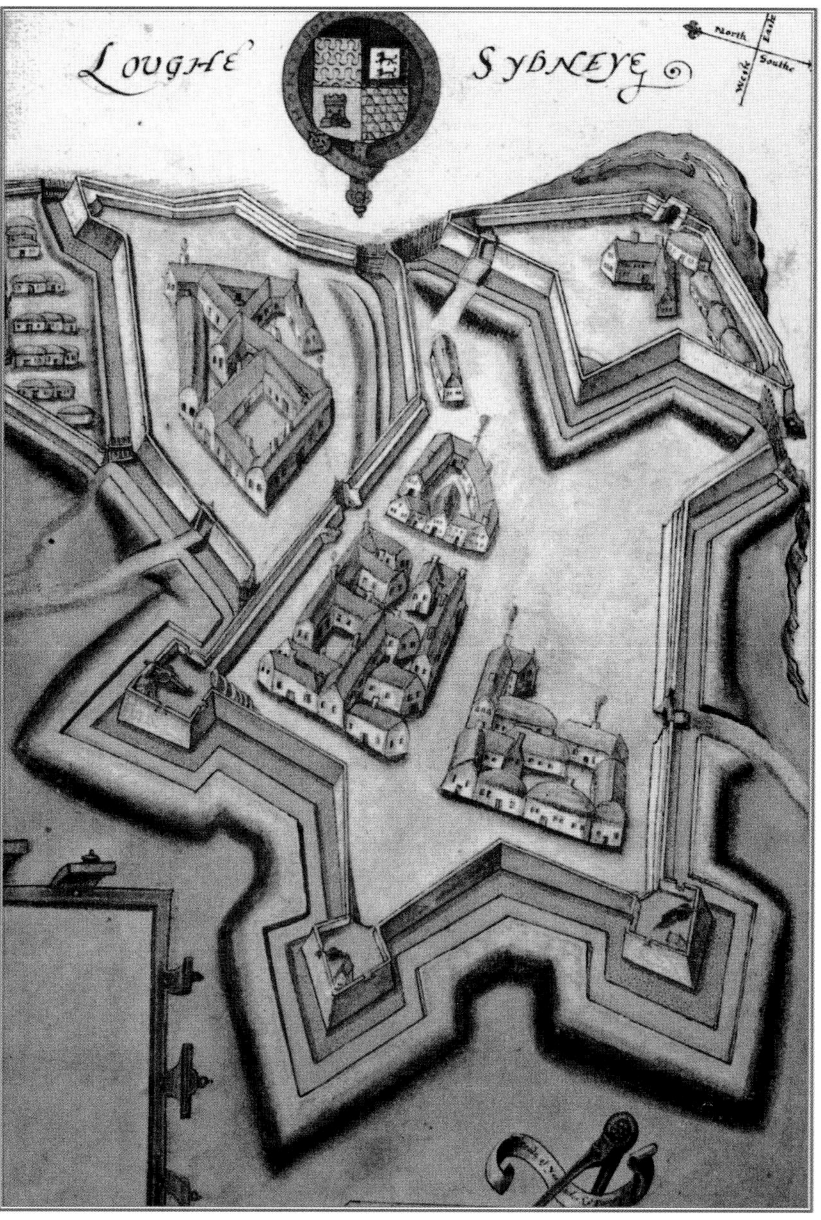

Plate 11. Mountjoy fort. G.A. Hayes-McCoy (ed.), *Ulster and other Irish maps c. 1600* (Dublin, 1964), between pp 14-5.

Plate 12. (a) Above: Monaghan fort, 1602; (b) Below: Unidentified lake and crannogs, 1602. NLI, MS 2656, ix.

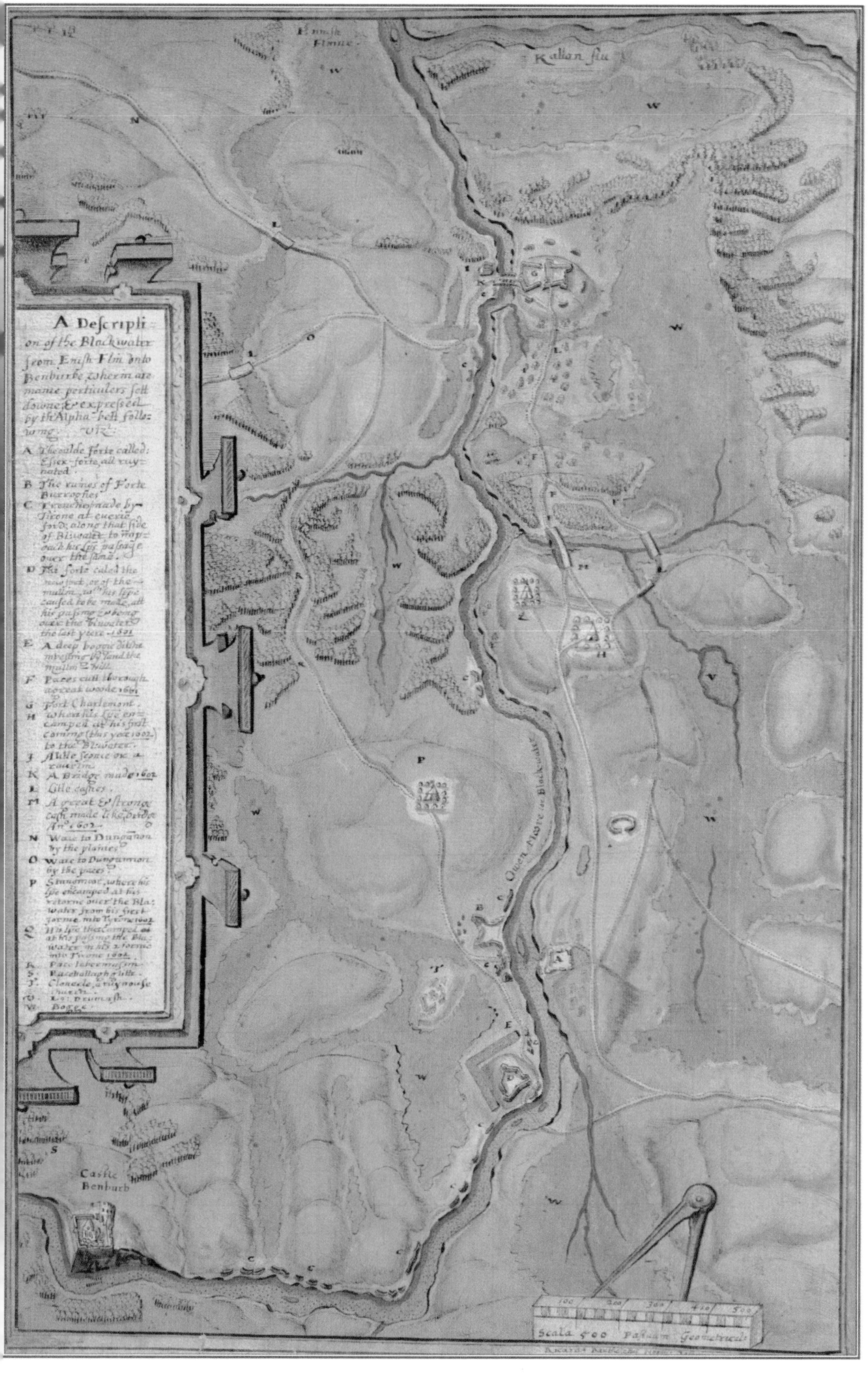

Plate 13. Blackwater valley, 1602. NLI, MS 2656, viii.

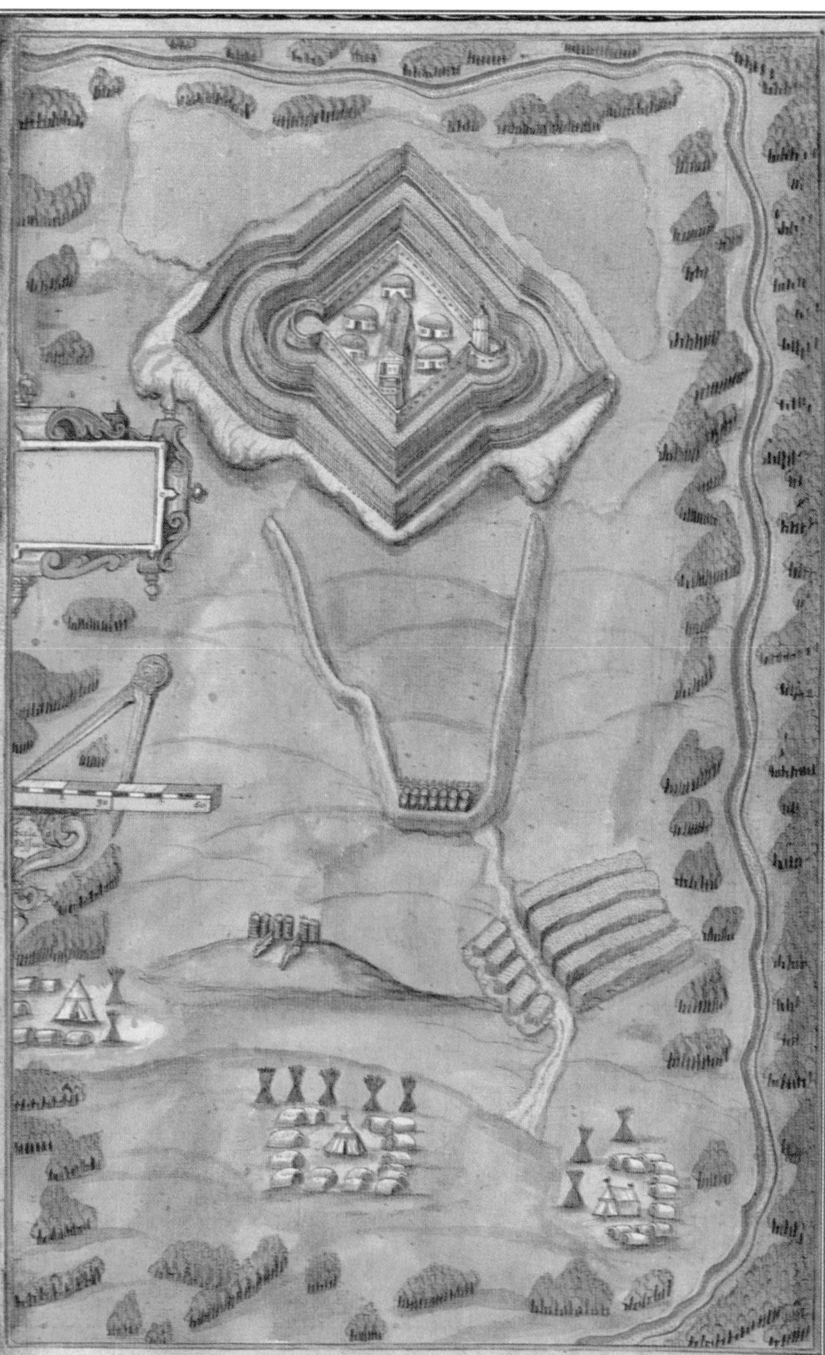

Plate 14. Inishloughan fort, 1602. NLI, MS 2656, vi.

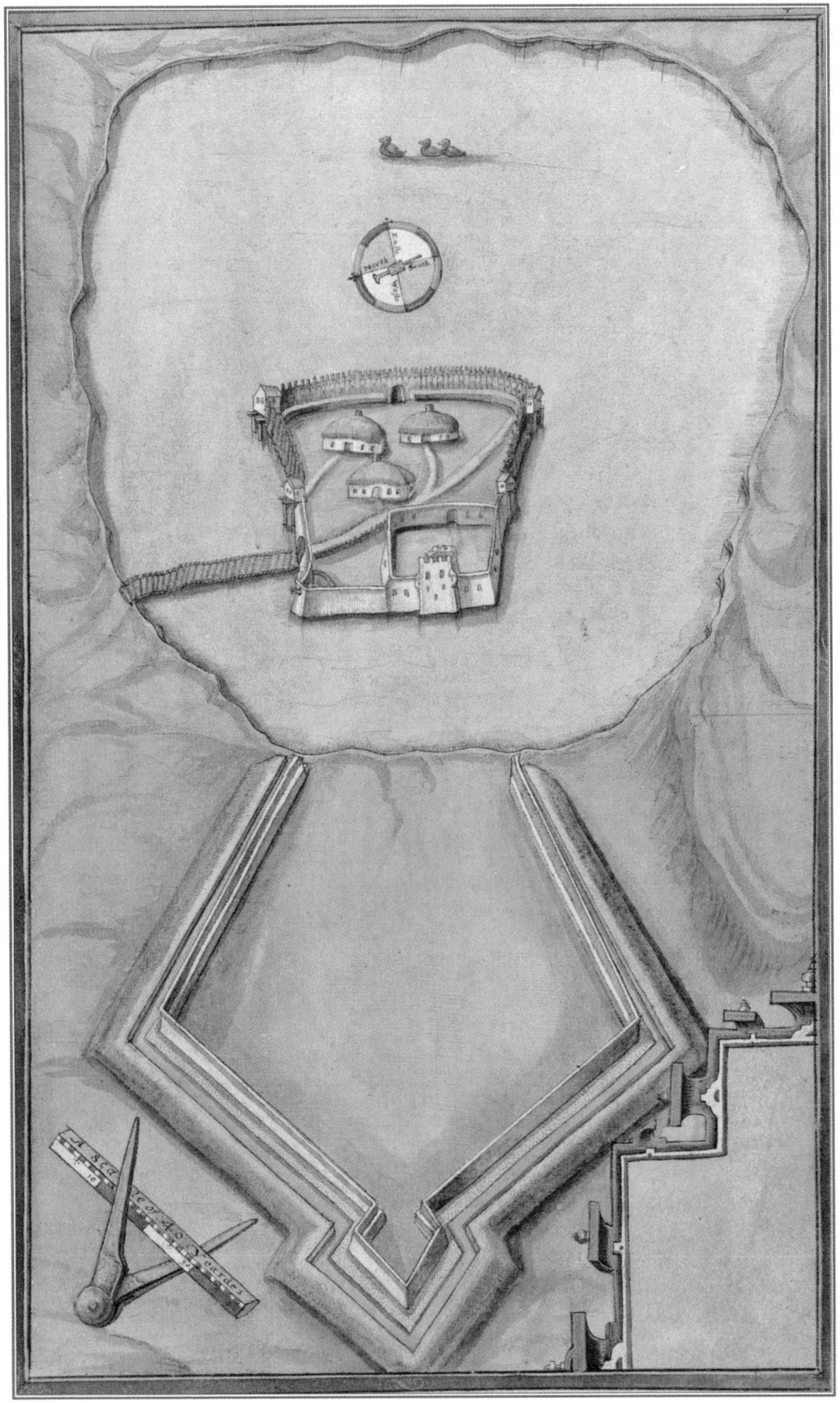

Plate 15. Augher island and fort, 1602. NLI, MS 2656, x.

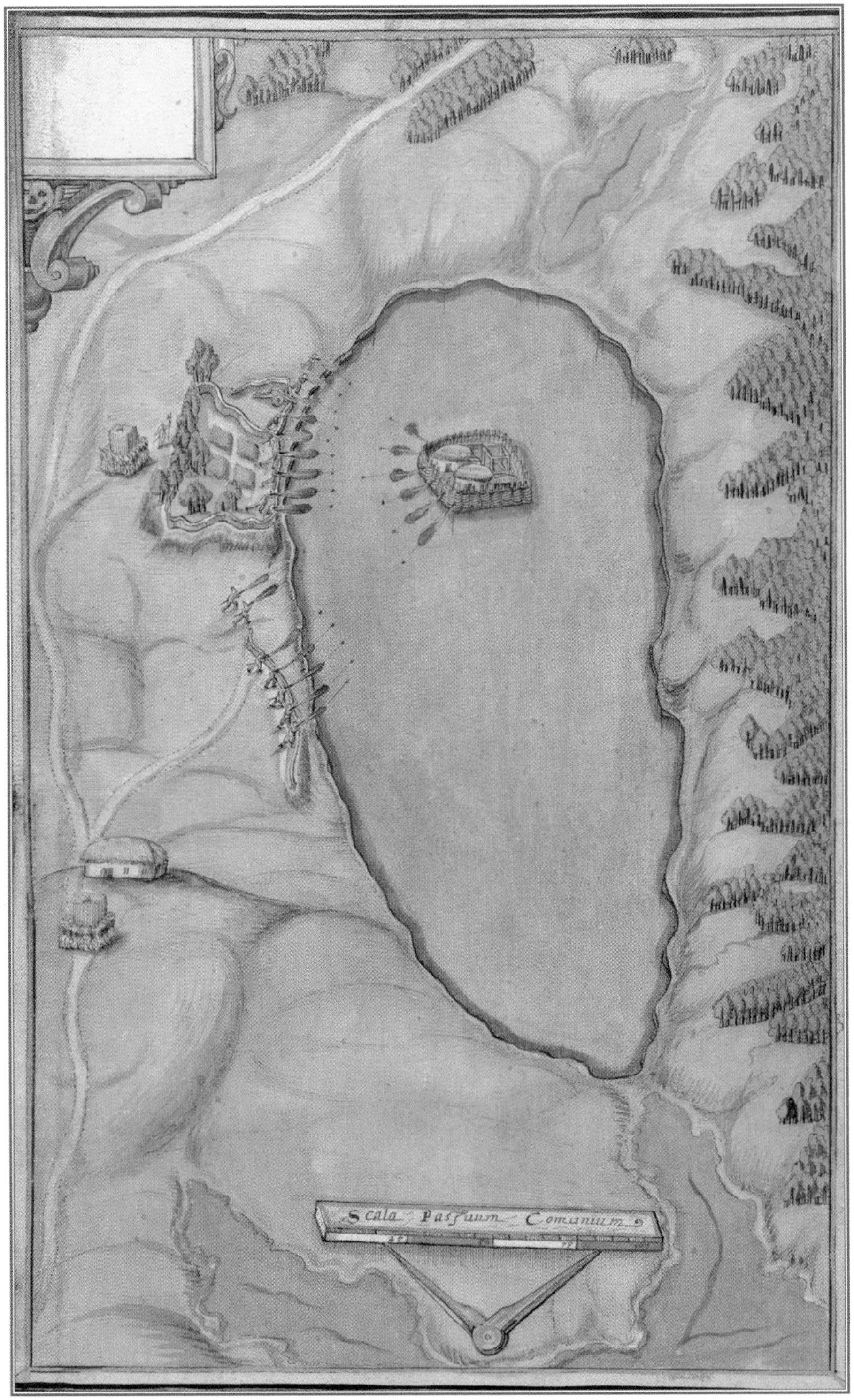

Plate 16. Unidentified lake and crannog, 1602. NLI, MS 2656, xi.

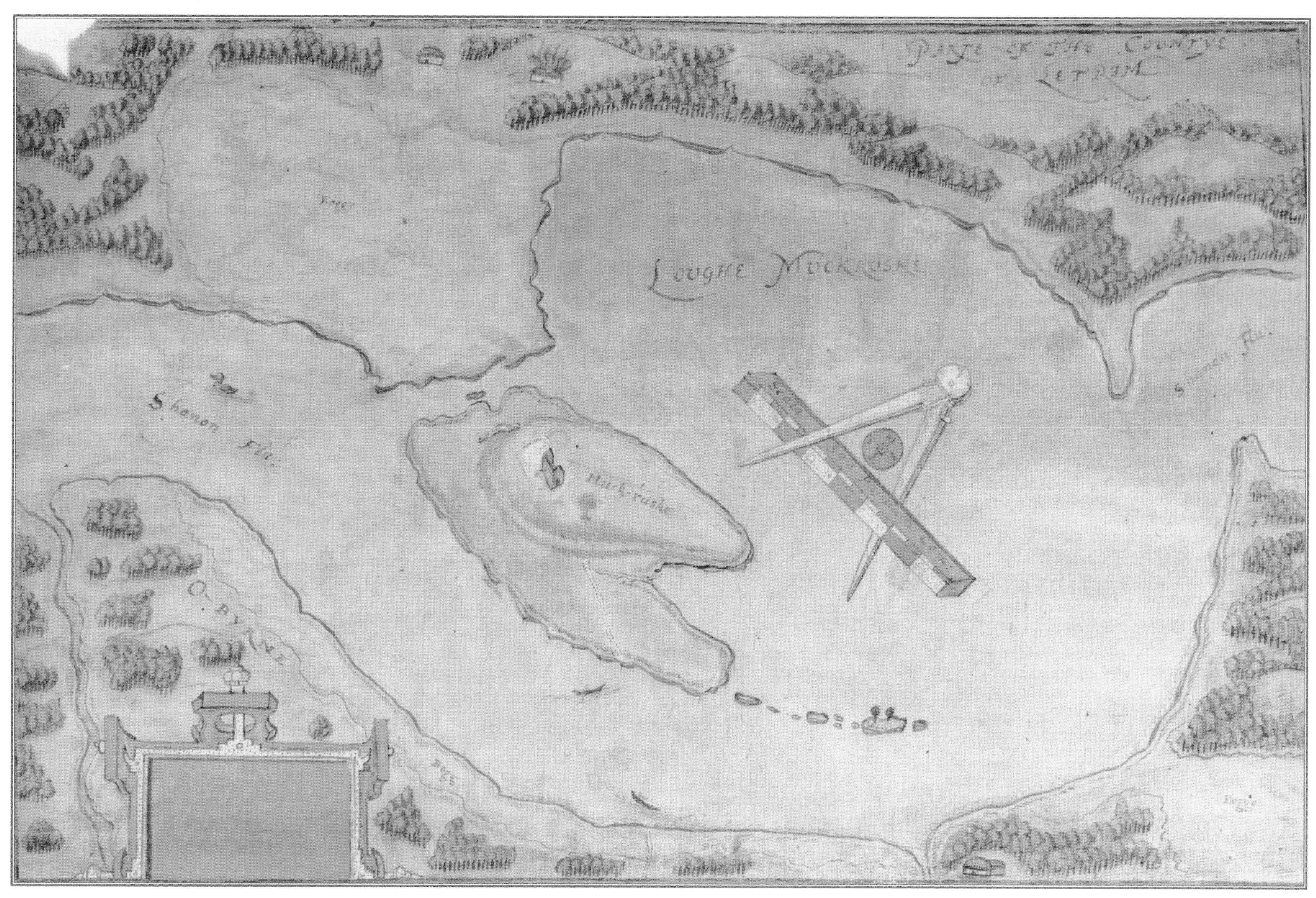

Plate 17. Lough Bofin, 1602. NLI, MS 2656, xii

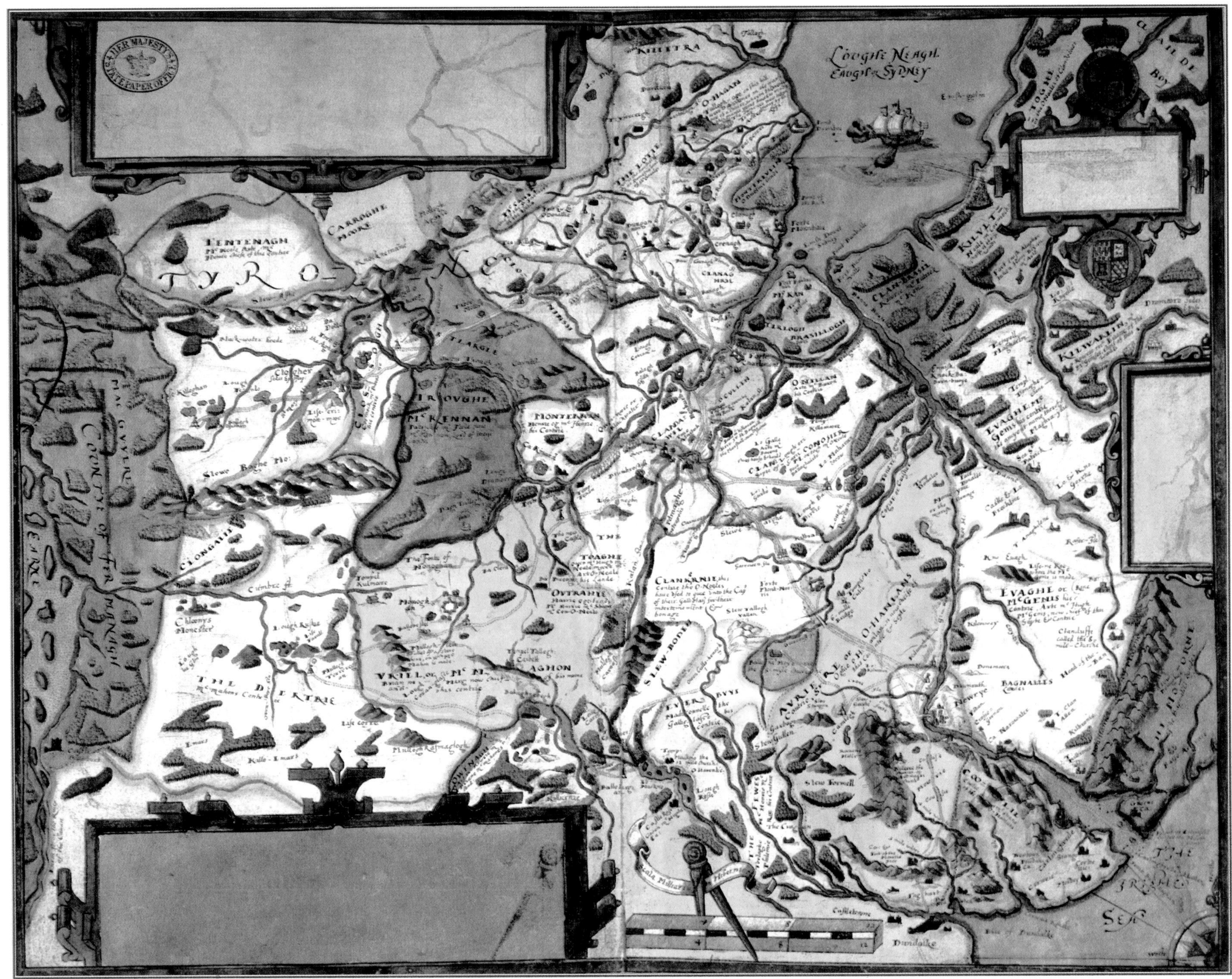

Plate 18. South-east Ulster, 1602-3. 'The campaign map'. PRO, MPF 1/36.

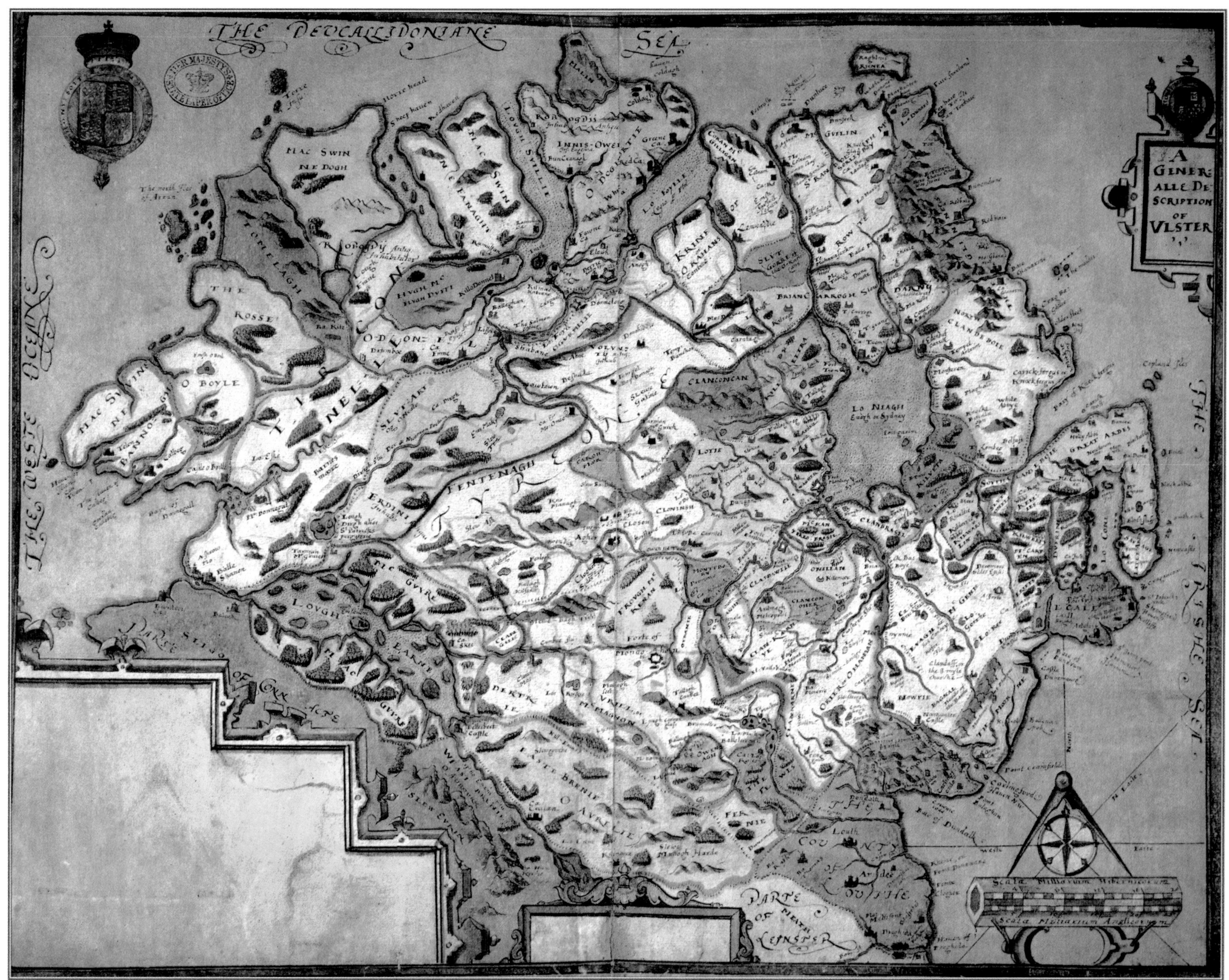

Plate 19. 'A generalle description of Ulster', 1602-3. PRO, MPF 1/35.

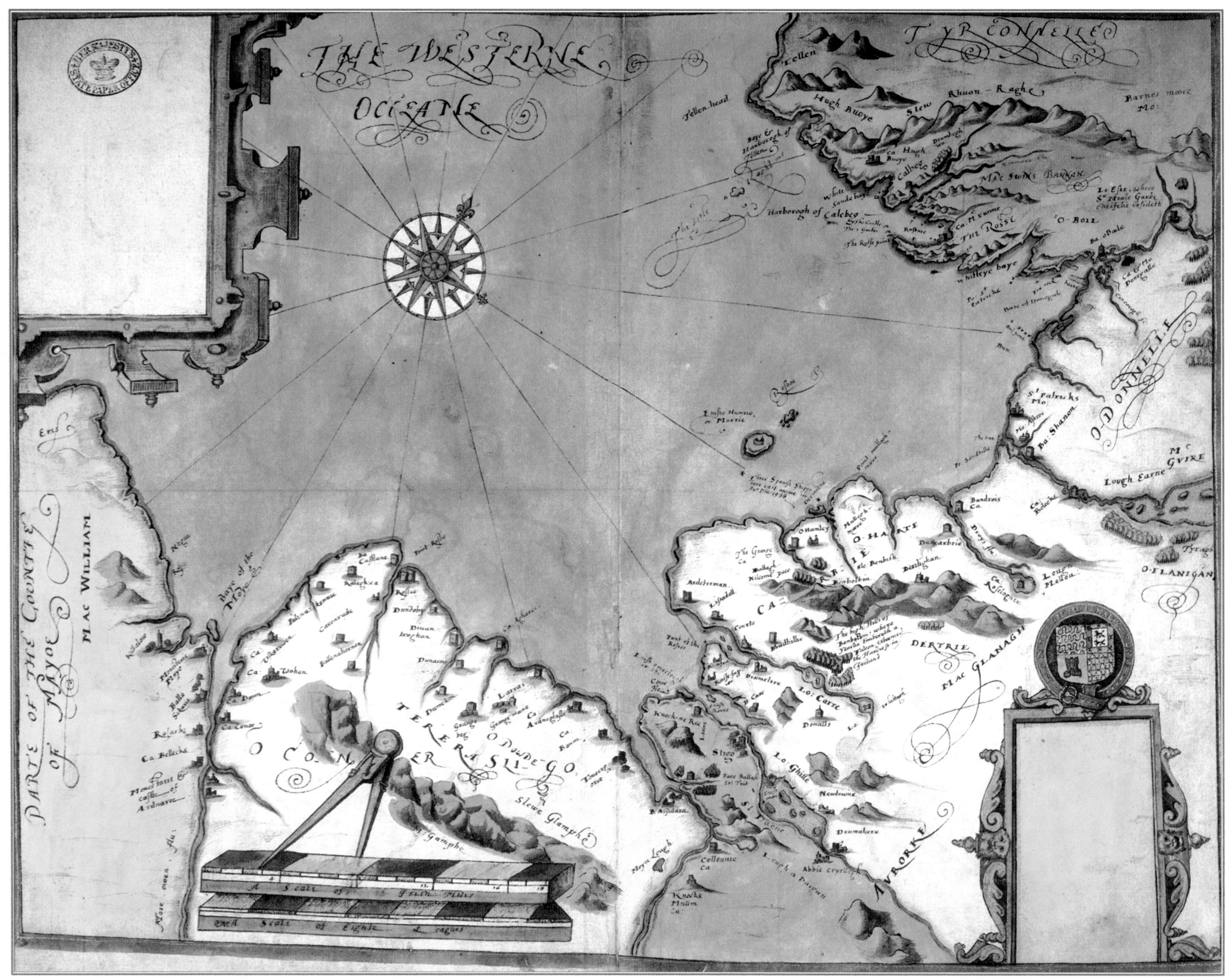

Plate 20. Donegal Bay and Sligo Bay, 1602-3. 'The Bays map'. PRO, MPF 1/37.

Index